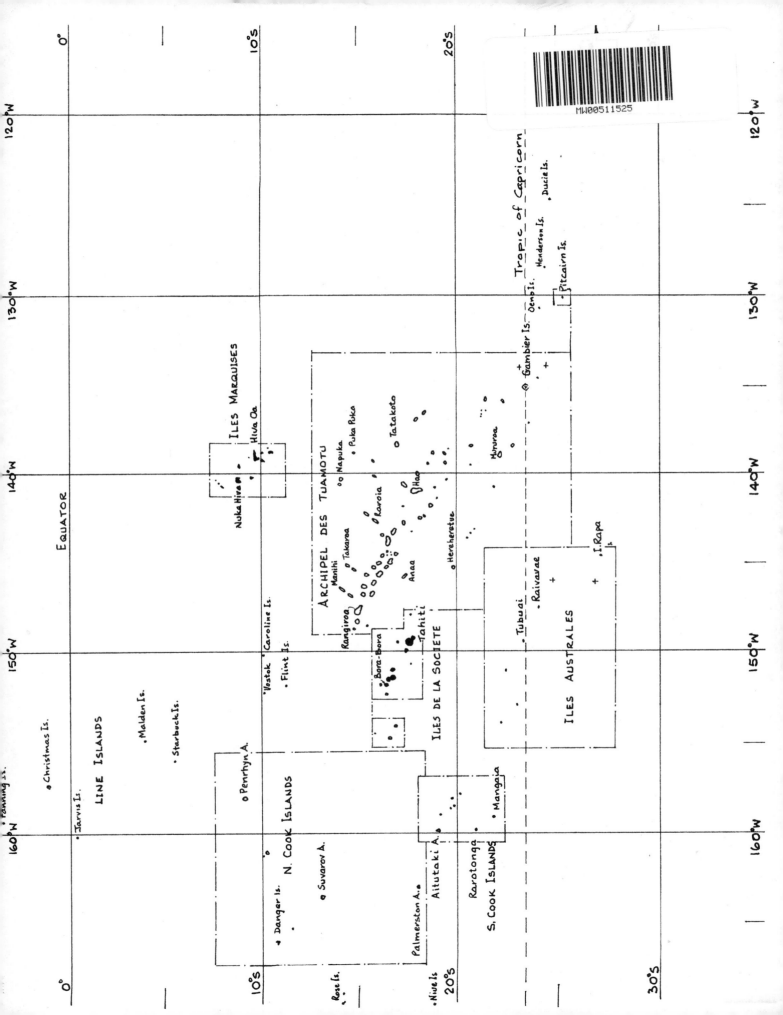

CHARLIE'S CHARTS CRUISING GUIDES

CHARLIE'S CHARTS North to ALASKA
CHARLIE'S CHARTS of the Western Coast of MEXICO ⎫ by Charles E. Wood
CHARLIE'S CHARTS of the HAWAIIAN ISLANDS ⎬
CHARLIE'S CHARTS of POLYNESIA ⎭
CHARLIE'S CHARTS of the U.S. PACIFIC COAST by Charles and Margo Wood
CHARLIE'S CHARTS of COSTA RICA by Margo Wood

Also written by Charles E. Wood:
BUILDING YOUR DREAM BOAT, published by Cornell Maritime Press
Numerous articles appearing in SAIL, CRUISING WORLD & PACIFIC YACHTING

Canadian Cataloguing in Publication Data
Wood, Charles E. (Charles Edward), 1928 - 1987
Charlie's Charts of Polynesia

ISBN 09697265-7-0
1. Pilot guides - Polynesia. 2. Boats and
boating - Polynesia - Maps. 3. Polynesia -
Description and travel. I. Title.
G2971.P5W6 1989 623.89'2996 C89-091553-9

Revised by Margo Wood   Photographs by Charles and Margo Wood
Edited by Christie Gorsline

Published by: CHARLIE'S CHARTS (Division of Polymath Energy Consultants Ltd.)
P.O. Box 45064   P.O. Box 1702
Ocean Park RPO   Blaine, WA
Surrey, BC V4A 9L1   98231-1702
CANADA   USA

TEL/FAX (604) 531-6292

PRINTED IN CANADA   ISBN 0-9697265-7-0

CHARLIE'S CHARTS

OF

POLYNESIA

(The South Pacific, east of 165°W. Longitude)

By

Charles E. Wood

ISBN 0-9697265-7-0

DEDICATION

This book is dedicated to the memory of the great navigators and explorers who went before us to make our way across the Pacific Ocean easier, and in particular to

Captain James Cook, R.N.

the greatest of them all. He was a seaman we could strive to emulate, a man ahead of his time (and ours) in meeting and treating with new peoples, of whom it was said that the Pacific Ocean was his memorial. As others have noted, his epitaph could well be read in the names of his brave little ships,

Endeavour, Resolution, Discovery and Adventure

ACKNOWLEDGEMENTS

Although my husband, Charles Wood, passed away in 1987 it had been his intention to continue updating and revising this cruising guide. I am happy to be able to continue his legacy to cruising sailors. Recently I have been fortunate in being able to make two trips to Polynesia to collect material first-hand as well as obtain current information from various sources.

Much credit is due to John Neal for the material he has provided as a result of the many months he spends each year in Polynesian waters. In addition, generous help in improving the accuracy of coverage of the Hawaiian Islands was given by Ian Birnie, the former District Manager of the Harbors Division for the Island of Hawaii. I gratefullly acknowledge invaluable information for Isles Australes sent by Harry and Mary Abbott of S.V. *Sugar Blues* and by Larry Richards for a mail forwarding address in Aitutaki, Cook Islands.

I would also like to thank the entire staff of the island freighter *Aranui* from Theodore, the Captain to Josephine, the laundry lady, toTino, the chief deckhand and especially Vivish Vaihere, a most charming and knowledgeable staff member—each of them contributed to my appreciation and understanding of the kind, friendly, happy and gentle people that are the Polynesians. My endless questions were always patiently answered with a smile.

Rose Corser of *Keikahanui Inn* in Baie de Taiohae, Nuku Hiva was most generous in giving local information as was Etienne Takihui Hodawpoko who kindlly sent me information and an invitation to cruisers to visit Ua Pou. Input from Dr. Robert C. Suggs whose detailed and precise information on place names and archeological data added accuracy to some of the misconceptions related to historical facts about the Marquises.

I am indebted to Anne-Maria Laroche of *Vaima Librairie* for providing assistance with travel arrangements and to Marius Luciani of *Librairie Klima* for helping with the acquisition of up-to-date information from local sources.

The painstaking representation and updating of "charts" is due to the efforts of two very patient brothers: David and Terry Law, each of whom deserve a commendation. Finally, I wish to recognize the painstaking job of editing done by Christie Gorsline, a retired English and journalism teacher and published writer. Her meticulous attention to detail has added polish where it was needed and I thank her for her enthusiastic input and effort.

DISCLAIMER

The word, "CHARTS," in the title of this publication is not intended to imply that these hand-drawn sketches are sufficiently accurate to be used for navigation. They and the accommpanying text are meant to act solely as a handy cruising guide to assist sailors in identifying and entering passes, harbors and anchorages. With the passage of time, new aids to navigation, marina development and other changes in the areas covered by this book make it inevitable that some of the material may become inaccurate and out-of-date by the time it is used.

The use of DMA (U.S. Defense Mapping Agency), British Admiralty, French or other official charts is mandatory for safe navigation. **DO NOT USE ANY OF THE DRAWINGS IN THIS BOOK FOR NAVIGATION.** CHARLIE'S CHARTS and POLYMATH ENERGY CONSULTANTS LTD. are in no way responsible for loss or damages resulting from the use of this book.

The coastline of many atolls and islands described in this guide have not been surveyed hydrographically as has been noted in the Marquises. Consequently, there could easily be many reefs, shoals and other dangers that are yet to be discovered. Cruisers are cautioned to be vigilant in recognizing and avoiding such hazards.

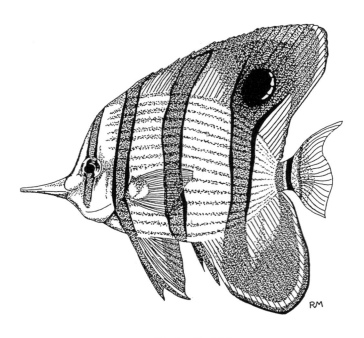

Butterfly Fish

Sunset in Paradise   *Charles Wood*

A dream come true — at anchor in Papeete Harbor, Tahiti

Charles Wood

CONTENTS

SYMBOLS

Recommended approach	Leading range and bearing
Anchorage	Reported anchorage
× Rock or reef underwater	Dangerous rock or reef
Barrier or fringing coral reef (exposed or awash)	Coral reef at shallow depth
Exposed coral heads	Submerged coral heads
Navigation lights	Beacons, not necessarily lit
Sector light	13°30' Lights in line with true bearing
Shoal	Sandy beach
6, 3f Depth in fathoms	Coconut palms
S Sand bottom	co Coral bottom
m Mud bottom	r Rocky bottom
Surf line	Cliffs of makatea
Breakwater	Rocky edge

INTRODUCTION

This guide is oriented to sailing from North America to the South Pacific. Thus the routes, weather and order of this guide through the islands are given for a westbound journey. However, the guide can be used by those approaching from other places, though it may not be convenient.

Some general introductory material on important facets of cruising the area is given first. Thereafter, each section describes a particular island group, and includes brief notes on history, weather, winds, currents and other data. These notes are a generalized summary of conditions and are by no means descriptive of what you might actually encounter—that lies with the gods. For additional information refer to the official Sailing Directions, Pilot Charts and other references.

The sketched "charts" illustrate anchorages and the approaches to them and are useful to the cruising sailor. The source material includes nautical charts, maps, other yachtsmen's comments, and my own material.

The South Pacific is the cruising sailor's dream. The area is politically stable, still fairly friendly, reasonably free of excessive strict regulations (a matter of opinion), and filled with an intrinsic beauty of land, sea, and weather that make it a Mecca for sailors.

Unfortunately, the polluting advance of "civilization" has begun to touch this once idyllic cruising haven. The lagoons adjacent to hotels in Tahiti and Moorea are not as clean as they once were and resorts operating on some atolls are degrading the knife-edge ecologies. In addition, a steady drift of people to Papeete is reducing out-island populations while the birth rate has been rising.

It is a major offshore voyage to get there, to cruise the many islands, and then a major voyage home again. Sailing Polynesia can be part of a Pacific circuit, a New Zealand hop, or a round-the-world odyssey. In any case it requires a large commitment in time to accomplish it; this is the criterion that does more to separate those who just dream of it from those who do it. Though a rushed voyage to the South Seas and back could be done in three months, enjoyment would be limited with such an itinerary. In fact, taking into account the controlling weather conditions, you should not plan on less than a year to allow for exploration and enjoyment.

PURPOSE and LIMITS OF THIS GUIDE

This guide identifies small boat anchorages in the eastern part of South Pacific. It is intended to assist the yachtsman in his choice of anchorages and to recognize approaches and hazards. Roughly, the area covered is that commonly known as the "Polynesian Triangle," with the exception of the Samoa Islands. Though the Hawaiian Islands are north of the Equator and are found in detail in *Charlie's Charts of the Hawaiian Islands*, they are considered here as part of the South Pacific so the Ports of Entry are included.

This guide helps the cruiser by showing small anchorages in larger scale and detail than most coastal charts. In the case of the South Pacific, the land masses are small, and the special difficulties of navigation in the area mean that there are more large scale charts available, though not as many as one would like.

The sketches are hand-drawn and are not meant to be accurate surveys or to be used for navigation. Nautical charts should be used for all navigational purposes and the sketches herein are intended to provide supplemental information only.

These sketches include information such as land form details in symbolic form, contour lines, depth lines or individual soundings, lights, some navigational data such as leading ranges, etc. In the geographic area covered by this guide, with coral reefs and low-lying atolls, the most important information is often the identification of, and detail of a pass through the reef rather than a specific anchorage. The practice of giving the view from seaward on approaching a coast is useful to sailors although it is disappearing from many current official charts as a consequence of an increasingly technological era.

Details cannot be shown of the complexities of coral heads and shoals once through the reef's pass. Navigation to an anchorage within a lagoon must be done by eye, in the best light, and from as high a position as possible. Thus a sketch might show the detail of an entrance and merely indicate the anchorage across the lagoon. This does not mean a yacht can go carelessly across as if traversing a channel. Passages may involve much maneuvering to thread a route through the coral heads and shoals. The responsibility for safely navigating your vessel through a pass and to any anchorage remains with the skipper, and this guide cannot be held responsible for the safety of a vessel in any way. A good seaman is always prudent.

When this guide was begun it was with the intent of describing all anchorages from personal experience, only. Sadly, this has not been possible and a few anchorages are included that I have not visited, e.g. some Tuamotu atolls, Niue, Pitcairn and Easter Islands. In such cases the information presented has been compiled from descriptions by fellow yachtsmen. Every effort has been made to present correct and current information, but changes in facilities are the norm. To update the section on the Marquises, Margo Wood's most recent cruise was in the spring of 1999 when all the islands were visited. As a result of communication with various cruisers passing through the area and John Neal, who spends much of the year in Polynesian waters, the addenda is regularly up-dated with current information.

PLANNING and PREPARATION

A South Pacific cruise is an offshore voyage that will last several months. The area is tropical, and inhabited by a warm and friendly people. It is, however, expensive, and much of the region is remote and isolated. Though connected by air and sea to the rest of the world to a far greater extent than previously, there are many deficiencies in the availability of supplies and facilities for repair and replacement of modern yacht equipment. In the regions covered by this guide only Honolulu, Papeete and Raiatea have reasonable facilities. Yachtsmen can find services further away in Whangarei and Auckland in New Zealand, Suva in Fiji, and Pago Pago.

Vessels bound for this region must be a well found and seaworthy. Your vessel will not only be your home but it will also be your primary means of survival and comfort. Sails and engine should be in good condition, as they are your method of transportation. Anchors and rodes are essential to the safety of the yacht. Most tropical anchorages are in fairly deep water, and since chain is the best to use in coral waters an anchor winch is essential. The vessel should be well ventilated, having opening ports and a wind scoop. A cockpit canopy or tarpaulin that can be rigged to provide shade is necessary.

Since credit cards are useful only in cities, carry enough traveler's checks (in small denominations) to cover the first major stage of the voyage. Limited cash should be taken, but it is useful to have some in US currency, for small payments and emergencies. Bank drafts and evidence of funds for transfer are the best way to handle the special demands for financial responsibility of some countries and for renewing funds for the next stage of the cruiser's itinerary.

Replenishing major food supplies is only possible in Hilo, Honolulu, and Papeete, though small quantities can be obtained in most villages. Supplies in small atolls are expensive and limited; you may be doing a disservice to local inhabitants by purchasing them in quantity. Coconuts, fresh fruits, and produce are available in season.

Water can be obtained in most locations, though amounts available and degree of purity will vary. All water taken aboard should he filtered and treated to ensure purity. Replenishment is best done at ports in the Hawaiian Islands or French Polynesia. Most atolls and small islands collect rain water for consumption; occasionally it is drawn from a well.

Fuel availability follows a similar pattern. Since supplies of diesel or gasoline at small centers cater primarily to local needs, there may be little left over for visitors. Major towns are the best places for refueling and it is recommended that you carry extra supplies.

Pilot Charts of the North and South Pacific are particularly helpful in planning the voyage. They provide information regarding weather, currents, storm patterns and other factors crucial to the area covered by the cruise.

Introduction

ROUTES and PASSAGE TIMES

The popular routes to the South Pacific are shown on the accompanying chart. From North America, the choices are either to go directly to the Marquises, or to proceed there from Hawaii or Mexico. Every year numerous vessels arrive from each direction. The choices are shown as (1A), (1B), and (1), (2), or ((3).

From Europe or South America the passage via the Panama Canal, or directly from South American ports, is illustrated as (4). Few travelers today follow the oldest sailing route around the Horn and then head for the Society Islands. The later explorers from Europe and the barques of the last century rounded the Cape of Good Hope, made their easting in the Roaring Forties and climbed up to the South Pacific Islands when once at their longitude.

From New Zealand, the passage is either directly to Papeete, or via Rarotonga in the Cook Islands, then to Papeete. Most modern vessels can make the windward passage adequately. The older route, sometimes still followed, makes the maximum easing south of, or around latitude 40°S to about 155°W before hauling northward into the trades and then going directly to Tahiti.

Passage times are merely guides based on averaging the past history of many different vessels traveling similar routes. There are many factors that can alter the traveling time, therefore, times are given only as an aid to planning the voyage. The following table lists an average time for a typical 35' to 40' sailing vessel. Skippers should allow for at least half again as much time in planning to provide for unforeseen delays and emergencies.

Route	Port of Departure	Destination	Distance in Nautical Miles	Average No. of Days
1A	Seattle/Vancouver	Hilo, Hawaii	2,400	27
1A	San Francisco	Hilo, Hawaii	2,050	22
1B	Los Angeles or San Diego	Hilo, Hawaii	2,200	23
1	Hilo, Hawaii	Iles Marquises	2,100	21
	Iles Marquises	Tahiti	750	7
2	Los Angeles or San Diego	Iles Marquises	2,850	28
	Seattle/Vancouver	Iles Marquises	3,650	38
3	Acapulco	Iles Marquises	2,900	27
3A	Acapulco	Tahiti (via Gambier) I	3,700	38
4	Panama Canal	Iles Marquises	3,850	40
5	Auckland	Tahiti	2,200	22
	Tahiti	Hilo, Hawaii	2,350	22
	Hilo, Hawaii	San Francisco	2,050	24
	Hilo, Hawaii	Seattle/Vancouver	2,400	27

*Approximate Great Circle distance not necessarily the actual distance via the route a yacht may follow to avoid the Pacific High Pressure areas

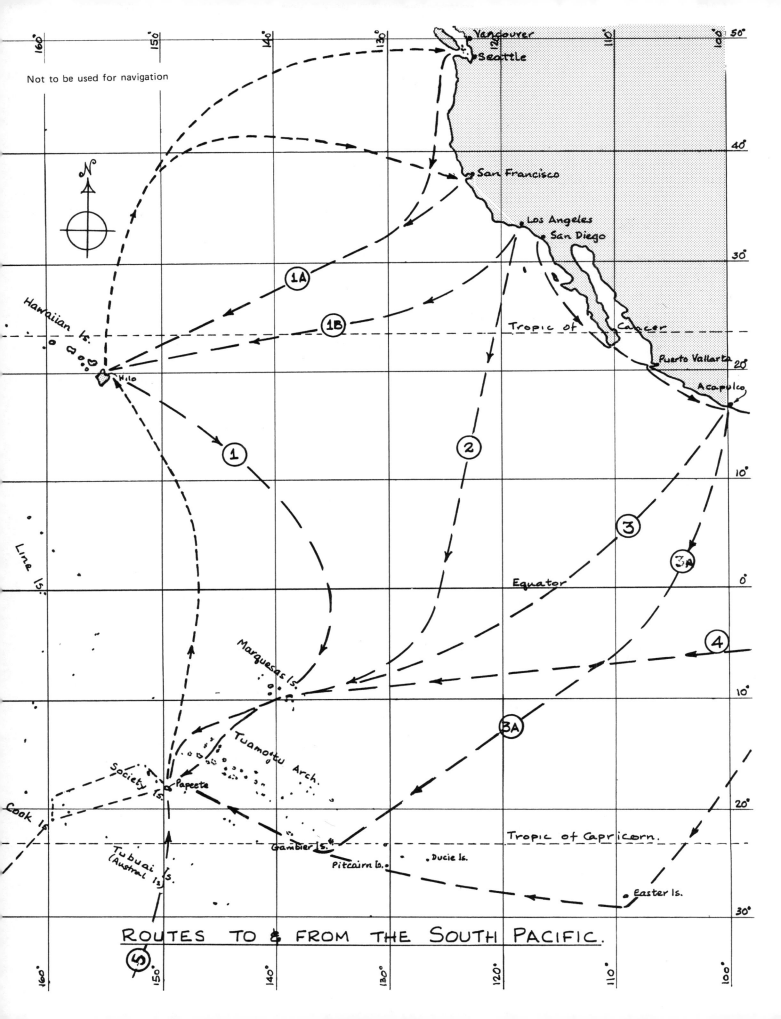

ROUTES TO & FROM THE SOUTH PACIFIC.

WINDS, WAVES and WEATHER

The main island groups of this guide are within the tropical zone, between the Tropics of Cancer and Capricorn. In this region, the trade winds predominate throughout most of the year, being mainly northeasterly to easterly in the Northern Hemisphere, and southeasterly to easterly in the Southern Hemisphere.

Generally speaking, north of the equator the NE Trades extend above 30°N at all times of the year within the area covered by this guide. They blow stronger during the northern winter, i.e. November to February. South of the equator the SE Trades normally extend at least to 20°S, but in the southern summer, i.e. December to February they may still be dominant as far south as 25°S. The strongest trade winds are experienced from June to September, the southern winter months.

There is an Inter-Tropical Convergence Zone where the two trade winds converge. This area is marked by extensive clouds and rain squalls with features similar to the doldrums.

The most significant weather factor in these areas (excluding major storms), is the location of the two dominating high pressure areas—the North Pacific High and the South Pacific High, and the intervening tropical low pressure area. The positions of these highs and lows shift in seasonal fluctuation with the sun. Their importance to most sailors arises from the need to avoid the actual high pressure area and find comfortable sailing weather by staying within isobars that offer good winds for passage making. There is an annual, somewhat predictable pattern of movement of the highs, and they are reasonably stable in average seasonal positions. But, there can be considerable actual daily variation in their positions that can be slightly confusing to the skipper trying to plot them from radio weather data in order to determine the vessel's best course.

Within the band of 20° on either side of the equator there is only a very small diurnal variation in pressure, and this is a twice daily 1.5 mb. above and below the monthly average. This is helpful, because any major change in this pattern, i.e. one exceeding 3 mb. from the monthly average, can be taken as a warning of an oncoming tropical depression or major weather change.

The overall, fairly stable weather patterns of this tropical area can be affected by tropical depressions. Among the smaller, slower moving disturbances in the pressure field are easterly waves, i.e. a small drop followed by a small rise then back to normal with the position of this surge moving from east to west. In some cases these develop into closed isobaric systems that become tropical depressions, with winds to Force 7 (33 mph). This is warm tropical air for there are no hot or cold fronts such as those found at higher latitudes. If they intensify to include winds of Force 8 to 11 (34 to 64 mph) they are tropical storms, and when they reach Force 12 (over 64 mph) they are called hurricanes, typhoons, or cyclones (all terms for the same weather phenomenon).

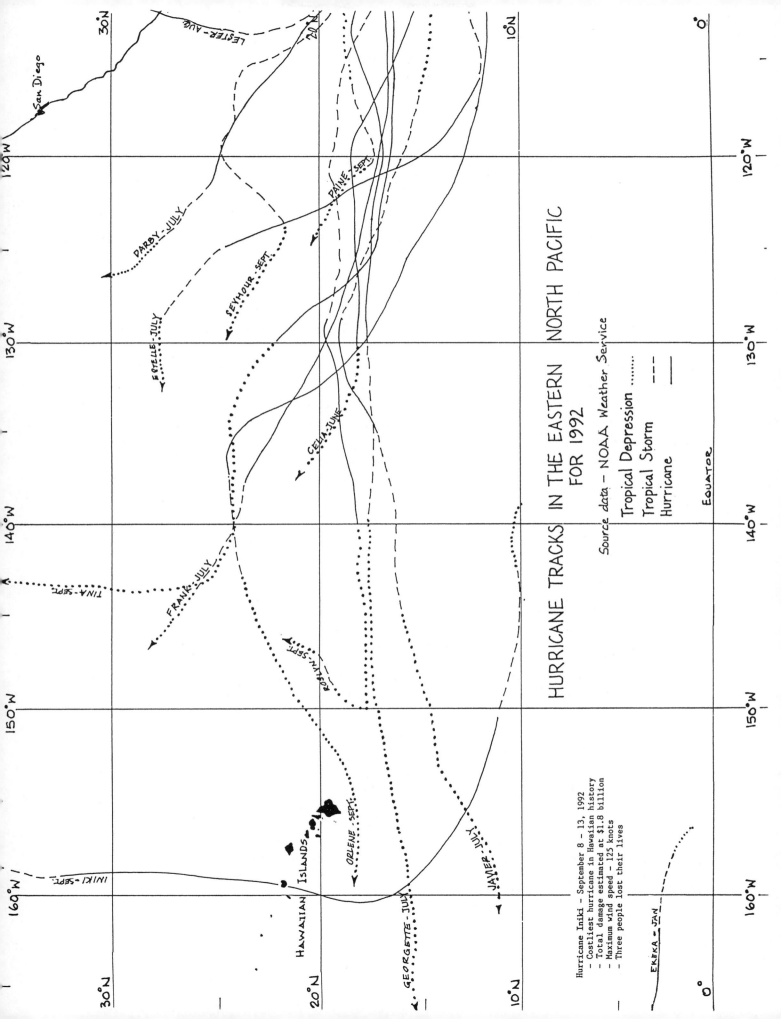

HURRICANE TRACKS IN THE EASTERN NORTH PACIFIC FOR 1992

Source data - NOAA Weather Service

Tropical Depression ⋯⋯
Tropical Storm – – –
Hurricane —————

Equator

Hurricane Iniki - September 8 - 13, 1992
- Costliest hurricane in Hawaiian history
- Total damage estimated at $1.8 billion
- Maximum wind speed - 125 knots
- Three people lost their lives

San Diego

Hawaiian Islands

LESTER-AUG.
DARBY-JULY
ESTELLE-JULY
SEYMOUR-SEPT.
PAINE-SEPT.
CELIA-JUNE
FRANK-JULY
TINA-SEPT.
ROSLYN-SEPT.
ORLENE-SEPT.
INIKI-SEPT.
GEORGETTE-JULY
JAVIER-JULY
EKEKA-JAN.

0°   10°N   20°N   30°N

120°W   130°W   140°W   150°W   160°W   0°

HURRICANES and CYCLONES

Major hurricane areas of the Pacific are:

1. On the eastern side of the North Pacific concentrated near the Mexican coast, generally curving northwesterly east of 140 W. A few penetrate further west.

2. On the western side of the North Pacific, generally well to the west of 180° and thus these "typhoons" are not included in this guide.

3. In the southwest corner of the South Pacific, they occur west of 180° and those that occur east of 165°W have been rare in the last 40 years. The following statement referring to Polynesia is excerpted from the Pacific Islands Pilot, Vol. II:

"Tropical storms are not frequent in this part of the Pacific, and hurricanes even less so. Parts of this area, however, are notable deficient in observations so that it is quite possible that storms have occurred that have not been reported. Tropical storms are not expected within about 40° of the equator. Moreover, they are not known to have occurred in the southern hemisphere east of longitude 135°W. Otherwise there is no part of this region where there is not some liability for such storms, even though over most of this region they are very rare."

A glance at most charts showing tracks of tropical cyclones and hurricanes supports the above view, and this benign situation has been an attractive feature for cruisers to this area. However, there has been a change in the overall weather pattern of these storms in recent years that might indicate some change in the expected pattern of weather, and it is best to be prepared.

During the last decade, several hurricanes originating near Mexico have traveled westward beyond 140°W. Several have reached Hawaiian waters where they were once rare occurrences.

An even more startling change has been seen in the South Pacific where, as the quotation above shows, cyclones were even rarer. A number have occurred in the last few years, some originating and passing east of 135°W. Tracks of these storms are shown on pages 7 and 9.

The cause of this change, which is related to the major climatological events occurring recently in many parts of the world, may be the weather phenomenon called "El Nino." This is a vast oscillation of air and water currents across the Pacific, known to have occurred about 10 times in the last 40 years. They are caused by a reduction in the drive of the currents westward, allowing a warming of the water in the eastern Pacific. One theory of meteorologists is that the cloud of dust released by large volcanic eruptions could weaken the heat received from the sun, slowing the trade winds and their associated currents sufficiently to trigger an "El Nino."

As a result of the erratic weather caused by El Nino and La Nina it was decided to illustrate the hurricane and cyclone tracks from years prior to this period so the frequency and direction of such storms could be seen during normal years. Prudent sailors must be prepared to face severe and unpredicted storms which can occur at any time, but particularly during El Nino and La Nina periods.

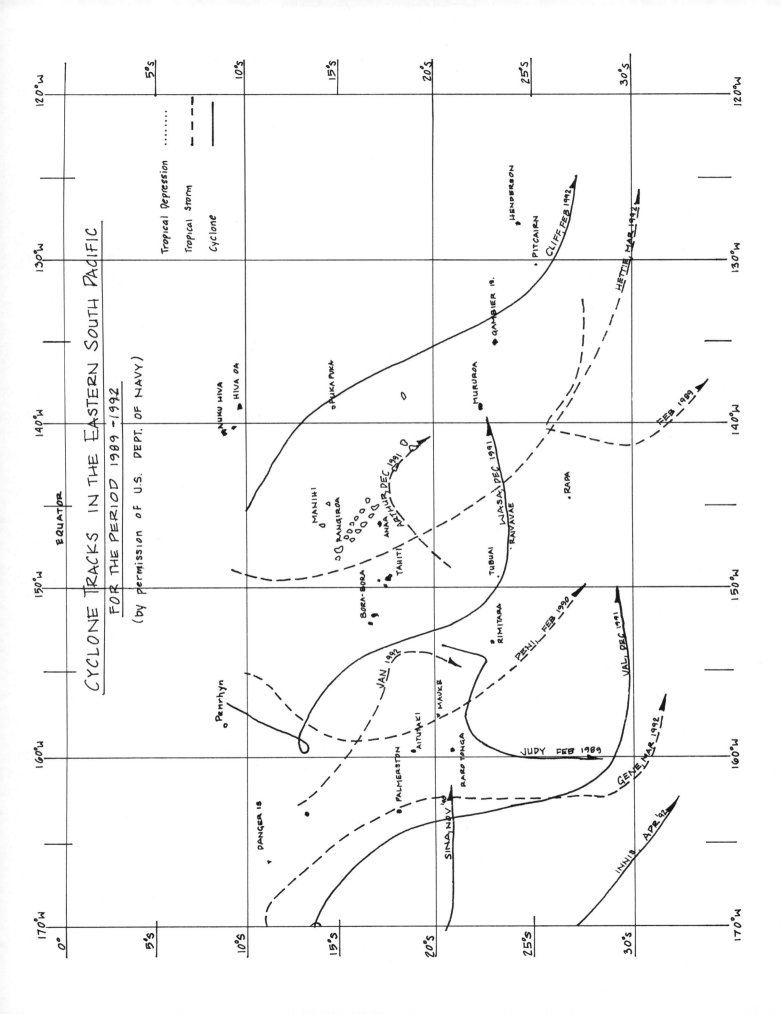

CYCLONE TRACKS IN THE EASTERN SOUTH PACIFIC

FOR THE PERIOD 1989 - 1992

(by permission of U.S. DEPT. OF NAVY)

Tropical Depression ·········
Tropical Storm − − −
Cyclone ——————

CURRENTS

The influence of the trade winds causes the oceanic currents in these tropical regions to flow westward across the Pacific forming the North and South Equatorial Currents. They are not equally spaced along the equator. The South Equatorial Current extends a few degrees north of the equator and between it and the North Equatorial Current is a region of the east-flowing Equatorial Counter-Current.

The limits of the counter current can be fairly firmly fixed at times, the southern edge being about 4° N Latitude all year, while the northern edge varies between 8° N and 10° N. However, the boundaries of the main equatorial currents are less defined and they tend to decline into variable currents as the latitude increases.

The North Equatorial Current moves at a fairly uniform rate of about 1 knot. The counter-current is also fairly steady at around 2 knots, but cannot always be assumed as running constantly easterly. The South Equatorial Current is less predictable. Rates of 1 knot are frequently exceeded and 2 to 3 knots have been noted. East of 136°W longitude some rates have exceeded 3 knots.

The general set of a current can be disturbed by an island group, often by being deflected and accelerated in its vicinity. In the Tuamotu, in particular, the currents can be irregular and the greatest caution and care should be exercised in approaching and passing through the area. Navigators in these waters should allow for a 1- to 2-knot current. The more open oceanic areas near the Society Islands and the Cook Islands have a steady westerly set and a rate of about 1 knot.

The major swell in this area is SW'ly, driven by the great winds and seas of the Roaring Forties. When this swell is heavy and it meets the strong outgoing currents from the atoll passes, it usually culminates in steep, heavy rips and tidal races at the entrances to coral reef lagoons.

NAVIGATION IN CORAL WATERS

Approaches

In the Tuamotu the sides of the reefs tend to be submerged or awash. They also constitute a lee shore because of the swell set in motion by the powerful storms of the Southern Ocean which crashes heavily on the reefs. It is a good idea to approach these atolls to a point 25 to 30 miles north of the destination, provided no other atoll or restriction is in the way. The ideal approach is to arrive at dawn to allow for a multi-body celestial fix to determine a fairly accurate position and, more importantly, to allow a daylight approach to the destination. A vessel can heave-to, drift, or use shortened sail to control position well off the destination and await dawn rather than press on. This procedure should be followed whether passing through atolls or approaching an anchorage when using celestial or GPS navigation.

Navigation in these waters requires special care because the Tuamotu are very low; the height of a coconut palm on an atoll will rarely exceed 15m (50'). From the deck of a yacht this means your horizon is not more than 3 miles away and for even the tops of the palms to be visible you may be as close as 7 or 8 miles. The high volcanic islands are visible much further away; a normal assumption for visibility is 20 to 25 miles, but in good conditions Tahiti can he seen 60 miles away and Hawaii, 100 miles. However, atmospheric and weather effects can drastically reduce visibility. Clouds and mist regularly obscure Tahiti's peaks, and it is astounding that you can sometimes be only 20 to 30 miles from the 4,560m (13,700') peak of Mauna Kea when it is hidden behind a light cloud and you seem to he sailing into an open ocean.

It is difficult to identify atolls because the palm-capped motus are similar in appearance. A combination of confidence in one's navigation and knowledge of the position of the atoll's perimeter or a glimpse of a village or other unique feature add up to a tentative identification. Sometimes long-lasting wrecks offer confirmation. It is often difficult to identify a pass into a lagoon and not all gaps between motus are navigable. An atoll must be positively identified before you can determine the location of a pass.

Running the Passes

The best time for entry through deep channels, assuming calm weather, is at slack low water. At this time reefs and shoals awash are readily seen and the channel is generally clearly defined. Furthermore, if you should go aground a rising tide will float the vessel free, although tidal variation is low.

Entry should not be attempted when a strong current is opposing the vessel's direction of travel, especially with an under-powered auxiliary motor with a low maximum hull speed. Strong currents are evident by breaking seas and rips which occur outside the entrance to a pass. Before entering a pass it is best to wait for slack water, or the beginning of the change to flood (as indicated by calmer sea conditions).

Once past the entrance to the pass, the turbulence diminishes and conditions improve for vessel and crew alike. It is necessary to maintain speed for control, especially when going with the tide and this results in rapid progress over the bottom. Since errors in judgment can result in damage it is better to err on the side of caution. Have the anchor ready with plenty of chain or cable free, to allow a quick drop in an emergency.

Estimating Slack Water

Tidal effects are small in the Tuamotu. The tides are predominantly diurnal and an amphidromic point (note where tides are almost negligible) is assumed in tidal calculations to be near Tahiti where spring tides are only about 12cm (8"). In some waters covered by this guide tidal currents can reach as much as 8 knots and when combined with an opposing wind dangerous seas can be created.

Introduction

It is essential to use a current edition of NOAA Tide Tables for Central and Western Pacific Ocean or the equivalent British or French publication. A formula, available from the Sailing Directions (Planning Guide), South Pacific Ocean (Appendix Atlas, p. 179) suggests that the minimum current is most likely to occur one hour after low tide and one hour after high tide as specified in the Tide Tables.

The estimated time of slack water could be altered by heavy southerly swells or strong prevailing winds, which by increasing the flow of water over the reef can alter the incoming and outgoing streams, even to the extent of sometimes maintaining a continuous outflowing stream for a considerable period of time.

Navigating by Eye

Once within the reef areas, the best piloting is accomplished by eye. The higher the position of the lookout the better, and the sun should be behind the observer or overhead (not in front). The best times are from about 2.5 hours after sunrise to 1 hour before local noon when going in a westerly direction, and the reverse (1 hour after noon to 2.5 hours before sunset) when going in an easterly direction. The quadrant of visibility is altered by the northerly or southerly position of the sun in relation to the observer.

The best position for conning on most vessels is at the first spreader. Since the lookout may spend some time looking ahead, gear should be arranged so that it is easy to get aloft and stay for some time. Ratlines on the lower shrouds enable a member of the crew to climb to a perch on a spreader, or for short passages to go up several feet. Ratlines may consist of rope lashed by seizing to the shrouds, or they can be oak strips clamped to the shrouds. Rope ratlines are easy to make, climb, and have less windage, but they are tiring to stand on for long periods as they sag and cut into the feet. A convenient perch made of oak can be placed part way up the shrouds.

Considerable glare is reflected off the ocean. Sunglasses prevent eyestrain and fatigue, and make it easier to see underwater obstacles. Polaroid sunglasses assist in making bottom features appear more defined. The choice of tints should help reduce ultraviolet and infrared rays, but should not alter color perception.

A hat or visor also help to block out unwanted glare and make conning easier. In tropical waters the heat of the sun on the head can be intense. Hats and visors should be well fitted to stay on in any breeze and be tied on. Binoculars should have safety straps and clipboards for maps or diagrams should he secured with a line and snap hook.

A flat, glassy calm is unsatisfactory for good conning since it is difficult to penetrate the surface glare; a slight ripple makes viewing easier. Perception continues to be good even with some wave action, unless there are whitecaps or the surface is quite disturbed. Deep water is seen as a deep blue (in some parts of the world, as a dark green). As the water becomes shallow, the blue lightens; light blue water normally indicates a water depth that is safe for most vessels. As the water appears whiter depths are decreasing to below 1 fathom. Pale white indicates very shallow water over white coral sand and is about .3m (1') deep.

Brown or purple patches mark coral heads. Reefs may be yellow or yellowish-brown. These colors signal danger and should be avoided, though it is often difficult to judge the true depth over coral heads. If a passage exists it is safer to thread a path following the clearer water.

The type of bottom and the amount of cloud overhead can affect conning. White sand bottom is the best for viewing. Black volcanic sand or olive green lava sand or rock can greatly reduce the amount of light reflected and reduce visibility. Clouds also cause similar effects as they cast shadows, so that when looking ahead to identify a reef, a cloud's shadow can be misleading. Shadows from clouds can darken the apparent water color and alter depth perception. The light becomes flat and colors weaken, sometimes to the extent that all ability to navigate by eye is lost.

Coral barrier reefs and atoll reef perimeters tend to be sharp in edge and outline, so that sometimes there may be deep water fairly close to them. On the other hand, uneven bottoms with many large spherical coral growths reaching toward the surface, occur within some lagoons and reef zones forming the most dangerous type of contours through which to find a passage. But many sailing vessels, often without power, have passed through coral waters without instrumentation other than the eyes of crew and a lead line.

MARKERS and BUOYS

Buoyage systems are not standardized around the world, so sailors must face the need to keep alert for changes when traveling. The United States uses a Modified Lateral System based on an International Conference of 1889. One might characterize this as "red right returning." Some European countries, including France (thus French Polynesia), use a Uniform Lateral System, recommended by a 1936 League of Nations committee, which can be characterized as "red left returning." There are other differences in shapes of buoys, topmarks, etc., but the difference in color of the buoys is of immediate significance to a mariner entering a harbor. The following synopsis notes the major points of each system. The skipper must review the system being used when entering a new area. The Uniform System includes some of the special features used in French Polynesia.

UNIFORM LATERAL SYSTEM

This system is used in French Polynesia, with some special features. The buoys are referred to and marked in reference to a vessel returning from seaward. See Appendix I.

Buoys marking the starboard side of a channel are conical and colored black or black and white checks. They may be numbered in odd numbers commencing from seaward, but this is often missing in Polynesia. Lights on them, if any, are white or green. They may have topmarks associated with them, generally conical (triangular), black, or diamond-shaped, on a black and white banded post. Diamond shapes are not used at the entrance to the pass or channel. Within a lagoon, these topmarks continue their significance and may be in combination. Some special topmarks are also used.

Buoys marking the port side of a channel are can-shaped and colored red, or red and white checks. They may be numbered with even numbers, commencing from seaward, and may often be unmarked in Polynesia. The light on them, if any, is red or white. Topmarks are can (square) or T-shaped, in red and mounted on red and white banded posts. T-shapes are not used at the entrance to a pass or channel. These shapes continue their significance within a lagoon, and may occur in combination, and some special topmarks are also used.

Middle ground marks are spherical buoys, or a circle when used as a combination topmark. The buoys are painted red and white horizontal bands, and the circles are red, if the channel is to the right, or if either channel is of equal importance. Topmarks allow differentiation: T or square for a preferred right channel, cross or circle if either channel is equal. When the main channel is to the left the spherical buoy is painted with black and white horizontal stripes, and topmarks are cone, diamond or circle, all black.

Mid-channel buoys or fairway marks vary in shape other than spherical, can, or conical, with vertical red and white or black and white stripes.

Wrecks are marked by green buoys, with green lights, whose shapes designate the channel. Can buoys are to be passed on the port hand; spherical buoys are to be passed on either hand, and conical are passed on the starboard hand.

Special Topmarks for French Polynesia

The standard can, T-shaped, vertical up-cone and diamond shapes are used at reefs as they would be for normal seaward approaches. In addition, once within the lagoon, the landward sides are marked by a red hemisphere (with the flat diameter downward) placed on a yellow and red barred spar; the reef side by a downward pointing cone (triangle), also on a yellow and red barred post. However, in many places in French Polynesia, these special marks or beacons, and the regular ones, are sometimes worn or appear unpainted and the colors indistinguishable. The shape of the topmark—if still in place—can be identified. **<u>Warning</u>: Beacons and markers mentioned in this guide and other sources are sometimes missing.**

Ranges and Entrance Beacons

A few of the major ports in this area have lighted ranges or colored sector beacons to indicate the correct approach through the pass. In Papeete, a pair of well-lit ranges mark the route through the pass and toward the quays. The green occulting (3) lights on red and white banded pylons have a white topmark for daylight use. The sides of the pass are marked by lit buoys.

Colored sector beacons mark the entry to Moorea, Fare (Huahine), Bora-Bora, Baie Taiohae (Nuku Hiva) and Autona (Hiva Oa). The bearings of each harbor light differ but they are arranged so that green is on the right of the correct white sector and red is on the left.

UNITED STATES SYSTEM OF BUOYAGE

Buoys are marked according to the side of a channel taken in reference to a vessel returning from seaward. Where channels may not be clear as to a seaward direction, there are certain arbitrary assumptions as to which is the correct orientation. This is taken in a clockwise sense, for vessels in channels proceeding south along the Atlantic coast, and north along the Pacific coast.

Buoys marking the starboard side of a channel, and buoys on wrecks or obstructions that must be left to starboard, are red and conical in shape with even numbers. The light may be white or red and have varied characteristics. Quick flashes indicate caution is needed.

Buoys marking the port side of a channel, or on wrecks or obstructions that must be left to port, are black, can-shaped with odd numbers. Lights on them are white or green and have varied characteristics. Quick flashes indicate particular caution is needed.

Buoys marking the center of a channel are painted in vertical black and white stripes and have variable shapes. They may be marked by letters, and if lit, will have a white light. They should be passed close-to.

Buoys marking a mid-channel obstruction, which has a channel to define on either side, are painted in red and black horizontal bands. A can buoy indicates the preferred channel is to starboard of the buoy, while a cone buoy indicates the preferred channel is to port (as seen from seaward).

Large buoys used for any purpose may not conform exactly as to shape but agree as to the color and markings. Special buoys are as follows:

White buoys mark anchorage areas
Yellow buoys mark quarantine areas
White buoys with green tops mark dredging or survey areas

PLACE NAMES

The spelling of place names used in different references varies considerably. An attempt has been made to use the spelling practiced in each area described while at the same time providing spelling used on nautical charts and other references. The use of the local name provides the reader with the words used within the country being visited so that communication with residents will be facilitated. For example, the French word "baie," meaning "bay" is used in French-speaking areas while the word "bay" is used in English-speaking countries.

Following the same pattern, the name "Iles Marquises" is used herein rather than the label "Marquesas Islands" normally found in many English references.

REFERENCES AND CHART LISTS

Books

The following books provide additional information about French Polynesia:

Chester, Sharon, Baumgartner, Heidy, Frechoso, Diana, Oetzel, James: *Mave Mai The Marquesas Islands* (1998)
Davock, Marcia. Cruising Guide to Tahiti and the French Society Islands
Fast, Arlow W. and Seberg, George (Editors) *Cruising Guide for the Hawaiian Islands*
Hinz, Earl. Landfalls of Paradise
House, Sheridan. Pacific Crossing Guide
McDavitt, Bob. Metservice Yacht Pack
Moorings Cruising Guide to the Leeward Islands in French Polynesia

Ottino, Pierre and de Bergh-Ottino, Marie-Noelle. *Hiva Oa, Glimpses of an Oceanic Memory*

Wheeler, Tony and Carillet, Jean-Bernard. *Tahiti & French Polynesia*

Wood, Charles E. Charlie's Charts of the Hawaiian Islands

These books have a wealth of information about offshore cruising:
Hiscock, Eric C.: *Cruising Under Sail*
Pardey, Lin and Larry: The Care and Feeding of the Offshore Crew
Worldwide Marine Radio Facsimile Broadcast Schedule, Published by Cortex

Charts and Official Publications

Since World War II, hydrographic departments have made continued efforts to chart the world. South Pacific sailors owe special thanks to the French Naval Schooner "*Zelee*" which made lengthy trips surveying the dangerous waters of the Tuamotu and was a familiar sight in Tahiti.

The selection of charts is an individual one and with many choices, cruisers should consider the advice of a chart dealer carefully. The following assessment is a personal one:

U. S. DMA (Defense Mapping Agency) charts and publications are good, and marked in familiar terms to North American sailors who are gradually learning metric measurements. They vary considerably in size and are printed on thin paper stock. Charts for US waters, which include Hawaii, are produced by NOAA (National Oceanic and Atmosphere Administration) and thus are numbered differently. Both are available from marine supply stores carrying charts.

British Admiralty charts and publications have advantages for waters outside the US. They are uniform in size and printed on heavy paper stock.

French charts are the most detailed for French Polynesian waters. Although some have been recently updated, there are many miles of coastline of the Marquises that have not been hydrographically surveyed. They use metric measurements and tend to be a little less expensive than British Admiralty charts.

Debris Harms Our Marine Life

Rex Herron

Brian Lawhead

Endangered species also suffer. Sea turtles mistake plastic bags for jellyfish.

Some 30,000 Northern Fur seals die yearly from entanglement in netting, a 50% population decline in 30 years has been noted.

Common items like six-pack rings, fishing line and strapping bands entangle and kill sea birds, fish and mammals. Plastics can last many hundreds of years, harming even large mammals like the gray whale.

Fishermen and boater safety is jeopardized when debris fouls propellers or causes engines to overheat. Heavy losses of time and money are reported from debris damage to vessels and equipment.

Jim Boeder

Pierce Harris

. . . AND THE ANIMALS ARE SUFFERING.

NASA

OUR BLUE OCEAN
IS BECOMING
PINK, YELLOW,
WHITE AND GREEN . . .

Dale Snow

Frans Lanting

Birds, fish and mammals mistake plastic for food. Some birds even feed it to their young!

With plastic filling stomachs, animals may die of starvation or poisoning.

George Antonelis

Plastics can last for hundreds of years in the ocean. A careless moment lasts generations.

Jim Boeder

You can help!
- Make it boat policy that no trash is discarded, washed or blown overboard.
- Minimize the amount of non-degradable products on board. Provision your vessel using bulk / refillable containers.
- Stow trash for disposal in port. Encourage your port to provide convenient refuse disposal facilities.
- Where possible retrieve trash encountered in the ocean.
- Share your concern with friends, fellow mariners and family.
- Participate in beach clean-ups, and leave the beach clean after visits.

DON'T TEACH YOUR TRASH TO SWIM!
WGM

THE PORT OF NEWPORT & FISHING FLEET
ENCOURAGE ALL BOATERS AND BEACH-GOERS
TO PROTECT THE MARINE ENVIRONMENT.

This material has been reprinted (by permission) from a brochure published by the National Marine Fisheries Service, Marine Refuse Disposal Project, Newport, Oregon.

CHARTS and SAILING DIRECTIONS

Pacific Ocean
  *BA 2683 (Coverage of a large area, good for planning)
Iles Marquises (Marquesas Islands)
  DMA 83207 Nuku Hiva
  DMA 83218 Hiva Oa, Tahuata, and Motane
  *BA 1640   Plans in the Iles Marquises
  French Charts 7352, 7353, 7354 and 7355 (excellent coverage of Iles Marquises)
Archipel des Tuamotu (Tuamotu Archipelago)
  DMA 83022   Ile Makemo to Ile Tatakoto (OMEGA)
  DMA 83023   Tahiti to Rangiroa and Makemo (OMEGA)
  DMA 83251   Archipel Des Tuamotu Iles Gambier
Iles de la Societe (Society Islands)
  DMA 83021   Manuae to Tahiti (OMEGA)
  DMA 83382   Approaches to Tahiti & Moorea
  DMA 83383   Moorea
  DMA 83385   Port of Papeete
  DMA 83392   Ile de la Societe - Iles Sous Le Vent Plans of Manuae, Maupihaa, & Mote One
  DMA 83397   Bora-Bora
  French chart 6002 Bora-Bora (recomended for travel within the lagoon)
Cook Islands
  DMA 83425   Islands and Anchorages in the Cook Islands
  *BA 979   Other Cook Is. Anchorages: Rakahanga, Manihiki, Danger Is.
  *BA 1174   Suwarrow Island
  *BA 997   Tongareva or Penrhyn Island
Hawaiian Islands
  NOAA 19320 Island of Hawaii
  NOAA 19324 Hilo Bay
  NOAA 19348 Island of Maui, Approaches to Lahaina
  NOAA 19347 Channels between Molokai, Maui, Lanai, and Kahoolawe
  NOAA 19381 Kaui
  NOAA 19383 Nawiliwili Bay
Sailing Directions
  SD 126 Pacific Islands (Enroute), Fifth Edition - 1996
* British Admiralty Charts
Tide Tables - Central and Western Pacific Ocean
North American cruisers may order French and British Admiralty charts from the following:

Bluewater Books and Charts	Captain's Nautical Supplies
1481 S.E. 17th Street	2500 - 15th Avenue West
Fort Lauderdale, FL 33316	Seattle, WA 98119
Tel (954) 763-6533	Tel 1-800-448-2278

Sailors transiting the Panama Canal may obtain British, US, Australian and New Zealand charts from Islamorada Internacional S.A., Balboa, Republic of Panama Tel (507) 228-4348.

In Papeete, nautical charts are sold at Librairie Klima which is located near the Cathedral.

Introduction

FORMALITIES

Each country covered by this guide has its own entry requirements, but there are some courtesies common to all.

Basic Entry Procedures

While visiting a country, yachts should fly a courtesy flag of the country at the starboard spreader. At the same time, a vessel should fly its own national ensign at the stern. Flag etiquette requires that the national ensign be hoisted at sunrise and lowered at sunset.

On first entry into a country, the yellow quarantine or "Q" flag should be hoisted under the courtesy ensign of the country being visited. This should be done whether the officials board a vessel for clearance, or the skipper goes ashore to inform them of the vessel's arrival. As soon as a vessel is cleared the Q flag can be taken down and need not be hoisted again while in that country.

Officials from Customs, Immigration, Health, Agriculture, Police and the Harbormaster or Port Authority may be involved in the vessel's clearance. In almost all countries an attempt is made to streamline the procedure. The crew and the vessel must be cleared first for health, then by Customs, Immigration, and Agriculture before any person other than the Captain can go ashore for any reason whatsoever. Detailed information is given on the following pages by country.

The documents that must be aboard include:

For the Vessel	For Each Person
Boat Registration or Documentation	Individual valid passports
Crew List	Visas or Tourist Permits (as required)
Outward bound clearance from the last port	Onward airline tickets or funds to cover such bonds as are required
De-ratization certificate (in certain areas)	

All firearms should be declared, and may be sealed and impounded by the authorities during the period of stay. The Customs inspector has the right to search the vessel to determine if it carries arms, contraband, or other prohibited items.

Anchor or moor in areas designated for entry purposes. The skipper should report the vessel's arrival by radio or shore telephone to the Harbormaster or controlling port authority (who may be the local gendarme). He will tell you how to get in touch with the other authorities in correct order or he may do this for you. To avoid overtime charges, entry should be made during normal working hours, Monday to Saturday.

Note:
1. The time zone in the Iles Marquises is one-half hour earlier than in the rest of French Polynesia, i.e. Z-9H30M.
2. Compass courses and bearings are given in True readings throughout the guide.

Departure Procedures

First, clear with the harbormaster and pay moorage bills. Secondly, clear with Immigration and retrieve passports; collect weapons from the Police (these are generally returned to you only within an hour of sailing), and lastly, clear with Customs and obtain the outward bound clearance (Zarpe) to be used for entry at the next country. If unable to depart within the hour, inform Customs and remain aboard. They may extend your period of stay; if the delay becomes excessive you may be required to re-enter.

SPECIAL REQUIREMENTS FOR DIFFERENT AREAS

French Polynesia

The entry system has been made flexible so that it suits down-wind travel routes for yachts. It is necessary to report to the local gendarme in any island group before cruising elsewhere. Although Papeete is the only true Port of Entry for French Polynesia, informal entry can be made by reporting to the local gendarme at the following subsidiary Ports of Entry:

Iles Marquises - Baie de Taiohae in Nuku Hiva, Atuona in Hiva Oa and Hakahau in Ua Pou

The Tuamotu / Gambier- Tiputa in Rangiroa and Rikitea in Mangareva

Society Islands - Uturoa in Raiatea, Fare in Huahine, Vaitape in Bora-Bora and Afareaitu in Moorea.

Iles Australes - Mataura in Tubuai, Moerai in Rurutu and Tairua in Raivavae

In contrast to previous years, the gendarme in Atuona, Hiva Oa does not object to vessels making a landfall in Fatu Hiva prior to landing in Atuona. The best sources of current information on changes in entry procedures, anchorages and weather conditions are the nets on SSB and HAM radio. SSB Radio nets include:

Russell Radio - Weather and daily check-in at	04:00 GMT on 12353
	04:30 GMT on 12359
Coconut Net - Weather and daily check-in at	19:30 GMT on 12365

All aboard a vessel must have a valid passport that will not expire during the term of your visit. Non-French citizens must also have an outbound air ticket or deposit a bond in a bank on arrival equal to the cost of air fare to the country of origin. Bonds can be returned at Papeete or at a bank in the island from which departure is taken. Banks charge a 1% administration fee. By notifying the bank ahead of time they will refund the bond in the currency that was deposited with them. Verify that there is a branch of the bank where the bond was deposited on the island from which departure is intended, usually Bora-Bora, the last port in the west.

Visitors Permits valid for 3 months are granted to citizens from EEC, Austria, Finland, Norway, Sweden and Switzerland. An extension for another 90 days can be applied for after 60 days by writing to Haut Commissariat/DRCL, Rue Jeanne D'Arc, BP 115, Papeete, Tahiti. Visitors Permits valid for 30 days are granted to citizens of Canada, USA, New Zealand, Japan, Singapore and some eastern European countries. A 3-month extension may be applied for by writing to the address given above. After receiving the 3-month extension you can apply for another 2-month extension, giving you a total of 6 months, equal to the time allowed cruisers from EEC.

The captain is responsible for the crew's bonds and completion of entry requirements. There isn't a standard form for a crew list but one should be prepared listing the date of arrival, last port of call, name of each person aboard and their position, date of birth, nationality and passport number. Prepare at least 4 copies of this information. All crew changes and boat moves from Papeete (further than Moorea) must be reported to the Maritime Office of Immigration /DICILEC.

Since March, 1999, boats have been allowed to stay in French Polynesia for 2 years without being subject to duty. The vessel can be put on the hard for 6 months during the cyclone season (November 1 - April 30), sailed for 6 months and hauled again. Favorable reports have been received by cruisers who stored their boats at Raiatea Carenage Services. Telephone (689) 66-2414. Their substantial cradles reduce but do not eliminate the risk of cycloone damage. Storage is also available in Papeete and monthly charges are vary from US$350 to $500 per month for a 10m (34') vessel.

When arriving in Papeete within 21 days of visiting Fiji, Tonga, Samoa, Cook Islands, and Central and South American Pacific areas, the yacht may be fumigated by the Port Authorities to prevent the introduction of the Rhinoceros beetle. It is best, therefore, to anchor out from the Quay on first arrival and clear all formalities before tying up at a moorage.

No special inoculations are required other than one for yellow fever if the vessel is arriving in Polynesia within 14 days of leaving, or transiting infected areas. It is advisable to have a polio booster, tetanus inoculation and a gamma gobulin inoculation for protection against hepatitis A. Filariosis (elephantiasis) and Dengue Fever are mosquito-borne diseases prevented by using mosquito repellent or covering up when ashore in mosquito plagued areas, securing all openings with fine mosquito netting and anchoring well offshore. There are several excellent hospitals in Papeete and some smaller medical centers in the outer islands.

Pets will be confined to the vessel for 6 months, counting from departure from your last port. Customs will advise you to contact the veterinarians at "Service de Developement Rural." If departing the country by air, you can take the pet but check with "Developement Rural" again and they will take the pet(s) to the airport and you will not be allowed to reimport them.

The Cook Islands

The official Ports of Entry are located on the islands of Rarotonga, Aitutaki, and Penrhyn. In Rarotonga all yachts must clear at Avatiu Harbor, flying the Q flag and remaining at anchor outside the small harbor. If the vessel is arriving from Tahiti, Fiji or areas considered infected by the rhinoceros beetle it will be searched and/or fumigated. Similar procedures are followed at Aitutaki.

Temporary visitor permits given after completing clearance allow a 14-day stay for the yacht and crew. Extensions for a longer stay have to be applied for at Rarotonga, and if granted, fees amounting to about $15NZ per passport are charged for the application. Evidence of financial ability may be requested in the assessment of this extension. Tourists arriving by air must have a valid return or on-going ticket and confirmed accommodations before arrival.

This is a healthy part of the world and no special inoculations are required. There is an excellent hospital in Rarotonga and smaller medical facilities are on some of the other islands. Firearms must be declared and will be impounded. The importation of firearms, cartridges and fireworks is expressly prohibited.

Yachts may be allowed to Med-moor to the concrete quay in the small basin harbor of Avatiu. The space for yachts is limited due to the small size of the harbor and the moorage required by inter-island vessels.

A small daily fee is charged for the use of the harbor, and it is collected by the Immigration officials when outward clearance is given. Showers, toilets and potable water are available dockside. Upon leaving the Cook Islands an exit fee of approximately US$20 per person is charged.

The Hawaiian Islands

All yachts, including US vessels, must enter the Hawaiian Islands at one of the following Ports of Entry: Hilo in Hawaii, Kahului in Maui, Honolulu in Oahu, or Nawiliwili in Kauai.

Procedures for entry and for leaving the Hawaiian Islands are essentially US standard procedures, but handled in a more detailed and consistent manner than on the mainland. It is important to comply with these formalities. Their purpose is to control illegal contraband that could enter the Islands.

Entry into United States occurs as soon as you have anchored or moored alongside and are in US waters. A vessel may not anchor at any place other than at a Port of Entry before completing official entry procedures. Considerable fines are imposed for violations. After entry, no person who is aboard can go ashore except for the skipper, or his representative, who reports the vessel's arrival to the Customs office. The skipper must return to the vessel immediately after reporting.

Customs will inform the other departments - Immigration, Agriculture, and Health and they will arrive to board the yacht. Generally the Customs officers handle immigration and health requirements at the same time. In Hawaii the forms and papers are the same for small and large vessels and those used on the US mainland. For US citizens the immigration procedure is simple and brief. All other persons are considered aliens and must have valid passports, with visas, where applicable. Complete requirements for entry into the US can be obtained from the nearest US Consulate, and visas obtained for citizens of those countries where the need applies. It is important for the skipper to realize that he is responsible for any alien crew member and he must ascertain that they have proper papers for entry or the skipper could be charged with aiding an illegal entry.

Agriculture is concerned with meats, citrus fruits and vegetables being imported. Most yachts have few problems in this regard since most boaters use all their fresh provisions enroute. There is a strictly enforced quarantine for pets. They are put into quarantine at the Animal Quarantine Center in Honolulu for 120 days. Shipping costs and daily charges must be paid in advance by the pet's owner. Pet owners who leave Hawaii before the 120-day period has elapsed may apply for a refund of the unused balance.

Introduction

The United States has reciprocal agreements regarding permission to cruise in territorial waters, provided that normal entry procedures have been followed. The countries include: Argentina, Australia, the Bahamas, Canada, New Zealand and West Germany. Cruisers on vessels from these countries are issued a cruising permit, valid for 6 months, which allows the yacht to travel in specific waters. The skipper must notify Customs by telephone when arriving at major ports. Vessels from other countries may not cruise in local waters but must make a formal entry and clearance only from designated Ports of Entry.

Firearms must be declared and registered in Hawaii even though they may be licensed in your own country or state. Permits for firearms are issued by the police.

To protect against unwarranted Customs duties, keep photocopies of receipts for items aboard the vessel such as cameras, navigational instruments and equipment so that proof of the country of purchase is readily available. If this is not done, you may be liable for a customs assessment on any item not clearly identified, and a duty may be charged prior to recovering it by application to the Customs Department.

When leaving the Hawaiian Islands, whether continuing to the US mainland or proceeding elsewhere, all vessels must clear with US Customs and obtain an "Outward Bound Manifest." It is important not to neglect this procedure, as failure to do so may cause the vessel to be subject to seizure when it arrives at the next port without having been properly cleared.

Pitcairn Island

There are no entry formalities for Pitcairn Island and all visitors are welcome. No health restrictions exist, but as the people are isolated, it is unwise for any yacht with an illness aboard or which has had recent contact with a major disease, to land and spread their germs.

Radio communication is possible with the island to inform them of your plan to visit, and thus to make arrangements to be landed by the Pitcairn surfboat. Attempts should not be made to land in rough weather using the vessel's dinghy. Lastly, when leaving, thank these generous people for their hospitality by performing some service, or by leaving useful material such as rope, blocks or school supplies (not ammunition or alcohol).

Easter Island

Easter Island (Isla de Pascua) is a colony of Chile, and it is administered by a Governor from the Chilean Navy, together with a local major of Hanga Roa. Spanish is the official language, but there are some people who speak a little English, French and German. The local language is a form of Polynesian.

There are few entry formalities. Valid passports are required for each crew member, but no visa is needed at present. Customs clearance and tourist cards can be obtained on entry at Hanga Roa, the Port of Entry. Report and clear with the same authority on departure.

PROVISIONING

Since groceries in French Polynesia (except for some fresh produce and meat) are shipped to the islands from various countries and are subject to high French tariffs, prices are approximately twice that found in North American supermarkets. Consequently, you should provision with as many non-perishable foods and paper products as is convenient before departure as well as fresh produce, baked goods and meat for as long as they are likely to be edible. Unsliced bread will last 2 or 3 weeks if it is wiped with a vinegar-soaked cloth and allowed to dry prior to storing in a plastic bag in a cool location. Mayonnaise will keep well if germs are not introduced into the bottle, so shake it out rather than scooping it out even with a sterile spoon or knife.

In French Polynesia groceries are found in general stores called magasins. Here you can find anything from aspirins to pareus and flashlight batteries to baguettes (30" long traditional French bread which has no preservatives and is of excellent quality). Rice is widely available and as it keeps well without deteriorating it is a basic staple for cruisers. Bring some tasty recipes using rice along with a variety of spices and be prepared to improvise. If you see an item you want to buy but it seems pricey, don't put off purchasing it for it may not be available at other locations.

Locally grown fruits such as sweet (green) oranges, limes, lemons and coconuts are widely available and are reasonably priced. A treat that shouldn't be missed is pompamouse, a sweet and juicy fruit that resembles a large grapefruit Bananas are a treat but once they start to ripen they tend to do so all at once. Take care to hang them in such a way that they don't become bruised for deterioration occurs quickly. Plantain resembles large bananas but must be cooked prior to eating. Taro root can be cooked like potatoes.

By including breadfruit in your diet your meals will have a new menu item. The following recipes have been developed by Pauline Dolinski of the yacht *Syrena*.

Breadfruit Chips

Peel about 1/4 of a medium firm breadfruit and cut into thin slices about 5cm (2") long. Discard the small dark seeds. Drop as many as will float freely in hot oil about 5cm (2") deep. Stir and turn until golden brown. Remove and drain on paper towels. Salt and pepper to taste. Eat as you would potato chips. If well sealed after cooling they will keep a few days.

Breadfruit Pancakes

Scoop well ripened, soft breadfruit away from the skin and mash it into a bowl. Add flour until it is firm enough to hold together. Drop into hot oil, flattening it with the back of a spoon to make a pancake. When golden brown, flip it over and finish cooking.

Breadfruit Fritters

Mash about a cup of soft, raw breadfruit into a bowl. Add an egg and mix in flour until it will hold together well. Drop by teaspoon into hot oil. Drain and serve with sauce or ketchup.

Breadfruit Salad

Boil and chill 4cm (2") chunks of breadfruit. Add mayonnaise, 1 tsp. lemon juice, 1 tsp. mustard, garlic salt and chopped onions. Serve like potato salad.

Breadfruit Cottage Fries

Slice finely, cooled, well drained, boiled breadfruit and fry in oil until brown and crispy. Serve with chopped fried onions and green peppers.

FISH POISONING (CIGUATERA)

A hazard of eating fish caught near coral atolls in parts of Polynesia is poisoning from those containing the toxin that causes ciguatera. No satisfactory explanation of the source and reasons for accretion of the toxins in particular fish has been determined. It appears to be related to the base of the tropical food chain, i.e. some of the algae, fungi or corals that are eaten by some fish. Another possibility is that food is chemically altered within the fish to become toxic. Added to the mystery is the fact that a particular species of fish is toxic near one atoll but the same fish in a nearby atoll may be unaffected while other species may be the culprits.

Though the source of the poisoning is unknown, some major facts are known:

1. This problem is present only in certain coral areas, and never occurs where the water temperature is below 20°C (68°F).
2. Pelagic fish, such as tuna, bonito and mahi-mahi, are seldom toxic, whereas, many species of reef fishes can be infected.
3. The toxin accumulates in affected fish and humans so that the larger the fish the more likely it is that it has accumulated enough toxin to be dangerous. In Polynesia, barracuda are not eaten, and selling them commercially is prohibited in the market place. Because smaller fish tend to be safe to eat, local fishermen usually keep only small grouper or other food fish measuring 45cm (15") or less. It is important to remember that size alone is not a fool-proof protection against poisoning if the fish are taken from a particularly toxic lagoon. Checking with local people will help identify which fish are most likely uninfected.

Symptoms

Between a few minutes to a few hours after eating a poisonous fish a tingling numbness (pins and needles sensation) around the mouth and nose and sometimes in the hands and feet is experienced. Contact with cold water intensifies the feeling until it resembles mild electric shocks or a burning sensation. These symptoms may intensify. Soon, vomiting and acute diarrhea are experienced, together with aching joints and muscle pains, especially in the legs. Itching that gets no relief from scratching may also occur. The affected person feels cold and weak; the pulse slows, and blood pressure drops, occasionally to the point where hospitalization becomes necessary. Later effects include continuing numbness and loss of skin on the hands and feet.

The symptoms continue for variable lengths of time, possibly depending on the amount of toxin ingested or accumulated. The person infected may have already ingested small amounts from other fish without apparent ill effect until a particular dose triggers the reaction. This is why Polynesians who eat a lot of fish, sometimes suffer severe reactions after a meal which doesn't affect visitors.

Introduction

Except in cases of low resistance or of a massive toxin intake, fish poisoning is not usually fatal. With rest and proper treatment, the patient will recover in a few hours or perhaps days. Severe cases may take weeks or even months for a full recovery.

Treatment

A doctor should be seen as soon as possible. Vomiting should be induced in order to void toxic material in the stomach. This may be accomplished by drinking salt water, syrup of ipecac or putting a finger down the victim's throat.

Epsom salts or sodium bicarbonate may help in neutralizing the poison, especially if some of it is of the scombroid type or due to spoiled fish. Strong allergic reactions may need the use of anti-histamines, which should be carried in every vessel's medicine chest. They may be taken orally or for faster results, by intra-muscular injection.

If the respiratory system is affected, efforts should be made to keep the patient breathing using artificial respiration. Adrenaline may be needed as a heart stimulant but is not advisable if the victim has heart problems. Strong pain relievers, or even morphine, may be needed for severe pain, but are advisable only with a doctor's advice.

The victim should have plenty of rest and avoid eating fish or highly seasoned food until recovery is complete.

Prevention

The only fool-proof prevention is abstinence from eating fish. But with caution and good judgment you can enjoy some fish following the precautions listed below.

1. If fish intake is to be limited, eat only pelagic fish (those which swim offshore)
2. Do not eat reef fishes more than 45cm (15") long or weighing more than 1kg (2 lbs).
3. Local advice should be obtained regarding "safe" fish to eat. Fish should not be eaten if there are any reports of poisoning in a certain area.
4. The liver and viscera are the most heavily contaminated; hence cleaning fish immediately after being caught helps to reduce any poisons present.

*Cigua-Check™ is a recently developed test kit which is intended to indicate the presence of ciguatoxin in a fish. It costs about US$20 for a kit containing 5 tests and has a shelf life of 6 months. The testing process takes 70 minutes.

MISCELLANEOUS MEDICAL CONCERNS

Puffer fish are highly poisonous and those eating it have a mortality rate of 60%. Though Japanese gourmets delight in flirting with death and consider it a delicacy, this fish should not be eaten. Herring and mullet in certain parts of the Pacific contain some poisons; local advice is worthwhile.

*For information about this product phone Oceanit Test Systems, Honolulu HI at 808-539-2345.

Filariosis (elephantiasis) is on the increase in French Polynesia. Clinics in Atuona, Hiva Oa and Papeete provide medication (pills) which give protection from this illness for six months.

Staph infection often results from scratches on coral, gravel, etc. To stop infection the cut must be washed regularly for at least two weeks with hydrogen peroxide or betadine, followed by application of an antibiotic cream.

ILES MARQUISES (MARQUESAS ISLANDS)

The Iles Marquises have a NW/SE orientation between 8°S and 1O°35'S between 138°25' W and 140°50'W longitude. W. Ten islands and several rocks and islets compose the group which has an area of 1,418 square miles (3,672 square kilometers). The northern group consist of Motu One, Hatutu, Eiao, Ua Huka, Ua Pou and Nuku Hiva (the largest). The southern group is comprised of Fatu Hiva, Mohotani, Tahuata, Fatu Huku and Hiva Oa (the largest). These high, volcanically formed islands have steep, black, cliff-edged coasts indented by many valleys. Their spectacular outlines are generally clearly visible from at least 20 miles at sea making them a navigator's ideal landfall.

The Marquises are the northernmost group of islands forming part of French Polynesia and they have their own distinctive setting and style. The total population is about 6,000, the descendants of proud and warlike Polynesian tribes that once numbered approximately 100,000 when Captain Cook visited the islands in the eighteenth century before they were decimated by western contact and diseases.

The earliest inhabitants are believed to have migrated from Melanesia at about the time of Christ. The population multiplied and the culture reached its maximum development from 1400 - 1790 AD. The first European to visit the islands was a Spanish navigator, Alvaro de Mendana in 1595 who named the islands. They were claimed by France in 1842.

Weather

The islands lie within the trade wind belt. The trade winds are predominantly northeasterly 80% of the year but swing east and southeast during the rainy periods. The rainy season begins in March and continues through October. The southern trades are not as steady as those in northern latitudes. Tropical storms and hurricanes are very infrequent. The wind can be dramatically disturbed in the vicinity of the high, steep islands causing frequent squalls and thunderstorms.

The Marquises have a sub-tropical climate with daytime temperatures averaging 86°F (30°C) throughout the year. The humidity is higher for two to three months in the middle of the year averaging 80% and annual rainfall varies between 1,000 and 3,000mm (40" to 120").

Currents

The South Sub-Tropical current passes through this region, generally moving in a westerly direction. The capes and points of the main islands alter currents slightly in their immediate vicinity, as do periods of strong winds.

Clearance and Travel Notes

The main administrative center of the area is at Baie Taiohae on Nuku Hiva, but entry can also be made at Atuona on Hiva Oa and at Hakahau on Ua Pou. Fly the Q flag on arrival and report to the gendarmerie. Because Fatu Hiva is to windward of the other islands it is tempting to stop there first but this is illegal and cruisers run the risk of being reported and fined. Once a vessel has cleared to leave it is illegal to stop at any other anchorages. It is well to remember that Papeete in Tahiti is the only true Port of Entry for French Polynesia.

Because of weather considerations in the Northern Hemisphere most vessels make the trip to the Marquises in the period from March to May. Cruisers tend to leave the Marquises for Tahiti or the Tuamotu at or near full moon. This should give the benefit of bright moonlight for the critical period of passage near the Tuamotu, but squalls which are typical at this time sometimes negate any advantage the full moon can have.

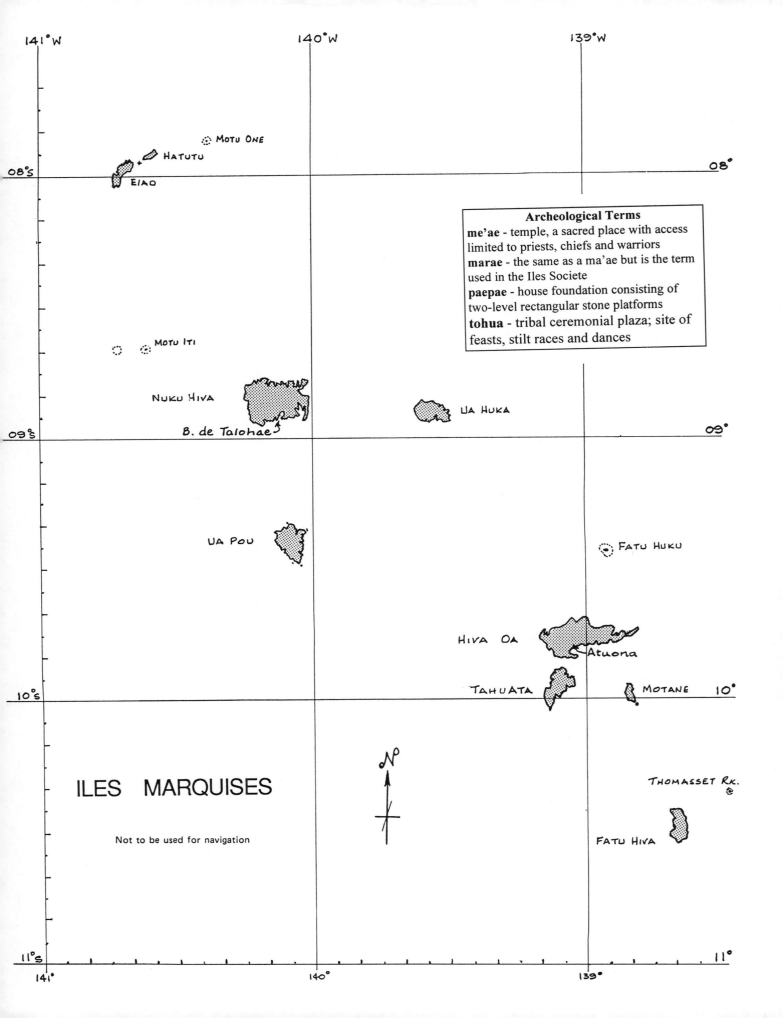

08°S · 141°W   140°W   139°W   08°

⊙ Motu One

Hatutu

Eiao

Archeological Terms

me'ae - temple, a sacred place with access limited to priests, chiefs and warriors

marae - the same as a ma'ae but is the term used in the Iles Societe

paepae - house foundation consisting of two-level rectangular stone platforms

tohua - tribal ceremonial plaza; site of feasts, stilt races and dances

⊙ Motu Iti

Nuku Hiva

B. de Taiohae

Ua Huka

09°S   09°

Ua Pou

⊙ Fatu Huku

Hiva Oa

Atuona

Tahuata

Motane   10°

10°S

N

ILES MARQUISES

Not to be used for navigation

Thomasset Rk.

Fatu Hiva

11°S · 141°   140°   139°   11°

ILE NUKU HIVA

This is the principal island of the Marquises and Taiohae is a **Port of Entry** where cruisers report their arrival to the gendarmerie. Nuku Hiva is precipitously high, with Takao the highest point, at 1,185m (3,888'). Other heights along the northern coast give rise to many beautiful waterfalls. Toovii Plateau is in the center of the island. Several bays are on the northern and southern coasts, many of which can be used as anchorages, depending on the direction of the wind and swell. Baie de Taiohae is the principal bay and a popular stop-over for cruisers.

Baie de Taiohae (Hakapehi)

Located about 3.5 miles eastnortheast of Baie Tai Oa, this is the safest and most important anchorage in the Marquises. At the entrance are two rocky islets (the Sentinels/Les Sentinelles) and a large white cross of crystalline rocks rises above the cliffs to the east. Rocky cliffs line each side of the bay; on the western side a steep-sided lava plug rises above the slopes. Within the bay, Pointe Arquee is a curved, bare, rocky spur that projects from the eastern shore. The remaining shores are covered with green growth except for a few black volcanic outcrops. This is where 23-year old Herman Melville jumped a whaling ship in 1842.

In the northeastern part of the bay a light on the hill near the ruins of Fort Collet defines the anchorage sector for large ships in the green sector. The best area for cruisers is on the west side of the head of the bay in 11m (6 fathoms), sand. Since swell often makes the bay uncomfortable, a stern anchor should be set to keep the yacht perpendicular to the shore and swell.

Taiohae is the administrative capital and the largest town in the Marquises. It lies in the open remains of a volcanic crater with the caldera walls surrounding the town. The red roofs of village buildings stand out on the eastern side at the head of the bay. Here, the ruins of Fort Collet are beyond a small, green hill which protrudes from the shore. Landing can be made either at the concrete wharf below the Fort (which is not visible on first approach) or at the concrete boat ramp inshore of the wharf. The town has a radio station, hospital, post office, satellite telephones, a few stores, a gendarmerie and other administrative offices. An airstrip at the northwest corner of the island can be reached in about 2.5 hours by boat or costs about $60 by helicopter. Points of interest include the Roman Catholic cathedral "Notre Dame des Iles Marquises," the Herman Melville memorial and two archeological sights.

Clearance for entry and permission to visit other islands of the group can be obtained here. Water may be taken on but it is often contaminated and should be boiled or purified before drinking. Taiohae is the only place in the Marquises where polluted water is a problem; it is caused by many goats and pigs which live in the catchment area. Hakatea, 5 miles to the west, is a much better place to fill your water tanks if they have enough to spare.

Fuel is available from the Total fuel dock on the east side of the bay. Drop a bow anchor and take a stern line ashore when taking on fuel. Propane tanks may be filled at the fuel dock or at Magasin Bigot. Butane burns satisfactorily but the gas in the tank is at a much lower pressure than propane. For many years a warm welcome for cruisers has been given by Rose Corser, the owner of *Keikahanui Inn* which can be used as a mail drop (B.P. 21 Taiohae, Nuku Hiva 98700, Iles Marquises, French Polynesia) or you can fax mail to cruisers at (689) 92.00.74 or telephone (689) 92.03.82. On the hill above, the bungalow-style hotel overlooks the bay.

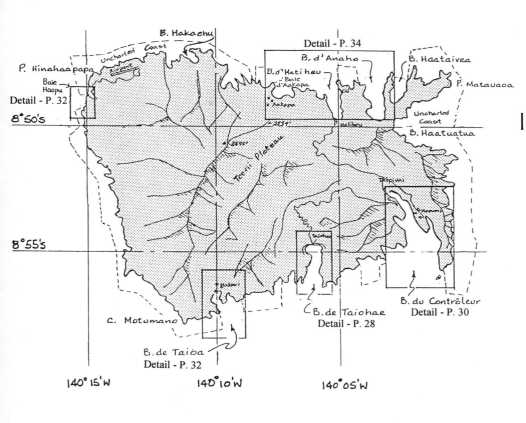

P. Hinahaapapa

Baie
Haopu
Detail - P. 32

B. Hakaehu

Uncharted Coast

8°50'S

Detail - P. 34

B. d'Anaho

B. d'Hati heu
Baie
d'Aakapa

B. Haataivea

P. Matauaoa

Hatiheu

Uncharted
Coast

B. Haatuatua

ILES MARQUISES

NUKU HIVA

Toovii Plateau

Taipivai

Hooumi

8°55'S

c. Motumano

B. de Taiohae
Detail - P. 28

B. du Contrôleur
Detail - P. 30

Not to be used for navigation

B. de Taiöa
Detail - P. 32

140°15'W

140°10'W

140°05'W

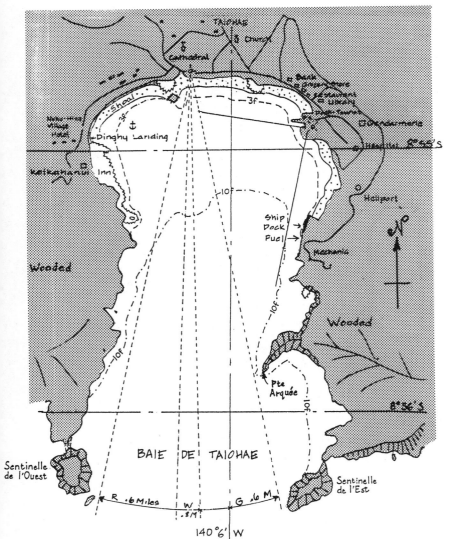

TAIOHAE
Church
Cathedral

Bank
Snack
Store
Restaurant
LIKANG
Dock Tohua
Gendarmerie
Headland

Nuku Hiva
Village Hotel

8°55'S

Shoal

Dinghy Landing

Keikahanui Inn

Heliport

BAIE de TAIOHAE

Wooded

Ship
Dock
Fuel

Machanie

-10F-

Not to be used for navigation

-10F-

Wooded

-10F-

Pte
Arquée

-10F-

8°56'S

Sentinelle
de l'Ouest

BAIE DE TAIOHAE

Sentinelle
de l'Est

R .6 Miles   W   G .6 M
.8M

140°6'W

RM

Baie de Controleur (Comptroller Bay)

This large bay is immediately west of the long, narrow projecting point of Cap Tikapo. Within the bay, two rocky points (one shorter than the other) divide the head of the bay into three narrow coves. Anchorage may be taken in good holding sand and mud near the head of each cove in 7 to 10 fathoms. Some swell may disturb the anchorages, though there is good protection from the prevailing winds. The westernmost cove, L'Anse Haka Paa. is the least affected by swell. It is advisable to set a stern anchor to keep the vessel perpendicular to the shore and swell.

The village of <u>Taipivai</u> is located a short distance up the river at the head of Anse Hakahaa, the middle and largest cove. A concrete loading dock in the village provides easy shore access and several excellent hikes can be taken from the village. A fifteen-minute walk north of the village, past a vanilla plantation, leads to a path which zig-zags up the hill. Located here are the ruins of an important archeological sight, Paeke, which has several large tikis and a huge maeae (ceremonial platform made from huge basalt blocks which was used only by priests and chieftans for worship, burials and sometimes human sacrifices). This maeae measures 170m by 25m (557' by 82'). A hike along the west bank of the river up the valley leads to two waterfalls. The dirt road linking Taipivai to Taiohae has many scenic viewpoints. Abandoned paepaes (ancient stone platforms that acted as house foundations) are beside the road from Anse Hanga Haa to Anse Hooumi. Insect repellant is necessary to guard against nonos.

Whaleboats (lighters) from the passenger-carrying freighter, *Aranui*, arrive every three weeks from Papeete. Its arrival gives an excuse for the local people to congregate at the dock and visit, while their wide-eyed children gaze quietly at the tourists. Freight is off-loaded and, similar to many villages in the Marquises, sacks of copra (dried nutmeat from which coconut oil is extracted), barrels of fermented noni, limes and bananas are taken on for delivery to Papeete.

It is interesting to note that this area is the setting for Herman Melville's well-known book, *Typee*. To get an appreciation for the rugged terrain on the island and the way of life prior to the inflluence of western civilization this descriptive book is a "must read."

* * * * *

*Noni (Morinda citrifolia) produces a green, pear-sized fruit with round, whitish markings. In contrast to coconut-producing palm trees, it grows quickly, does not need special care and is easy to harvest. The fruit is loaded into barrels and shipped to Papeete in a fermented state. The pulp is then shipped to the Morinda juice factory in Salt Lake City, Utah where it is processed and mixed with various fruit juices. The final product is promoted as an elixir for various ailments. Since 1996 the sale of noni has added an economic boost to the Marquises. Thus it is interesting to see the proliferation of 4 x 4s and other late-model vehicles on islands which have only a few miles of roads.

One of the problems of producing coconuts are rats living on the islands. A band of zinc around the trunk of coconut palms prevents them from climbing up to the coconuts and destroying the fruit.

ILES MARQUISES
ILE NUKU HIVA

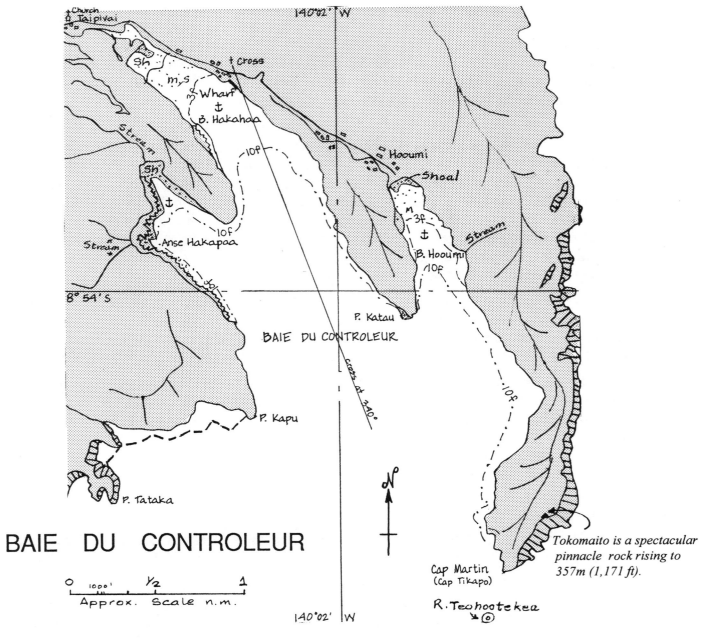

140°02' W

Church
& Taipivai

† Cross

Sh

m,s

3 Wharf
‡
B. Hakahaa

10f

Stream

Sh

‡

10f

Stream

Anse Hakapaa

10f

Hooumi

Shoal

m
3f
‡
B. Hooumi
10f

Stream

8° 54' S

P. Katau

BAIE DU CONTROLEUR

cross at 340°

P. Kapu

P. Tataka

BAIE DU CONTROLEUR

0   1000'   ½   1

Approx. Scale n.m.

Not to be used for navigation

10f

N

*Tokomaito is a spectacular
pinnacle rock rising to
357m (1,171 ft).*

Cap Martin
(Cap Tikapo)

140°02' W

R. Teohootekea
↘ ⊙

DANGER
*Teohootekea Rock is marked by heavily breaking
seas. Pass well to the south when in the vicinity.*

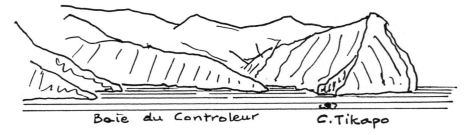

Baie du Controleur   C. Tikapo

Baie de Taioa (Tai 'oa or Hakatea)

The southernmost point of Nuku Hiiva is Pointe Motumano. One and a half miles eastnortheast is the small bay of Baie Taioa. It provides good anchorage and is less affected by swell than is Baie de Taiohae which is 5 miles to the east. On some charts it is called Baie Hakatea, though this name is more correctly applied to the eastern lobe of the bay. It is also known as Daniel and Antoinette's Bay, after the friendly Marquisan couple who have lived here for over 60 years. A river exits from the Hakaui valley, a spectacular, precipitous area often viewed by tourists on sight-seeing helicopters flying from Taiohae.

The opening to the bay is difficult to identify from seaward since the entrance points overlap. The west side is a steep, 488m (1,600') mountain, that to the east is a lower, black cliff with a flat-topped point. There is often a rough sea at the entrance and surf breaks on the eastern point, but you can motor in to find a calm anchorage with white sand beaches at its head. The western cove, L'Anse Hakaui is shallow, and the better anchorage is in the eastern cove, L'Anse Hakatea, in about 1 m (6 fathoms), midway into the bay. Swinging space is restricted if there are several boats in the anchorage. Though the bay is calm, strong squalls sometimes blow down the two valleys. Landing can be made on the rocky shore east of the beach. Nonos are a pest that infest the beaches and sometimes affect the anchorage.

If you need water, go ashore with a gift and ask if some water can be spared. Return to your boat for jerry cans which may be filled at the water spigot located next to the cooking shed on the beach. It would be most discourteous to go ashore and help yourself to the precious water without first asking for permission and giving a gift or making a contribution of some kind.

Boats can land near the river at the eastern head of L'Anse Hakaui. Close behind the beach are the ruins of the old village and a church with some very old statues. A walk through the coconut palms and up the slope leads through the valley to Vaipo waterfall, a spectacular, high and narrow waterfall cascading from the 610m (2,000') plateau to the valley floor below. The hike takes 2.5 hours but it is well worth the effort for this is the third highest waterfall in the world. There are also many ruined paepae and some tikis in the valley.

Baie d'Haahopu

This bay is 1.7 miles south of Pte. Hinahaapapa, the norwestern extremity of the island. Anchorage in good holding sand can be taken inside the entrance of the bay where there is protection from easterly winds.

A boat dock is at the terminus of a road linking the bay to the Nuku-Ataha airport, the only airport on NukuHiva. *Le Truck* shuttle service operates between the airport and the boat dock where passengers board a boat for the one-hour trip to Taiohae. Air Tahiti operates three regular flights per week between Tahiti and Nuku Hiva.

Tent Olive
(Oliva porphyria Linne)

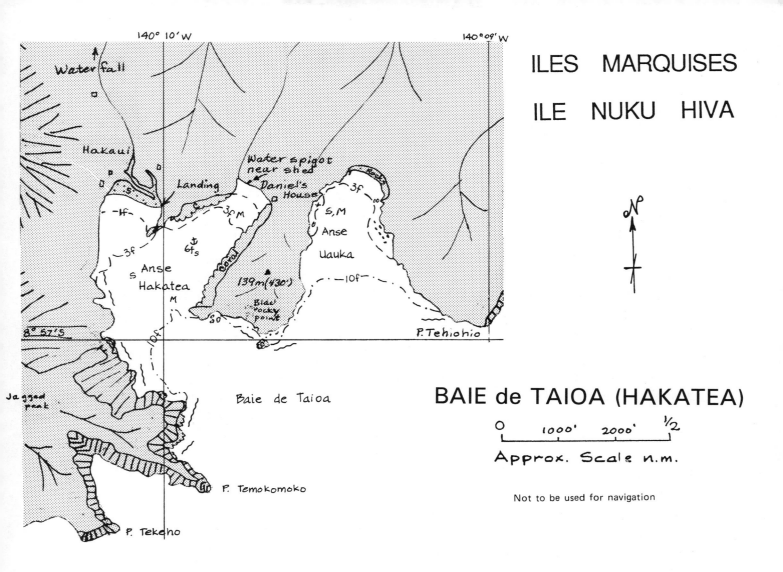

ILES MARQUISES

ILE NUKU HIVA

Waterfall

Hakaui

Water spigot
near shed

Daniel's
House

Landing

3f

S,M

Anse
Uauka

3f M

Anse
Hakatea
M

6fs

139m(430')

Black
rocky
point

P. Tehiohio

8° 57'5

Jagged
peak

Baie de Taioa

BAIE de TAIOA (HAKATEA)

0   1000'   2000'   ½

Approx. Scale n.m.

Not to be used for navigation

P. Temokomoko

P. Tekeho

BAIE HAAHOPU

0   100 200 300

Approx. Scale yds.

Not to be used for navigation

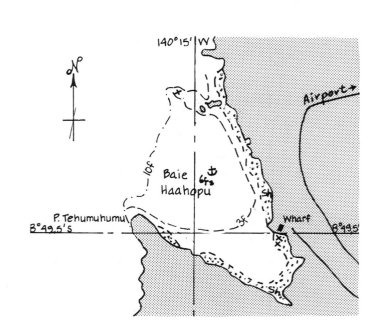

140°15' W

Airport →

Baie
Haahopu

6fs

P. Tehumuhumu

Wharf

8°49'5

8°49,5's

Sh.

Baie D'Anaho

This large bay on the north coast near the eastern end of the island, is one of the calmest anchorages in the Marquises. On one side is a long, narrow peninsula and on the other is a steep mountain about 305m (1,000') high. The bay indents the coast by about 1.5 miles and provides a sheltered anchorage from the prevailing trade winds and swell. But for periods of the year when the wind moves northerly, the swell can enter the bay and be bothersome. The low pass on the east side near the head of the bay lets easterly squalls through in bad weather.

The entrance to the bay is clear and open. Pointe Tekea and Pointe Mataohotu project from the western side about a mile into the bay, narrowing it slightly. Some coral reefs are on the western side and at the head of the bay; the eastern side is clear and steep-to. Small vessels anchor in the shelter given by Pointe Mataohotu on the western side in about 10 fathoms, fine sand bottom, in a position keeping the entrance open and avoiding the coral.

Landing can be made through an gap in the coral near the huts on the western side. A dirt road with a view of Baie D'Anaho traverses Teavaimaoaoa Pass (200m/650ft.) and leads to Baie D'Hatiheu. A short hike along the beach to the east, passing rocks at the point, then crossing sand dunes, leads to one of the oldest archeological sites in the Marquises at Haatuatua. A road over the saddle leads to the village of Taipivai at the head of Baie du Controleur.

Baie D'Hatiheu

Two miles west of Baie D'Anaho is Baie D'Hatiheu where good anchorage may be taken in 9m (5 fathoms) with easy landing on a wharf to the east. Bordering the waterfront is a collection of tikis and intricately carved arches which add a special ambience. A craft center and museum are in the village. High up on one of the spires over-looking the village, is the *Madonna of Hatiheu*, a white statue built in 1872 by Frere Blanc. The unique crown on the Madonna is made of branch coral. The village of Hatiheu was a favorite spot for Robert Louis Stevenson.

One of the best restaurants in the islands, *Chez Yvonne*, (owned by the town's mayor) is famous for cooking pork in an earthen oven (umu). The pig and bananas are wrapped in ti leaves and placed on hot rocks, covered with banana leaves, burlap, and earth and left to cook for six hours—the results are tender and delicious!

Three archeological sites within easy walking distance are in the vicinity. The most important one is the tohua (public plaza) Hikoku'a, a large, well-restored ceremonial center consisting of stone platforms. A local dance group periodically performs dances in this exotic setting. Two other significant sites are just up the hill at the me'ae (temple) to the goddess Tevanaua'ua'a where a huge sacred banyan tree is located. Further up the hill is tohua Kamuihei with petroglyphs of turtles, human figures and fish tiki faces. Mosquitoes and nonos abound.

Baie Hakaehu

Baie Hakaehu, six miles west of Baie D'Hatiheu, provides good anchorage in 6 fathoms, sand bottom. Fresh water is available from the inhabitants of Pua who welcome cruisers. **Caution**: Since this part of the coast has not been hydrographically surveyed cruisers must give the coast a safe clearance and maintain a sharp lookout for unmarked reefs or other dangers.

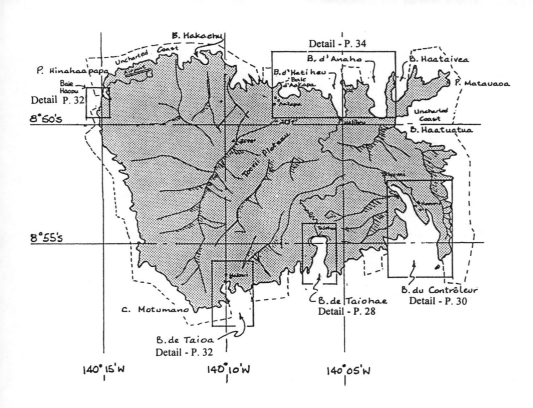

ILES MARQUISES

NUKU HIVA

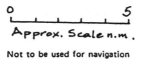

0   5
Approx. Scale n.m.

Not to be used for navigation

BAIE D'ANAHO & BAIE D'HATIHEU

0   1000'   ½   1
Approx. Scale n.m.

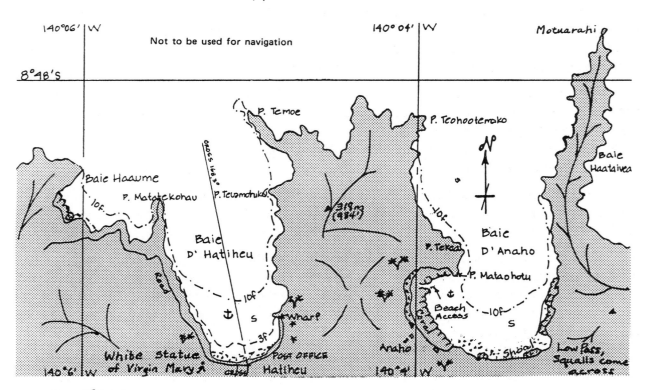

UA HUKA (pronounced wa-huka)

The smallest of the inhabited islands in the northern group, Ua Huka lies about 24 miles east of Nuku Hiva. This crescent-shaped island is topped by a high ridge which splits at its western end forming two valleys. A curved line of peaks form the spine of the island, the highest of which is Mount Hitikau (1,800'/852m). Near its base is a vast plateau with arid, desert-like topography and scrub brush which resembles California's Big Sur country or Ireland's rural landscape. Few yachts visit this beautiful island which has much of interest to enjoy.

The island is overpopulated with more than 1,500 horses and 3,000 goats which have almost deforested the landscape. With less than 600 people living on the island, the combined population of horses, goats and cattle outnumber the population by about ten to one. Plans are underway to reduce the numbers of horses and goats to a level that the island's vegetation can support.

The island gives good radar returns for up to 30 miles distant. All available anchorages are on the southern side and include Baie de Vaipaee, Baie d'Hane, and Baie Haavei.

Baie de Vaipaee (Invisible Bay)

About a mile east of Pointe Tekeho, the southwestern point of the island, is the narrow bay of Baie de Vaipaee. It is aptly named, for it is very difficult to identify until directly opposite the entrance when the beach at its head is visible. The steep, black walls at the entrance appear forbidding, and a rough sea always seems to exist here, but once inside, the water is calm.

The head is shoal and anchorage in about 5.5m (3 fathoms) is found about two-thirds of the way in. As swinging room is limited, use bow and stern anchors to hold the vessel into the swell. In northerly or easterly winds the bay is a satisfactory anchorage. If the wind sets southeasterly, the swell sets into the bay, making it very dangerous and departure can be difficult.

Landing can be made at the concrete boat launching ramp and jetty, or on the beach at the head of the bay, where the village of <u>Vaipaee</u> is located. The best museum in the Marquises, located in the Mayor's office, is well worth a visit and it features a 300-year-old canoe. Two small stores, an attractive church and very friendly people are in this village. The villagers are excellent wood carvers and numerous craft shops attest to the skill of their handiwork.

About a mile west of the entrance to the bay is the steep, cliffy southern tip of the island at Cap Tekeho. The huge sea caves in the cliffs are ancient burial sights which are now used as nesting sites for seabirds.

Two small islands, Ilots Hemeni and Teuaua, .5 miles west of Cap Tekeho and .25 miles offshore are known as Bird Islands. Hundreds of petrels, terns, tropicbirds, boobies and frigatebirds can be seen soaring above the islands while the cacophony of their calls is heard. A rope hanging down the cliff on Ilot Teuaua aids in the collection of tern eggs reported to have a red yolk and a distinctive fishy flavor.

A one-and-half hour hike to Vaikivi archeological site is where 50 stone carvings can be seen, one of which is a unique sailing canoe. Several old stone carvings can be seen on the side of the beautiful beach at Hatuana.

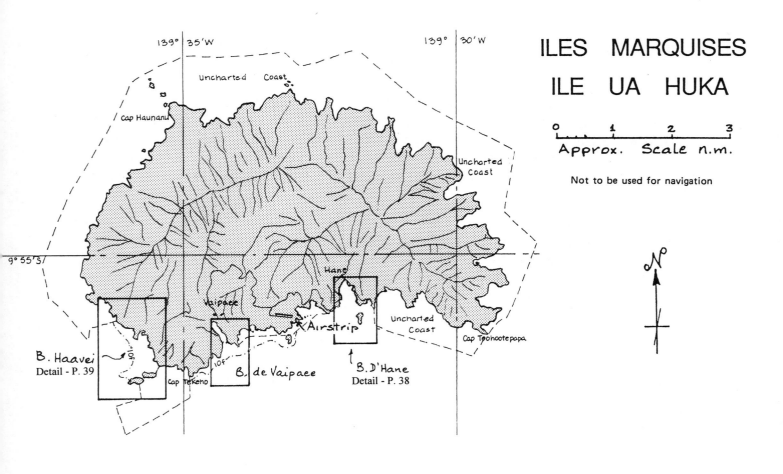

ILES MARQUISES
ILE UA HUKA

0   1   2   3

Approx. Scale n.m.

Not to be used for navigation

139° 35' W   139° 30' W

Uncharted Coast

Cap Haunanu

Uncharted Coast

9° 55' S

Hane

Vaipaee

Airstrip

Uncharted Coast

Cap Teohootepapa

B. Haavei
Detail - P. 39

Cap Tekeho

B. de Vaipaee

B. D'Hane
Detail - P. 38

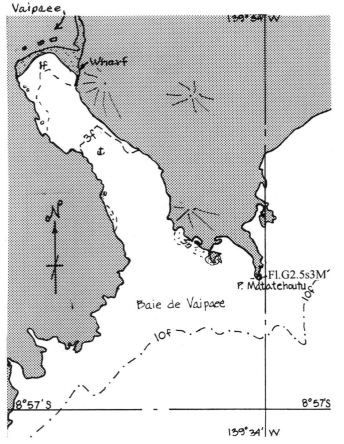

Vaipaee

139° 34' W

Wharf

Baie de Vaipaee

Fl.G2.5s3M'
P. Matatehoutu

8° 57' S   8° 57' S

139° 34' W

BAIE DE VAIPAEE

0   ¼   ½

Approx. Scale n.m.

Not to be used for navigation

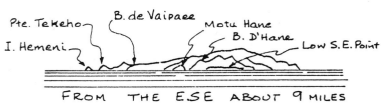

Pte. Tekeho

I. Hemeni

B. de Vaipaee

Motu Hane

B. D'Hane

Low S.E. Point

FROM THE ESE ABOUT 9 MILES

Baie d'Hane

Two miles to the east of Baie de Vaipaee is Baie d'Hane, recognizable by the 155m (508') reddish-purple rocks of Motu Hane lying to the east of the entrance. The bay is a little wider than Baie de Vaipaee and good anchorage can be taken in 14 - 18m (8 to 10 fathoms) about midway into the bay. Strong gusts sometimes blow off the hillside and some swell enters the bay. Landing on the beach through the surf can be challenging; the best place for going ashore is in the northwest corner.

Near the stream at the head of the bay is the village of Hane which has stores and a bakery. In the annex of the city hall is an arts and crafts center and next door is a small maritime museum. The archeological site of Meaiaute is well worth the somewhat strenuous walk up the valley beyond the village. Of particular interest are several interesting tiki, one which is headless and another has a tattoo on its face. Be prepared for abundant mosquitoes in the area.

A scenic, winding road links Hane to the town of Vaipaee. Along the route is a massive botanical garden featuring hundreds of plants found in Polynesia. In addition to the wide variety of flora many birds can be seen in the arboretum such as the beautiful and rare ultramarine lorikeet, Marquesan reed-warblers, iphis monarchs and fruit doves. Beyond the airfield is an area of reefs and rocks marking the location of an abandoned archeological site which has a spectacular setting.

The coastal road continues eastward to the small village of Hokatu. The selection and quality of wood carving of everything from bowls to walking sticks as well as replicas of axes, javelins, etc. is by far the best to be found in Polynesia and the prices are most reasonable.

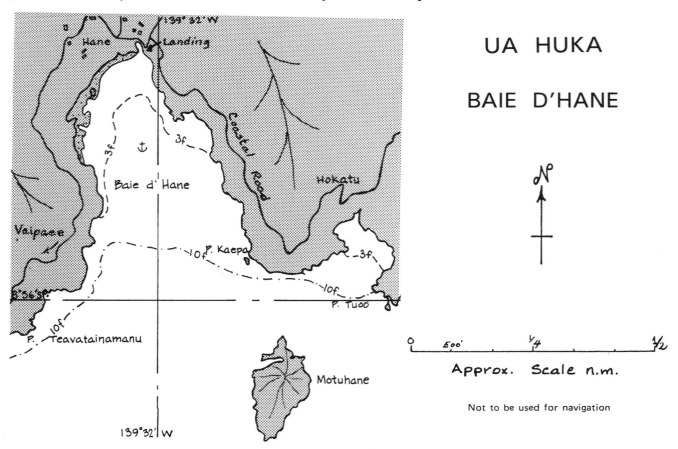

UA HUKA

BAIE D'HANE

Approx. Scale n.m.

Not to be used for navigation

Baie Haavei (Baie Chavei, Baie Blanche, Shaveb Bay and Shavay Bay)

This open bay near the southwestern part of the island is about a mile northwest of Cap Tekeho. Two islets, Hemeni and Teuaua help to protect it from wind and swell. Anchorage is off a beautiful sandy beach, with Ilot Hemeni lying a little east of south from the vessel.

The bay is owned by the influential Lichtle family which founded the Community Museum of Ua Huka in Vaipaee and the arboretum on the Vaipaee-Hane road. The valley is like a tropical garden park, and since it is private land, permission is needed before walking around. Landing on the sandy beach may be difficult because of the surf.

There are two archeological sites in the vicinity that can only be reached by sea. In Hatuana Bay, west of Haavei there are petroglyphs depicting tiki faces and geometric designs carved in the lava flow. At low tide foot prints in what is known as the Ghost Cave of Anavenihae are reported to be seen in the floor of the cave.

The coast of Ua Huka is pock-marked with sea caves and are the perfect habitat for spiny rock lobsters. These often appear in the menus of local restaurants as langouste. Because of the prolific goat population on the island the islanders have developed a tasty variety of recipes which include barbecued goat, stewed goat and curried goat served in coconut milk. By the way, when helping yourself to coconut milk be aware of the fact that generous servings act as a laxative. However, by eating several guavas the results of over-indulgence in coconut milk can be overcome.

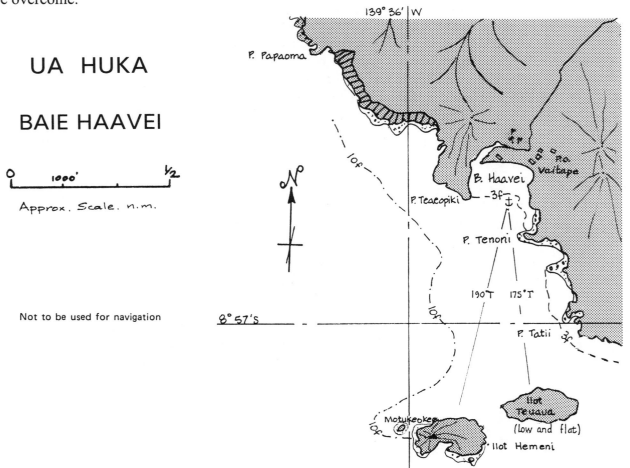

UA HUKA

BAIE HAAVEI

0   1000'   ½

Approx. Scale. n.m.

Not to be used for navigation

UA POU (Ua Pu or Hua Pou, pronounced as wapoo)

This diamond-shaped island lies about 25 miles south of Taiohae Bay on Nuku Hiva. It is about 10 miles long and 7 miles wide and has a spectacularly serrated skyline. It has countless soaring mountain spires and towers, the highest being Oave, a volcanic plug reaching 1,200m (4,040'). Often shrouded in cloud, it is an awesome sight when visible. Many bays indent the coastline, but only those most useable by for small craft are described. A dirt road circles the central part of the island and has spectacular views.Good radar returns are received for distances up to 26 miles.

Baie d'Hakahau

This bay lies midway on the northeast coast and is thus exposed to NE winds. A large white cross is prominent on top of a hill to the east of the harbor. The village of Hakahau is the main settlement and the 1,000 residents are half the island's population. A breakwater/wharf combination extending out from the east side of the bay affords yachts considerable protection from the swell. Landing on the surf-free, sandy beach is easy, making this a convenient place to visit. Boats visiting Ua Pou should check in with the gendarmerie before visiting other anchorages on the island.

This is the third most populated village in the Marquises (following Taiohae and Atuona) and has a post office, gendarmerie, stores, bakery and infirmary. Hakahau is noted for the beautiful wood, stone and coconut shell carvings done by local craftsmen. The spectacular use of stone and local woods in the construction of Eglise Saint-Etienne is amazing. The pulpit is a massive block of tou meticulously carved in the shape of a boat's prow on a huge base of detailed symbolic carvings. Nearby is *Rosalie's Restaurant*, featuring Marquisan foods such as poisson cru (fish marinated in lime juice and soaked in coconut milk), breadfruit, curried goat, barbecued rock lobster, taro, octopus, green mango, tapioca and sweet red bananas.

Beyond the school is a restored paepae where a replica of a typical Marquisan house has been built. Sometimes wood and coconut shell carvings are sold here and occasionally local dancers perform traditional dances.

On the ridge to the east is a large, white cross overlooking the bay. An easy trail leads up the hill giving a nice view of the bay. The last part of the trail is overgrown with shrubs but with some scrambling the cross can be reached. Part way down the hill the road branches to the east, leading to a beautiful sandy beach at the head of Anaho Bay. Except in June and July when jelly fish sometimes invade the bay, the waves are great for surfing once you have run the gauntlet of swarms of nonos.

A road further to the east leads to what was once a thriving and vibrant community at Hakamoui. Known as "The Valley of the Kings," when it was inhabited over a hundred years ago, only a few people live in the area and the archeological remains are neglected.

Some of the many spires on Ua Pou, Marquesas Islands, (Iles Marquises)   *Margo Wood*

The Bay of Virgins (Baie des Vierges) on Fatu Hiva in the Marquesas Islands   *Margo Wood*

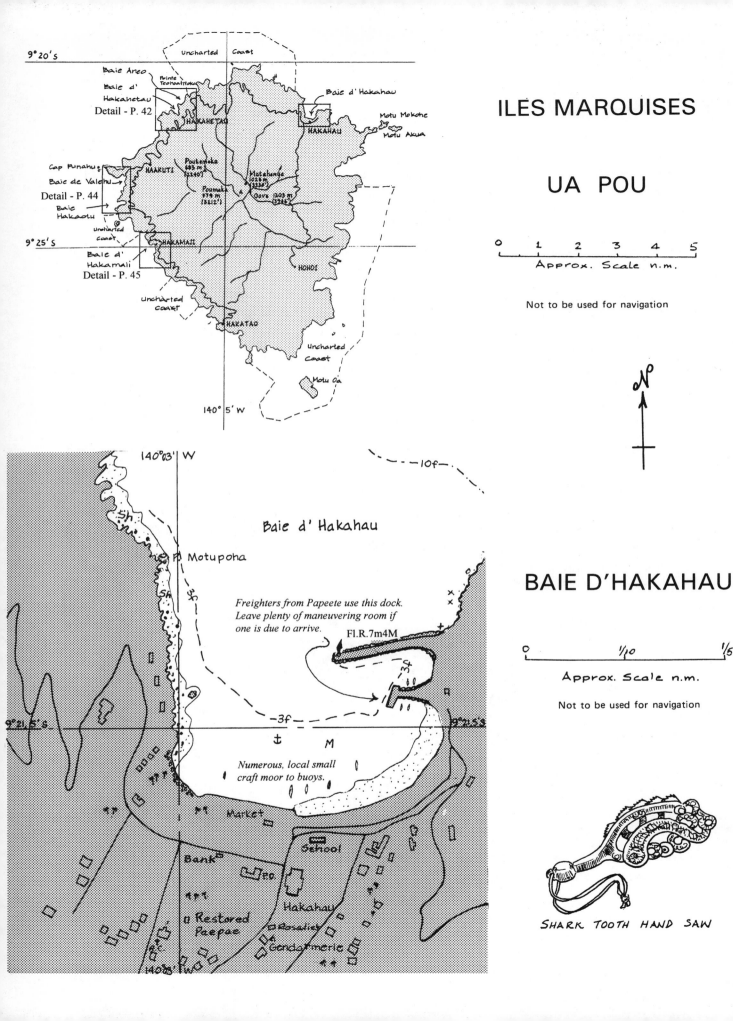

ILES MARQUISES

UA POU

0   1   2   3   4   5
Approx. Scale n.m.

Not to be used for navigation

BAIE D'HAKAHAU

0   1/10   1/5
Approx. Scale n.m.

Not to be used for navigation

Map labels (top map)

9°20'S

Uncharted Coast

Baie Aneo
Baie d'
Hakahetau
Detail - P. 42

Pointe Teohaatiuku

HAKAHETAU

Baie d' Hakahau
HAKAHAU

Motu Mokohe
Motu Akua

Cap Punahu
Baie de Valehu
Detail - P. 44

HAAKUTI

Baie
Hakaotu

Uncharted
Coast

Poutemoka
683 m
(1140')

Poumaka
379 m
(3212')

Matahenua
1026 m
(3336')

Oave 1203 m
(3266')

9°25'S

HAKAMAII

HOHOI

Baie d'
Hakamaii
Detail - P. 45

Uncharted
Coast

HAKATAO

Uncharted
Coast

Motu Oa

140° 5' W

Map labels (bottom map — Baie d'Hakahau)

140°03' W

10f

5h

Baie d' Hakahau

Motupoha

5f

3f

*Freighters from Papeete use this dock.
Leave plenty of maneuvering room if
one is due to arrive.*

Fl.R.7m4M

3f

9°21.5'S

3f

9°21.53'

M

*Numerous, local small
craft moor to buoys.*

Market

Bank

School

PO

Hakahau

Restored
Paepae

Rosaries

Gendarmerie

140°

Uncharted

SHARK TOOTH HAND SAW

Baie D'Hakahetau

This bay lies about midway along the northwest coast of the island and has several identifying features. A whitish patch can be seen on the spectacular volcanic cliffs on the eastern shore. Below the cliffs is Motukoio and farther out, Rochers Rouges. At the center of the head of the bay is a conspicuous rock, Rocher Anapuai, with an island, Motukivi, in front. Coral reefs line the eastern shore and extend past Rochers Rouges. The western point, Pointe Tehena, has a coral patch before it. The red roof of the church and a long, aluminum-clad open market stand out from the luxuriant, green vegetation. A broad valley opens up beyond the town, overseen at the far end by a sharp, pyramid-shaped spire.

Anchoring can be taken about 11m (6 fathoms), sand. Though this is a rolly anchorage, it is the best spot to minimize the effect of the swell. The swell is never completely absent, though you can land on a cement dock, east of a reddish islet at the head of the bay. The steps are quite slippery and the swell can make going ashore difficult. The village of Hakahetau welcomes cruisers and has made an effort to provide services. Located behind the beach and palm trees, the town has a post office, church, store with fax service and school. Fresh water and showers are available on the pier and arrangements can be made for laundry service. In season, cruisers may purchase fresh produce from the owner of a large vegetable garden in the village.

Arrangements can be made for guided tours or horseback riding. The interior of the island can be explored by renting a 4 x 4 car, taking a guided tour or by horseback. This part of the island has a luxuriant variety of flora and a wealth of bird life.

Etienne Hokaupoko, the Marquisan mayor/school teacher is very knowledgeable about history and is involved in establishing a museum on Ua Pou. Fluent in English, French and Marquesan, he enjoys visiting with cruisers and extends a warm invitation to visit the village. He has offered his address for cruiser mail: Hokaupoko, Etienne Takihiu, B.P. 120, Ua Pou, Iles Marquises, French Polynesia.

DISTANT VIEW UA POU FROM ENE

Baie Aneo

This bay lies about 2.4km (1.5 miles) northeast of Baie d'Hakahetau. It has a wide entrance split in two by a reddish rock, Rocher Tauna, which is surrounded by coral. Though you may enter on either side, the western entrance is easier and deeper. When using the eastern entrance stay about 91m (300') from the eastern shore to avoid the coral patch near the island, and watch the current setting at the entrance.

Anchorage can be taken in 6 fathoms southwest of Rocher Tauna, where swinging room is available. Landing can be made ashore, but the swell can make this anchorage somewhat uncomfortable.

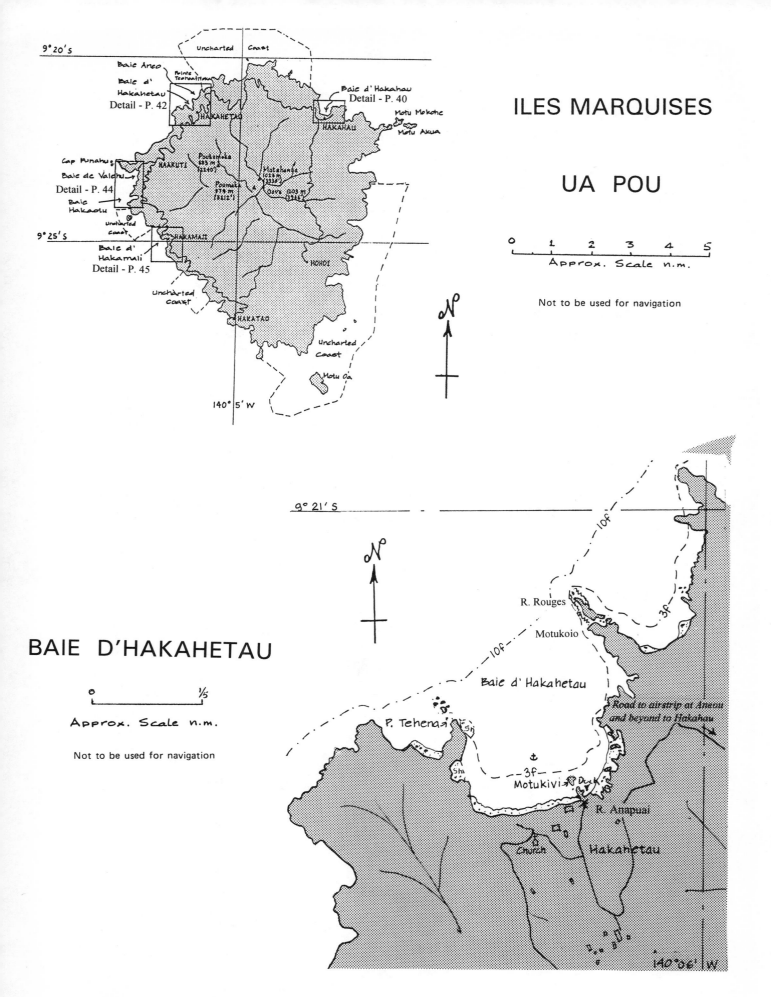

9° 20'S

Uncharted Coast

Baie Aneo
Baie d'
Hakahetau
Detail - P. 42

Pointe Teohaatitoue

HAKAHETAU

Baie d' Hakahau
Detail - P. 40

Motu Mokohe
Motu Akua

ILES MARQUISES

UA POU

Cap Punahu
Baie de Valehu
Detail - P. 44
Baie Hakaohu

HAKAHETAU

Poukemoka
685 m
(2240')

Poumaka
779 m
(2412')

Matahenua
1025 m
(3355')

Oave 1203 m
(3945')

Uncharted coast

9° 25'S

HAKAMAII

Baie d'
Hakamaii
Detail - P. 45

HOHOI

Uncharted coast

0   1   2   3   4   5
Approx. Scale n.m.

Not to be used for navigation

N

HAKATAO

Uncharted Coast

Motu Oa

140° 5' W

BAIE D'HAKAHETAU

0   1/5
Approx. Scale n.m.

Not to be used for navigation

9° 21'S

N

10f

R. Rouges

10f

Motukoio

Baie d' Hakahetau

3f

Road to airstrip at Aneou
and beyond to Hakahau

P. Tehenai

Sh

Sh

3f

Motukivi   Dock

R. Anapuai

Church   Hakahetau

140° 06' W

Baie de Vaiehu (Vaieo Bay)

This is a large, open bay at the westernmost part of the island, between Cap Punahu on the north and Pointe Motukoio, with its prominent obelisk, on the south. Anchorage can be taken in the northern part of the bay close to shore in about 14.5m (8 fathoms), where there is good protection from easterly winds. Swell is a factor and thus the other bays are generally preferred. Baie de Vaiehu is uninhabited, but a short hike over the ridge to the north leads to the village of Haakuti and further along to Hakahetau. The coastal road to the south leads to the village of d'Hakamaii. Landing is easiest in the NE corner of the bay.

Baie Hakaotu

A small indentation between Pointe Motukoio and the peninsula where the prominent landmark of Pain de Sucre (Sugarloaf) is located is Baie Hakaotu. Snug, protected anchorage can be taken with limited swinging room, necessitating fore and aft anchors. Landing is easiest in the northeast corner of the bay.

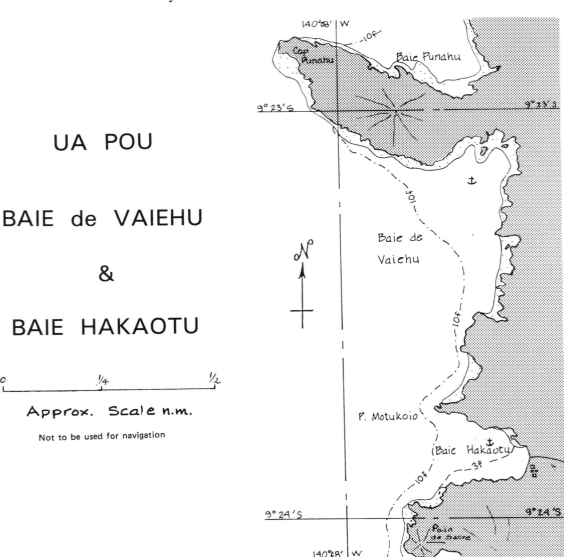

UA POU

BAIE de VAIEHU

&

BAIE HAKAOTU

0   ¼   ½

Approx. Scale n.m.

Not to be used for navigation

Baie Hakamaii (Baie Haka Maii)

This small bight lies 2 miles SSE of Baie Vaiehu (1.5 miles SE of Sugarloaf) and has traditionally given cruisers a warm welcome. The yellow, blue and red painted panels on the front of the stone church resemble large stained glass windows when viewed from the sea. Good holding anchorage may be found about 180m (200 yds.) from the head of the bay, midway between the southern shore and a large, low, black rock near the northern side of the entrance. It may be necessary to set a stern anchor to keep the yacht perpendicular to the swell at night when the wind changes direction. Landing on the beach at the head of the bay must be well timed, depending on sea conditions.

The tiny village is quite isolated and the people use traditional canoes for fishing. The sale of wood and stone carvings and copra support the local population. A trail inland from the village of <u>Hakamaii</u> follows the river where mosquitoes are a pest.

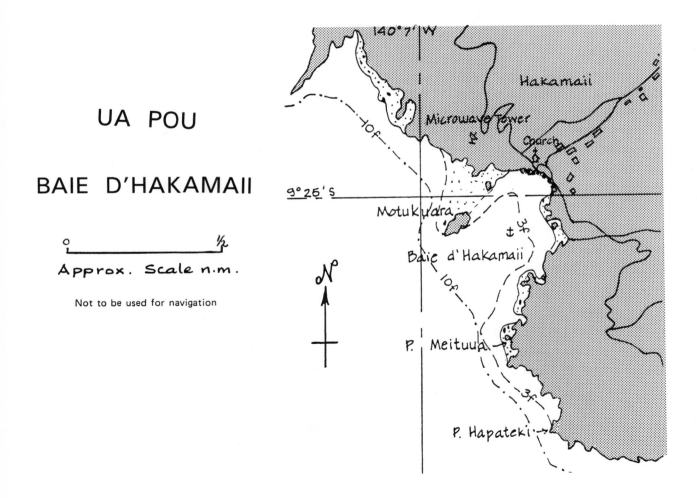

UA POU

BAIE D'HAKAMAII

9°25'S

Approx. Scale n.m.

Not to be used for navigation

HIVA OA (Dominica Island)

Hiva Oa, the largest of the Iles Marquises, is the main island of the southern group of four islands of this archipelago. It lies east-west, and the land falls to the indented coastline from a central ridge of high mountains reaching 1,067m (3,5OO') at the eastern end. Much of the coast is composed of steep cliffs. Pointe Teaehoa stretches to the south forming a large bay, Baie Taaoa (also called Baie Vipihai or Traitor's Bay). At its northern end is a smaller bay, Baie Atuona and the **Port of Entry** of <u>Atuona</u>. South of Hanakee, Baie Taaoa is open to the prevailing winds and seas. Several bays along the northern coast can be used as anchorages. The current generally sets westward along the southern coast.

Baie Atuona and Baie Tahuku

These two adjacent bays indent the northern part of Baie Taaoa, otherwise known as Traitor's Bay. They are separated by a small rocky point, Pointe Feki, on which there is a light. Between Pointe Feki and Ilot Hanakee to the south is the open bay of Atuona (Traitor's Bay). A somewhat rolly anchorage may be had within the mouth of the bay in 8 to 10 fathoms or you can anchor in the breakwater-protected area and Med-tie to the breakwater. Leave adequate maneuvering space off the breakwater for freighters/passenger ships from Papeete which dock at the wharf regularly.

The largest town on Hiva Oa is <u>Atuona</u> where entry permits for the Marquises can be obtained at the gendarmerie located downtown. With a population of over 1,500, Atuona is the administrative center for the southern Marquises. It has a radio station, bank, hospital, church, bishopric, hotels and restaurants. International telephone calls and faxes may be sent from the post office. In addition to water and various groceries, beef and excellent goat meat are available at stores in the town (closed from 1130 to 1430). Fresh fruit and vegetables are usually difficult to find, but on the road west of the village there are some market gardens which may sell produce in season. The airstrip, with connections to Tahiti, is on the plateau north of the village.

The French artist, Paul Gauguin lived in Atuona. He and Jacques Brel, a songwriter, are buried in the Calvary Cemetery, on a hill overlooking the bay, about a one-hour walk from town. The Gauguin Museum features copies of his art and various memorabilia.

It is a one-hour hike to the site where Jacques Brel planned to build a house (Belvedere). Here, a memorial in his honor has been erected where the view of the town and bay is spectacular. In addition several sights of interest are in the vicinity, in the valley behind the anchorage where petroglyphs can be seen or by walking or hitch-hiking to the village of <u>Taha'a</u> (5 miles west of Atuona) where you can find a tiki and some paepaes.

Baie Tahuku

This bay is immediately to the east of Pointe Feki. Narrower than Baie Atuona, both its orientation and a breakwater near its mouth greatly reduce the effect of the swell, though backwash effects do occur. Anchorage may be taken between the concrete steps and a concrete wharf, in 5 fathoms, good holding, sand bottom. Landing can be made at either the steps or the wharf where showers and fresh water are available. The head of the bay is shoal and swimming is inadvisable because of the large shark population.

ILES MARQUISES
ILE HIVA OA

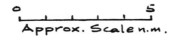

Approx. Scale n.m.

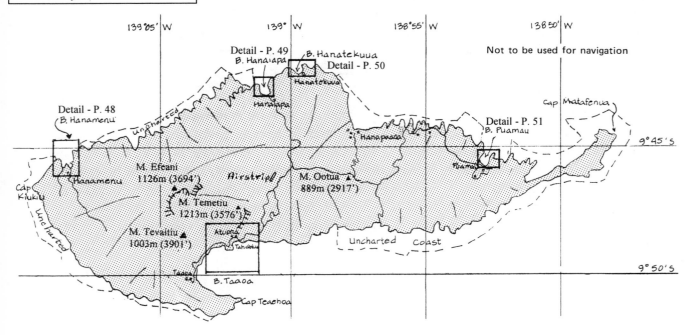

Not to be used for navigation

BAIE TAAOA
(Traitor's Bay)

BAIE ATUONA
&
BAIE TAHUKU

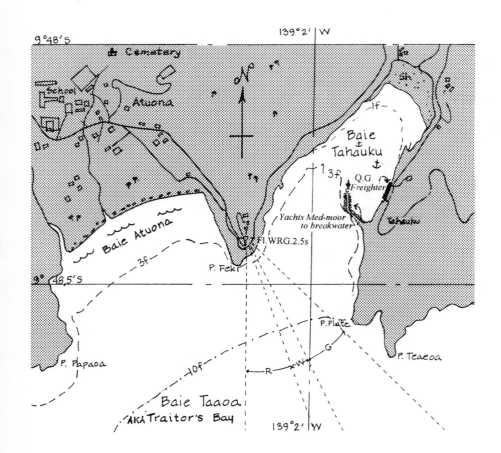

Approx. Scale n.m.

Not to be used for navigation

Baie Hanamenu (Hana Menu)

A double-lobed indentation is at the northwestern end of Hiva Oa, between Point Kaunakua (Point Gaussin) on the east and Point Matatana (Point Bonnard) on the west. The bay is divided into two by the steep-sided peninsula terminating with Point Matahau marked with a steep, massive dark rock, Grosse Tour, 112m (368') high. Anse Tanaeka (Hanaheka), the western bay is shallow and open. Baie Hanamenu is the eastern bay. It is deeply indented with steep, almost overhanging cliffs on the western side and on the east are the slopes of a mountain ridge. The head of the bay is shoal with a lovely beach and a coconut palm plantation beyond.

Vessels may travel well into Baie Hanamenu, anchoring toward the head in about 6 fathoms, sand bottom. It is a good idea to buoy your anchor to assist is retrieving it in case sunken tree trunks on the bottom foul the vessel's anchor. Northerly winds make the anchorage rough and squalls may sometimes be felt off the steep walls. A strong onshore breeze often comes up in the afternoon, making landing through the surf difficult. The bay is occasionally visited by wild pig and cattle hunters. The small village of Hanamenu at the head of the bay has no facilities but water reported to be of excellent quality is available from the stream at the eastern end of the beach.

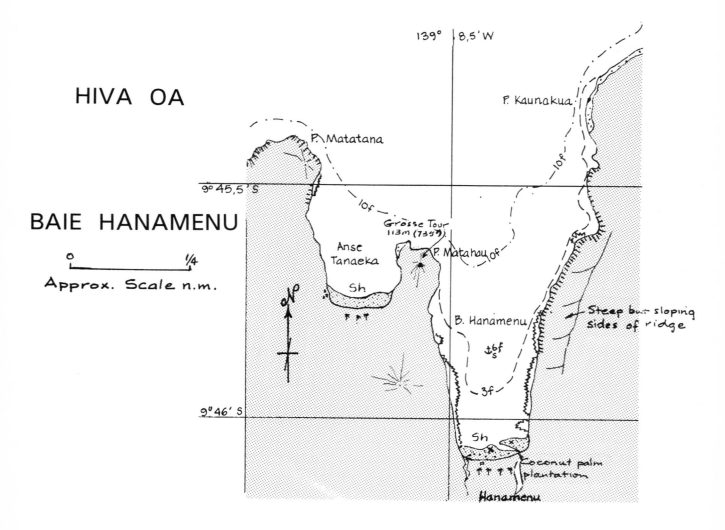

Baie Hanaiapa

Located on the north coast of Hiva Oa, Baie Hanaiapa is between Pointe du Dome on the east and Pointe Jouan on the west. Excellent protection from easterly winds and anchorage in good holding sand in 7 to 10 fathoms can be taken in the middle of the bay. Do not proceed far into the bay as some coral is found and a very shallow spot extends northwest of the little peninsula extending from the head of the bay. This is the best anchorage on the north side of the island.

A rough concrete wharf on the east side of the bay is joined to the village of <u>Hanaiapa</u> by road which leads on to Atuona and Puamau. The tiny village stretches for more than a kilometer (.6 miles) and the luxuriant variety of colorful flowers make visiting it a treat. A well kept paepae is featured in the center of the village. The harvesting of copra is the mainstay of people in the area. The copra-drying sheds with their removable covers attest to the showers frequently experienced.

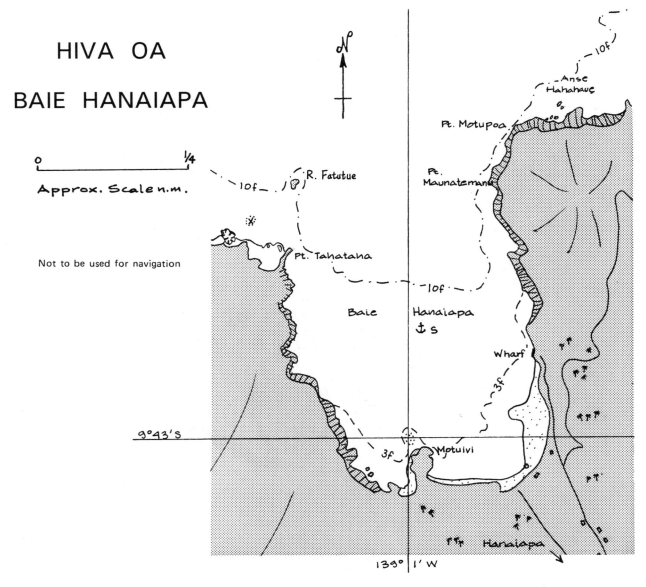

HIVA OA

BAIE HANAIAPA

0 ————————— 1/4

Approx. Scale n.m.

Not to be used for navigation

9°43'S

139° 1' W

BAIE HANATEKUUA

Baie Hanatekuua is five miles west of Pointe Mautau. The French Hydrographic Service states that vessels may find suitable anchorage about 250m (800') from the NE point of the bay when it has a bearing of 054° or closer to the coast in 5 - 6 fathoms, sand. There are no facilities at the small village of Hanatekuua.

HIVA OA
BAIE HANATEKUUA

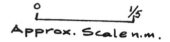

Approx. Scale n.m.

Not to be used for navigation

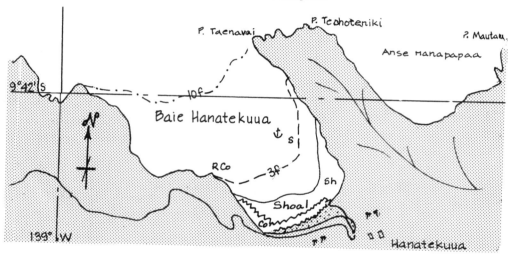

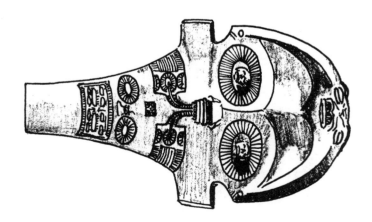

MARQUESAN WAR CLUB

Baie Puamau

Open to the northeast, Baie Puamau is between Pointe Mataai on the west and Pointe Obelisque on the east. The hill on this point is surmounted by a natural obelisk composed of two vertical rocks separated by a fissure. Two coral-fringed motus in the eastern part of the bay are difficult to identify when approaching from the west and should be given safe clearance. Anchorage in good holding sand can be taken in 6 - 8 fathoms in the center of the bay or you may also anchor closer to the eastern shore where the effect of the swell may be less noticeable. Landing may be made at the concrete wharf in the southeast corner of the bay where a road leads to town. The swell combined with slippery steps can make landing on the wharf quite difficult and extreme care must be taken. The bay is exposed to the north and with fresh breezes from northeast to northnorthwest the anchorage become unfenable; the current enters the bay and a strong northwesterly set develops. Because its exposure the bay is always affected by swell making it a rolly anchorage.

For those who are interested in archeological sites, Puamau must be near the top of the list since this is the location of one of the most extensive archeological sites on the island. It is a half-hour walk through the town to Iipona where Takaii, the largest tiki in the world, standing at 2.43m (8') can be seen. In addition, massive terraces, petroglyphs and various statues on the site make it truly a spectacular place to visit. A road links the Puamau to Atuona.

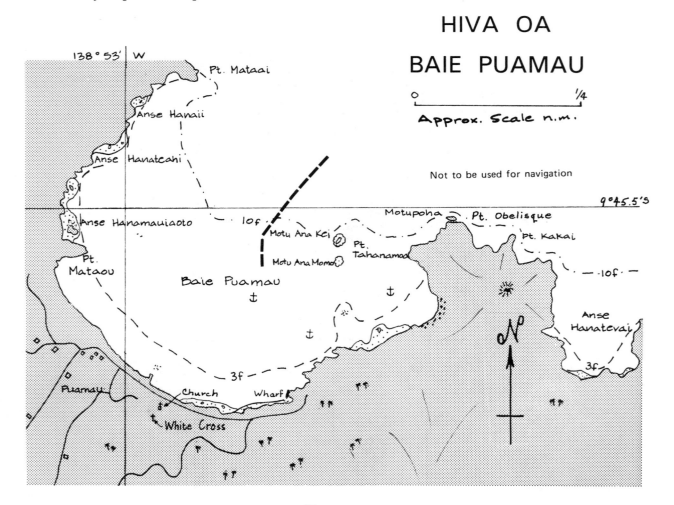

HIVA OA

BAIE PUAMAU

0   1/4

Approx. Scale n.m.

Not to be used for navigation

TAHUATA

This island lies south of Hiva Oa across the 4km (2.5) miles width of Canal du Bordelais. Here, as is normal in narrow passages between high islands, the wind and sea are usually more intense. A 2 - 3 knot westerly current is typical in this passage unless there have been several days of westerly winds. The center of the island is a 457m (1,500') mountain chain, radiating out in steep ridges and valleys to the coast. It is well worth sailing around the island to see the southern coastline which is rugged and has spectacular scenery. The principal villages of Vaitahu and Hapatoni are on the west coast. The population of the island is about 600.

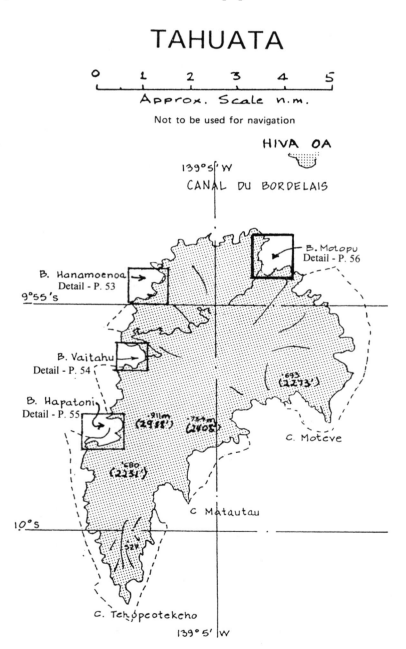

TAHUATA

0   1   2   3   4   5
Approx. Scale n.m.

Not to be used for navigation

Baie Hanamoenoa (Hana moe noa)

This is the most popular anchorage on Tahuata. It is 3.2km (2 miles) NNW of Baie Vaitahu and is the third sandy bay visible after coming around the corner from Atuona. Anchorage may be taken in the middle of the bay in 5 fathoms, good holding sand. The clear water provides excellent diving and shelling although the beach has many nonos. Eric Hiscock rated this as one of the three most beautiful anchorages in Polynesia.

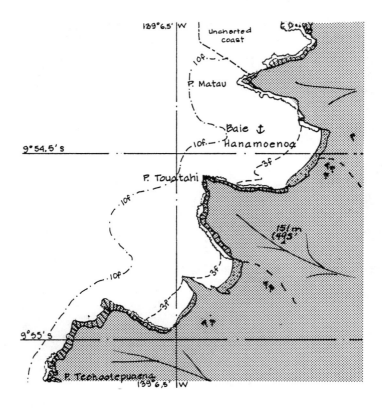

BAIE HANAMOENOA

Approx. Scale n.m.

Not to be used for navigation

Baie Vaitahu

Situated 3.2 (2 miles SSW) of Hanamoenoe, this is the site of <u>Viatahu</u>, the largest village on the island. As an anchorage the bay has some shortcomings. Though protected from the prevailing winds, it is fairly open and has such a steeply sloping bottom that it is not dependable. Squalls blowing over the mountains into the bay may cause dragging, so it is advisable to set two anchors off the bow. Northerly winds and swell also make the anchorage untenable. Landing can be difficult on the beaches and may have to be made at the concrete wharf.

The town has an infirmary, radio station, telephone, post office and a small museum. several sights of interest in the village. A monument in the center of the village proclaims the true Marquisan name for the islands–Fenua Enata (Land of Men). Eglise Sainte Marie de L'enfant Jesus, a Catholic church built near the shore, was built in commemoration of the 150th anniversary of the arrival of Catholic missionaries to the islands. The structure has been designed to artistically combine local wood with discarded stones used as ballast for 19th century trading ships. A beautiful stained glass window graces the altar. Several archeological sites can be visited in the valley beyond the village. Bone carvings are sold at a studio near the church where tattoos can also be obtained

Viatahu has been the site of several historic occurrences in the past. It was that the first European visitors disembark: the Spaniard Mendana in 1595 followed by James Cook in 1774. In 1842 Admiral Dupetit-Thouars signed the treaty linking the archipelago to France.

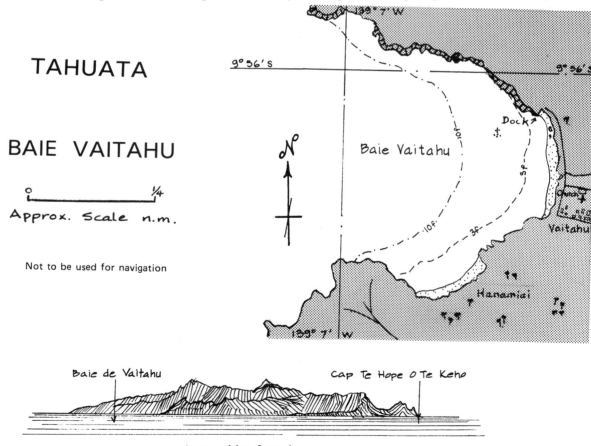

Approaching from the west

Baie Hapatoni

This beautiful bay is 2.4km (1.5) miles south of Baie Vaitahu, is the southern part of a double-lobed indentation between Pointe Fakaua on the north and Point Vaioteoho on the south. The village of Hapatoni is one of the friendliest and most attractive in the island group. The villagers welcome visitors with a sincerity that is heartwarming. Landing at the concrete wharf can be difficult when surf is present and care must be taken to avoid an accident. When the sea is calm excellent snorkeling can be enjoyed in the shallows near the dock.

The anchorage area is directly off the village; it is quite deep, sometimes rolly, and has many coral heads on which the anchor can be snagged. The tree-lined road through the village leads to a large, recently restored archeological site consisting of huge stone platforms (maeae) which is near a Christian cemetery. Handicrafts sold in the covered marketplace adjacent to the bay include beautifully carved wooden bowls and replicas of javelins, necklaces and bottles of locally made fragrant coconut oil scented sandalwood (Pani Puahi).

Baie Hanatefau

This uninhabited bay is the next bay to the north, separated brom Baie Hapatoni by rocky Pointe Matautu. It is a better anchorage and has some of the best snorkeling in the Marquises with good visibility and excellent coral formations..

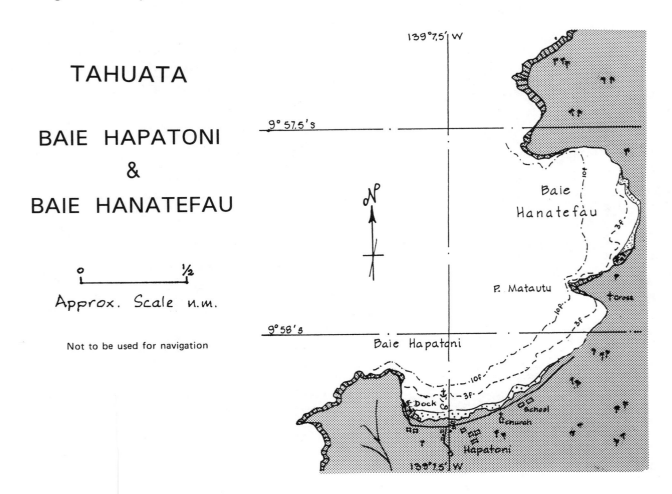

TAHUATA

BAIE HAPATONI
&
BAIE HANATEFAU

0 ——— ½
Approx. Scale n.m.

Not to be used for navigation

Baie Motopu

Situated southeast of the northern extremity of Tahuata, Baie Motupu is an open bay entered between two points bordered with steep, rocky cliffs. Point Paona divides the shoal areas at the head of the bay in two. Avoid the shoal patch almost awash located a short distance northeast of the point.

Good anchorage in sand and coral may be taken in 6 - 7 fathoms sand and coral. The bay is seldom visited by cruisers and a stop-over would likely be met with a warm welcome.

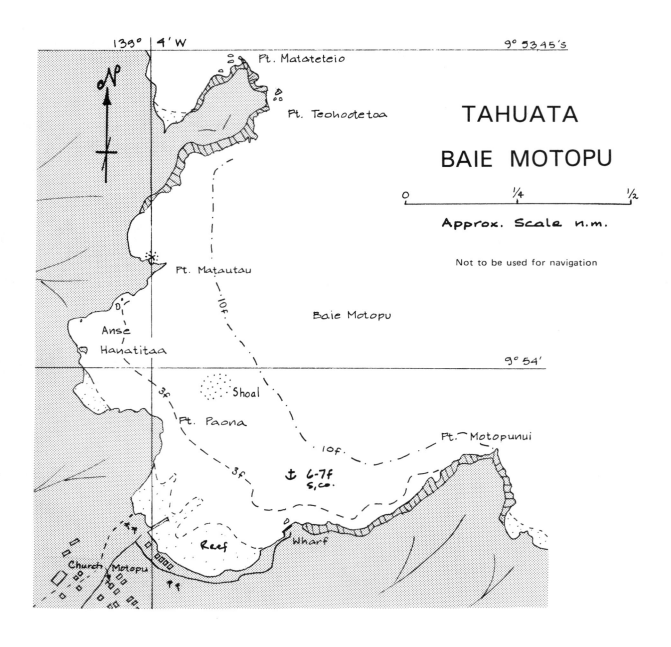

FATU HIVA (FATU-HIVA, FATUIVA or FATU 'IVA)

The southernmost island of Iles Marquises, Fatu Hiva lies about 35 miles south of Hiva Oa. With its heavy rainfall and lush vegetation, it is the most beautiful island in the Marquises. Featured in Thor Heyerdahl's book of the same name, it is the only island without an airstrip and is therefore the most unspoiled. The central range of mountains runs north-south, reaching 960m (3,150') at the south end. The eastern side is steep, precipitous and pounded by heavy surf; only on the western, lee side, are there useable anchorages. The most practicable for small vessels is Baie des Vierges. It is tempting to make Fatu Hiva the first stop in the Marquises, before reporting in at Atuona. Although some cruisers have done this without facing any consequences others have been reported to the gendarme in Atuona where a fine has been levied.

This is the only island where tapa cloth (produced from the inner bark of trees) is still being made. This time-consuming process is interesting to observe and several of the crafts-women are pleased to demonstrate the how it is done. The source of the bark determines the color of the tapa cloth; off-white bark comes from the mulberry tree, medium brown is from the breadfruit tree and dark brown comes from the banyan tree. Because many cruisers visit this bay, the inhabitants have become market-wise, demanding realistic returns for their tapa.

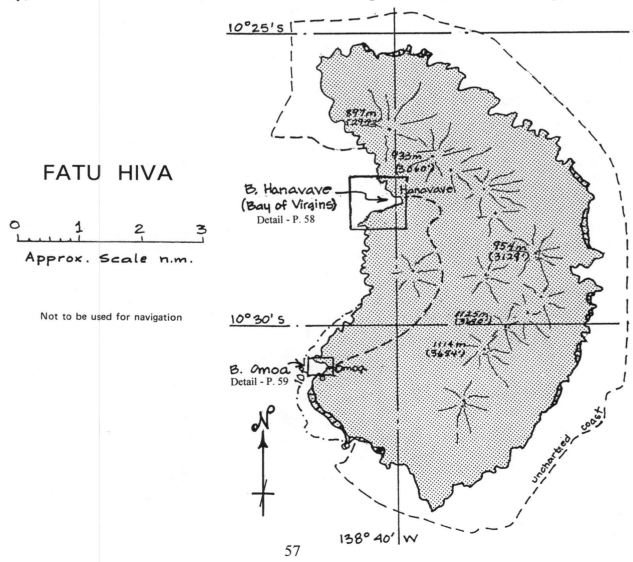

FATU HIVA

0   1   2   3

Approx. Scale n.m.

Not to be used for navigation

10°25' S

897m
(2922')

433m
(3660')

B. Hanavave
(Bay of Virgins)
Detail - P. 58

Hanavave

954m
(3124')

1125m
(3660')

10°30' S

1114m
(3654')

B. Omoa
Detail - P. 59

Omoa

N

Uncharted coast

138° 40' W

Baie Hanavave/Baie des Vierges (Bay of the Virgins)*

This incredibly beautiful bay lies about 2.5 miles SSE of Pointe Teaitehoe, the northern end of the island. The rocky spires near the head of the bay are the most noticeable feature. On either side and beyond are dark green cloaked, steep-sided mountains creating a spectacular view which is made more dramatic when highlighted by the setting sun. It has a .5 mile wide opening which narrows to a beach at the head of the bay. The bottom is steeply sloping and the 18m (10-fathom) curve is well within the bay. Though swells are tolerable, gusty winds sweeping down the steep slopes can cause a vessel to drag. In archaic Marquesan, Hanavave means "strong surf bay," a name that is most appropriate at times.

The bay is entered by lining up a steep pinnacle rock on the north side with a whitish peak halfway up the slope behind. Small vessels can then proceed toward the head of the bay to anchor in 11m (6 fathoms), good holding mud and sand. At the north end of the beach is the village of Hanavave where landing can be made at the concrete wharf at the north end of the bay. The dock is usually affected by an ever-present swell; consequently, care and heavy fenders are needed to make a safe landing. The village is famous for its many graceful outrigger canoes which are used for fishing and visiting Baie d 'Omoa.

About an hour's walk behind the village, is a spectacular 61m (200') waterfall, or you may take a hike to Omoa, about 16km (10 miles) distant, which takes 4 to 5 hours. Along the way orchards of cashew trees and noni plantations can be seen. Beyond the highest part of the trail windfall mangos provide a tasty snack in season where the road is covered with a blanket of dried mango seeds. Water in the former swimming hole in the river is polluted.

*It has been rumored that the bay was originally named "Bay des Verges" (Bay of the Phalli) by early explorers because of the shape of the rocky pillars. Supposedly the missionaries disapproved, and inserted an "i" making it "Bay des Vierges" which translates to Bay of the Virgins.

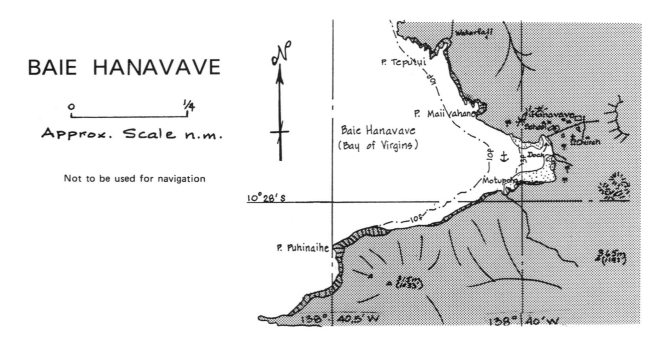

BAIE HANAVAVE

0   ¼

Approx. Scale n.m.

Not to be used for navigation

Baie Omoa

This bay, 3 miles south of Baie des Vierges, lies between Pointe Matahumu in the north and Motutapu (30m/100'), a dark, rocky spire to the south. Beyond the head of the bay is a conspicuous slender pinnacle, Pierre Bonhomme (104m/336'). To enter the bay steer 095°T for Pierre Bonhomme.

Anchorage in about 12m (6 - 7 fathoms) may be taken when the northern entrance point of the bay bears north. This bay is not well suited for small vessels as it is uncomfortable due to swell and poor holding. In addition, strong winds affect the bay and heavy gusts sweep down from the mountains. Landing is possible on a slippery concrete dock where the swell makes this a difficult and sometimes dangerous operation. Alternatively, if conditions permit, landing can be attempted on the northwest point or in the southeast corner of the bay, near the village.

Near the chapel there is a good museum that is well worth visiting. A few petroglyphs may be found in the vicinity.

Occasionally it is possible to trade for tapa, wood carvings or other crafts. In addition to being items of interest for trading, the following may also be used as gifts: small bottles of perfume, sunglasses, fishing gear, toys, earrings for pierced ears, hair clips, tools or T-shirts. An indication of the wide-ranging influence of television is the fact that figurines of well known landmarks such as the Eiffel Tour, Statue of Liberty and London Bridge are prized trading items in these remote islands.

BAIE OMOA

Approx. Scale n.m.

Not to be used for navigation

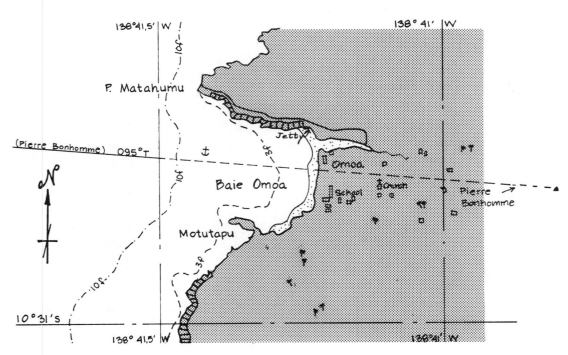

NORTHERN ISLETS

Two groups of small, uninhabited islands are located west and north of Nuku Hiva. One group is Motu Iti, the second group is comprised of Eiao, Hatutaa, and Motu One. This group is about 52 miles northwest of Nuku Hiva. **WARNING**: Fish poisoning is reported to be prevalent around the islands; trolling well offshore from the area does not have the same hazard.

Motu Iti

Motu Iti is a cluster of three rocky islets. The largest islet is a sheer, 220m (722') rock 23 miles WNW of Nuku Hiva. Deposits of guano on the smaller rocks gives a whitish appearance from a distance.

Eiao

Eiao is about 7 miles long and rises to about 579m (1,900') at its northwestern end. The south coast is steep and inaccessible; the north coast has several small bays. About midway up the island is Baie Vaituha, the largest bay, where vessels anchor in 22m (12-13 fathoms) near its head. Landing is possible on the sand and stone beach but the swell can make going ashore troublesome and the stay uncomfortable. At one time the island was inhabited but now only sheep and goats live on the island and are gradually destroying the vegetation.

Hatutaa

Hatutaa is smaller than Eiao and is an uninhabited island which rises to 427m (1,400') about 3 miles ENE of Eiao. The channel between the two islands should not be used.

Motu One (Ile de Sable or Sand Island)

Motu One consists of two small islands 11 miles ENE of Hatutaa. The sea breaks heavily on the banks surrounding the islands.

SOUTHERN ISLANDS

MOTANE (San Pedro Island)

This small island, 518m (1,700') high lies about 12 miles east of Tahuata and is south of Hiva Oa. Hunters from Hiva Oa and Fatu Hiva visit the island to kill the wild goats and mouton sheep which roam the island, almost denuding it of its vegetation There is little incentive to visit Motane for it has no harbors or anchorages though landing is possible in the lee of the NW side.

FATU HUKA

This small, cliff-edged islet, reaching 361m/1,184' is 32 km (20 miles) north of Hiva Oa and 65 miles east of Ua Pou. The sea breaks over two rocky heads 2 miles NNW and 1.25 miles NE of it.

ROCHER THOMASSET

This dangerous, solitary rock lies 14 miles ENE of the northern extremity of Fatu Hiva.

TATTOOS

The ancient art of tattooing has been practiced for centuries in many parts of the world and throughout Pacific islands. Marquisan tattoo artistry is considered to be the ultimate because of the intricacy and quality of the designs.

In the South Pacific distinctive patterns are unique to each area and are clearly recognizable. At one time, even newborn infants were given a small tattoo and as the child matured more were added. In some cases the entire body was completely covered. Tattoos were considered elegant and were believed to give the bearer additional power and status. The use of geometric patterns in Marquisan tattoos is supplemented by stylized motifs such as these:

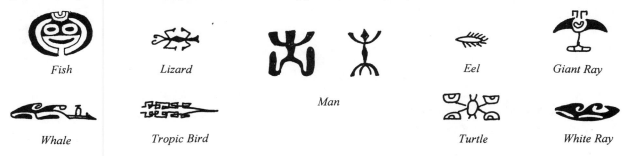

Fish	*Lizard*		*Man*	*Eel*	*Giant Ray*
Whale	*Tropic Bird*			*Turtle*	*White Ray*

TAPA CLOTH ARTISTRY

This example of a tapa cloth from Fatu Hiva illustrates the intricate and beautifullly designed use of patterns similar to those used by tattoo artists. The actual size of the tapa shown here is 42cm x 33cm (16" x 13"). It was done on the dark brown bark from a banyan tree; some of the texture of the tapa shows through.

ARCHIPEL DES TUAMOTU (TUAMOTU ARCHIPELAGO)

This group of 78 islands, all but two being coral atolls, lies spread across 150° of longitude and extends almost 1,000 miles in a NW-SE direction. In contrast to the lush vegetation of the Marquises, the atolls have little greenery except for palm trees and short grass. Together with the Marquises and Society Islands they form French Polynesia, administered from Tahiti.

These islands have justifiably been called the "Low or Dangerous Archipelago." because of their low-lying character, making them visible from a yacht only when the vessel is within 8 miles. Typically, the motus (islets) on the reefs are clustered to a greater degree on the northern and western sides while the southern sides are often bare, awash coral reefs. This is very dangerous, since even in daylight the reef cannot be seen until close-to and the sound of the wind and sea often masks the sound of the breakers.

Not so long ago, most cruising plans aimed at only sighting and passing the Tuamotu safely. Today, a few atolls are regularly visited and are included in cruising itineraries. But do not underestimate the dangers of traveling in these waters; the increased number of yachts lost and stranded on reefs attests to the hazards.

The atolls most often visited are Manihi, Ahe, Takaroa and Rangiroa, since they are close to the usual route to Tahiti. Occasional visits are made to Arutua, Apataki, Aratika and Fakarava; sketches of these and other atolls follow, but this does not infer that they are easy to visit, nor that the Tuamotu may be cruised with greater safety than previously.

Routes Through the Archipelago

The Tuamotu may be avoided by steering well to westward of Mataiva, the westernmost atoll, before reaching down to Tahiti. The most direct, and most used, route through the archipelago makes a landfall at Takaroa and then passes through the 20-mile gap between Rangiroa and Arutua. An alternate route through the Chenal de Fakarava provides the most direct route to Tahiti from the Panama Canal. Alternatively, one may stop at Raroia or Makemo and leave the Tuamotu for Tahiti from Tahanea.

French Nuclear Tests

The testing of nuclear weapons in the southeastern part of the Tuamotu archipelago ended in January, 1996 but the area south of 17°20'S Latitude and east of 145°25'W Longitude continues to remain off limits to cruisers unless prior permission has been obtained.

Spider Conch
(Lambis lambis Linne)

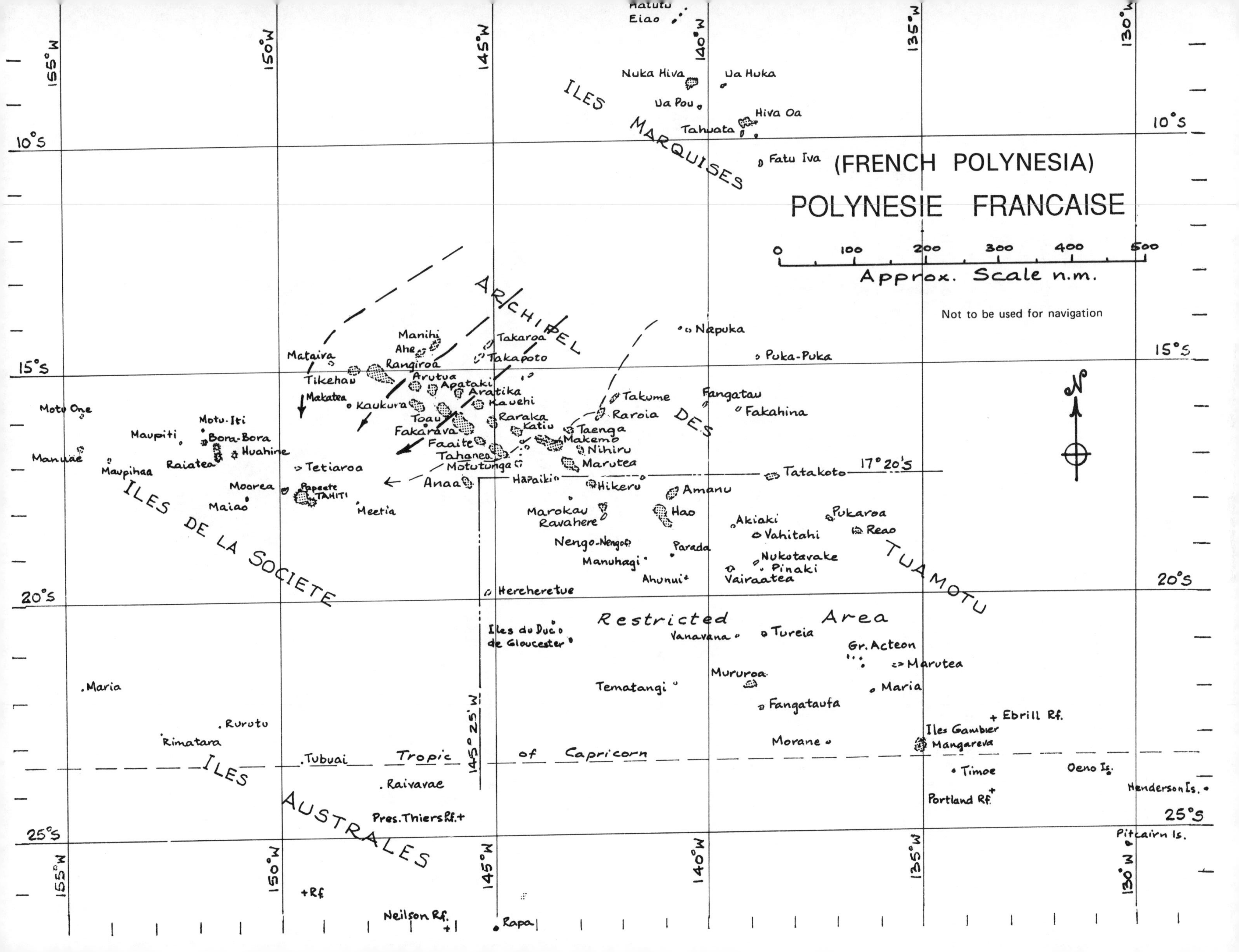

POLYNESIE FRANCAISE
(FRENCH POLYNESIA)

Approx. Scale n.m.

Not to be used for navigation

0   100   200   300   400   500

ILES MARQUISES

Aatutu
Eiao
Nuka Hiva
Ua Huka
Ua Pou
Tahuata
Hiva Oa
Fatu Iva

ARCHIPEL DES TUAMOTU

Napuka
Puka-Puka
Fangatau
Fakahina
Takume
Raroia
Taenga
Makemo
Nihiru
Marutea
Takaroa
Takapoto
Arutua
Apataki
Aratika
Kauehi
Manihi
Ahe
Rangiroa
Raraka
Katiu
Toau
Fakarava
Faaite
Tahanea
Motutunga
Anaa
Haraiki
Hikeru
Amanu
Hao
Parada
Ahunui
Marokau
Ravahere
Nengo-Nengo
Manuhagi
Hereheretue
Akiaki
Vahitahi
Nukotavake
Pinaki
Vairaatea
Pukaroa
Reao
Tatakoto   17° 20'S

Mataiva
Tikehau
Makatea
Kaukura
Tetiaroa
Meetia

Iles du Duc
de Gloucester

Restricted Area
Vanavana
Tureia
Tematangi
Mururoa
Fangataufa
Morane
Gr. Acteon
Marutea
Maria

Tropic of Capricorn   145° 25'W

ILES DE LA SOCIETE

Motu One
Maupiti
Motu-Iti
Bora-Bora
Huahine
Maupihaa
Raiatea
Moorea
Maiao
Papeete
TAHITI
Manuae

ILES AUSTRALES

Maria
Rimatara
Rurutu
Tubuai
Raivavae
Pres.Thiers Rf.
Neilson Rf.
Rapa
Rf.

Iles Gambier
Ebrill Rf.
Mangareva
Maria
Marutea
Timoe
Portland Rf.
Oeno Is.
Henderson Is.
Pitcairn Is.

10°S   15°S   20°S   25°S

130°W   135°W   140°W   145°W   150°W   155°W

ATOLL MANIHI (Wilsons Island)

This atoll and its companion, Ahe, together with the other pair of Takaroa and Takapoto, are the northernmost of the Tuamotu. As a result, they are close to the usual route followed by the majority of cruisers and are likely to be visited. For this reason they are described in more detail than other locations. Manihi and Ahe lie close together about 40 miles WNW of Takapoto.

Passe Tairapa is an easily identified, well defined pass on the southwest side of Manihi. The village of <u>Manihi</u>, on the eastern side of the pass, is visible from offshore and is a good landmark for identifying the pass. On its western side is a long, curving island where an airstrip is about 2.5 miles northwest of the village. Two sandy patches on either side of the entrance offer temporary anchorage if you are waiting for improved conditions before entering the pass. The coral reef is close to shore on the ocean side, but on the lagoon side the reef awash extends inward for some distance.

The pass is about 75m (250') wide, decreasing at the inner end to 40m (130'). The half-mile passage is straight, and the western side is deeper. Though a strong current runs out of the pass, it is usually possible to enter and proceed to the lagoon. Within the pass is a straight concrete wharf on the village side. Two large trees are in the little square behind the wharf; casuarina bushes are on the other side of the pass.

Once clear of the coral reef beyond the entrance, anchorage may be taken in the bight about .5 mile beyond the village. Vessels with very shallow draft can moor at the small boat basin at the village, but check water depths before entering. Another pretty and protected anchorage is further to the east in the lee of the long motu that is separated from the village motu by a small islet with four or five palm trees. A sandy bottom with coral patches provides good holding, and the motu acts as a windbreak against the constant strong trade winds which blow across the atoll. There is good shelling on the outer side of the motu.

Other anchorages can be found in the lagoon, but a passage must be threaded through coral heads and suitable swinging room found between them. Such an anchorage is in the curved bight with a white sand beach about .5 mile west of the pass. Another spot is off the Kaina Hotel, but caution is advised for this is a lee shore.

Most of the lagoon can be explored but there are shallow spots and many coral heads to be avoided. The underwater visibility is excellent and diving is superb. A pearl culture station for black-lipped oysters operates on the atoll. WARNING: fish poisoning has been reported here.

ARCHIPEL DES TUAMOTU
AHE & MANIHI

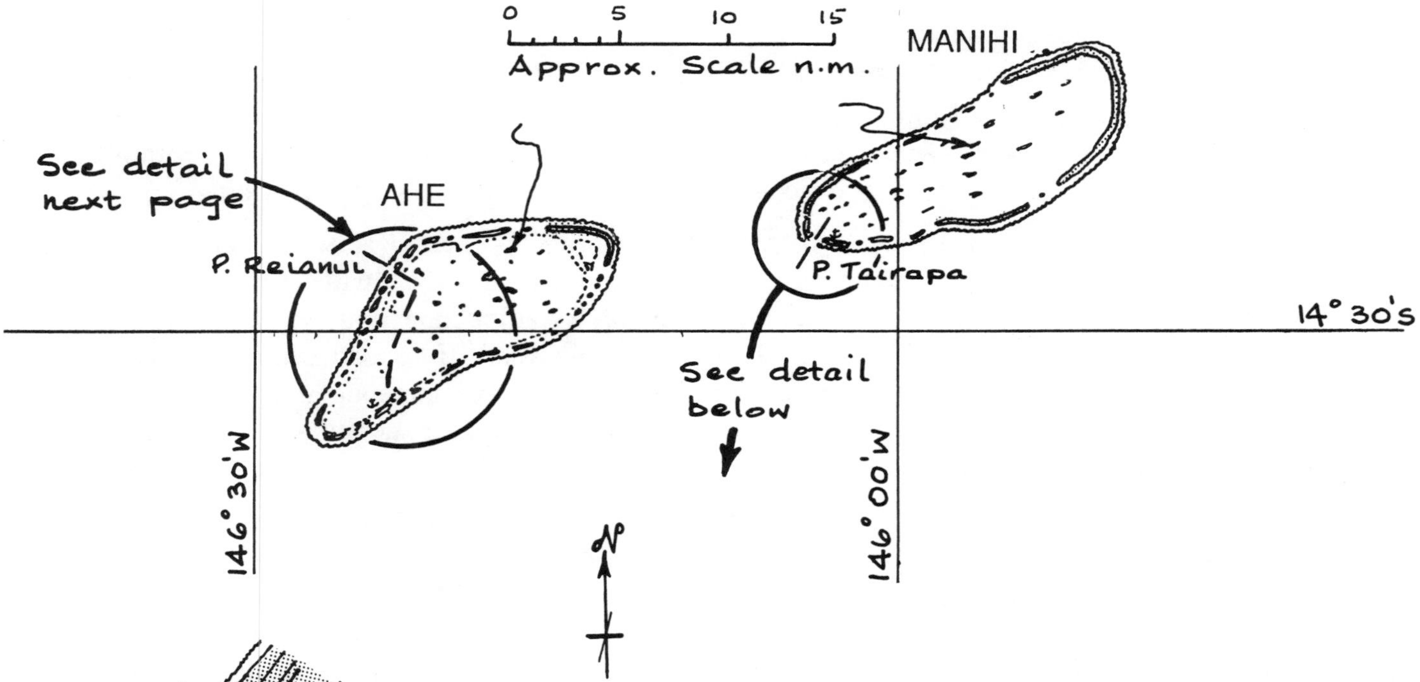

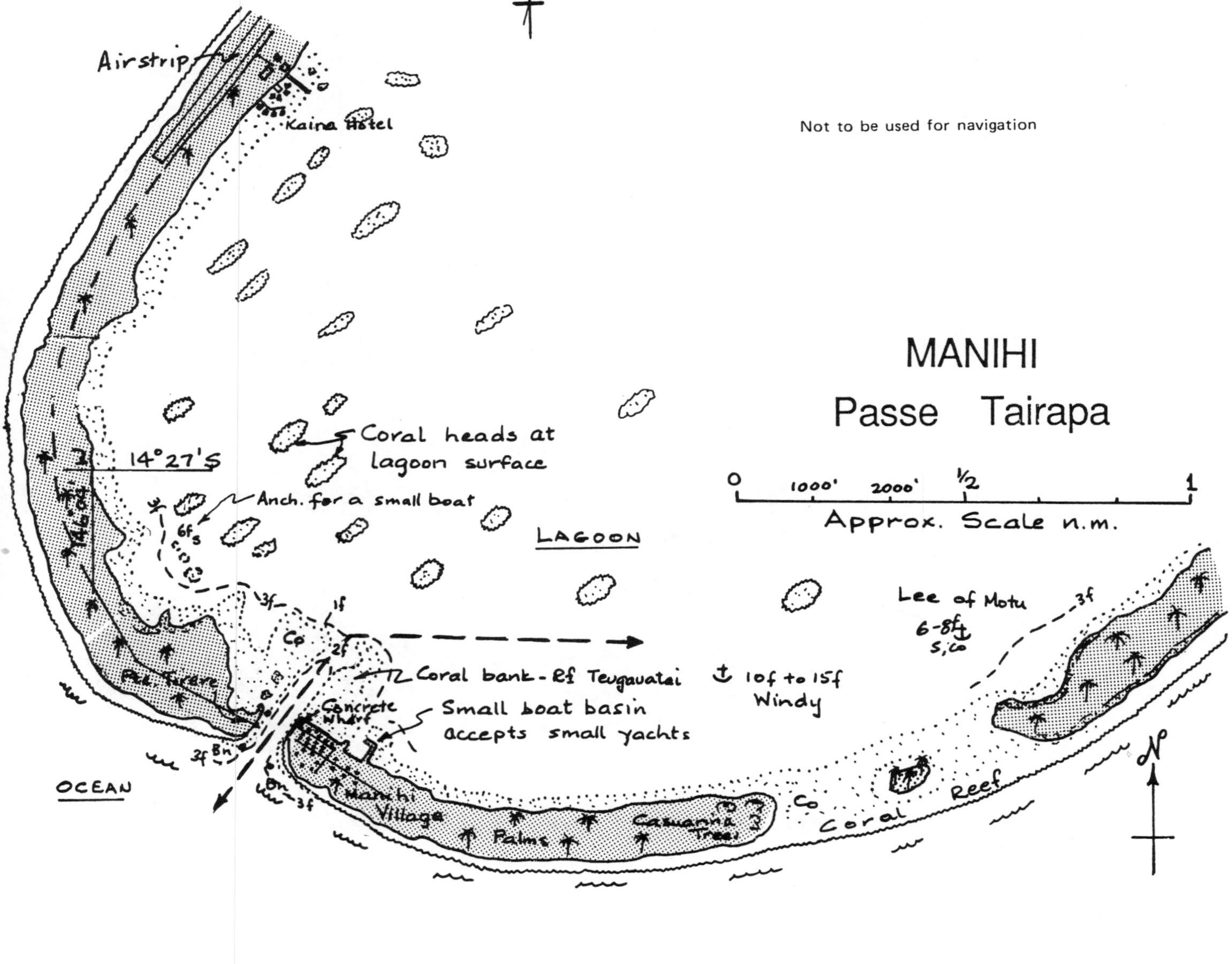

0   5   10   15
Approx. Scale n.m.

MANIHI

AHE

See detail
next page

P. Reianui

P. Tairapa

See detail
below

14° 30'S

146° 30'W

146° 00'W

Airstrip

Kaina Hotel

Not to be used for navigation

14°27'S

2

Coral heads at
lagoon surface

Anch. for a small boat

6fs

LAGOON

MANIHI
Passe Tairapa

Lee of Motu
6-8f
S,Co

3f

0   1000'   2000'   ½   1
Approx. Scale n.m.

3f

1f

Co

2f

Coral bank-Rf Teugauatai

Pt. Terere

Concrete
wharf

Small boat basin
accepts small yachts

10f to 15f
Windy

3f Bn

OCEAN

Co   Coral   Reef

3f

Village

Palms

Casuarina
Trees

Co

N

ATOLL AHE (Peacock Island)

This wooded atoll, 13 miles long and 5 miles wide is about 13km (8 miles) west of Manihi. There are less than 200 inhabitants in the village located on the southwestern part of the atoll. Good radar readings can be received for distances up to 19 miles. The water within the lagoon is clear and the diving is magnificent; the area has been the site of pearl farming.

Passe Reianui is the only pass into the lagoon and is located about 3.2 km (2 miles) southwest of the northwestern point of the atoll. It is about 137m (450') wide at the entrance but is reduced to a navigable width of approximately 26m (85') at the inner end, where the bar limits use to vessels having a draft of less than 3.6m (12'). Entry should be made during slack water since strong tidal currents affect the pass. It is important to have someone aloft to identify the deeper water over the bar and spot coral heads. With the sun overhead, conning is made easier by the exceptionally clear water.

Inside the lagoon are many coral heads exposed and awash between which a route can be threaded to an anchorage. South of the pass is a series of beacons set on coral heads which mark a route to the village of Tenukupara. Anchorage can be taken either outside a coral bar in 22m (12 fathoms), sand and coral bottom, or with care, a boat can pass between the heads to Med-moor to the concrete wharf. Many yachts have visited Ahe and the villager's hospitality is well known. Unfortunately, the great increase in traffic in recent years has placed a heavy load on the resources of the atoll and as a result the once exuberant welcome has been toned down.

Anchorage can also be found off the motus near the entrance in about 15 fathoms. In addition, there is good, but isolated, anchorage at the partially shoaling northeastern end of the atoll.

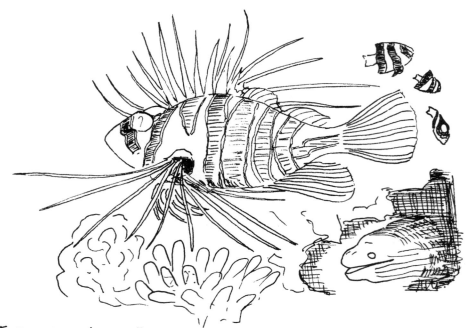

EVEN THE MORAY EEL AVOIDS THE POISONOUS LION FISH.

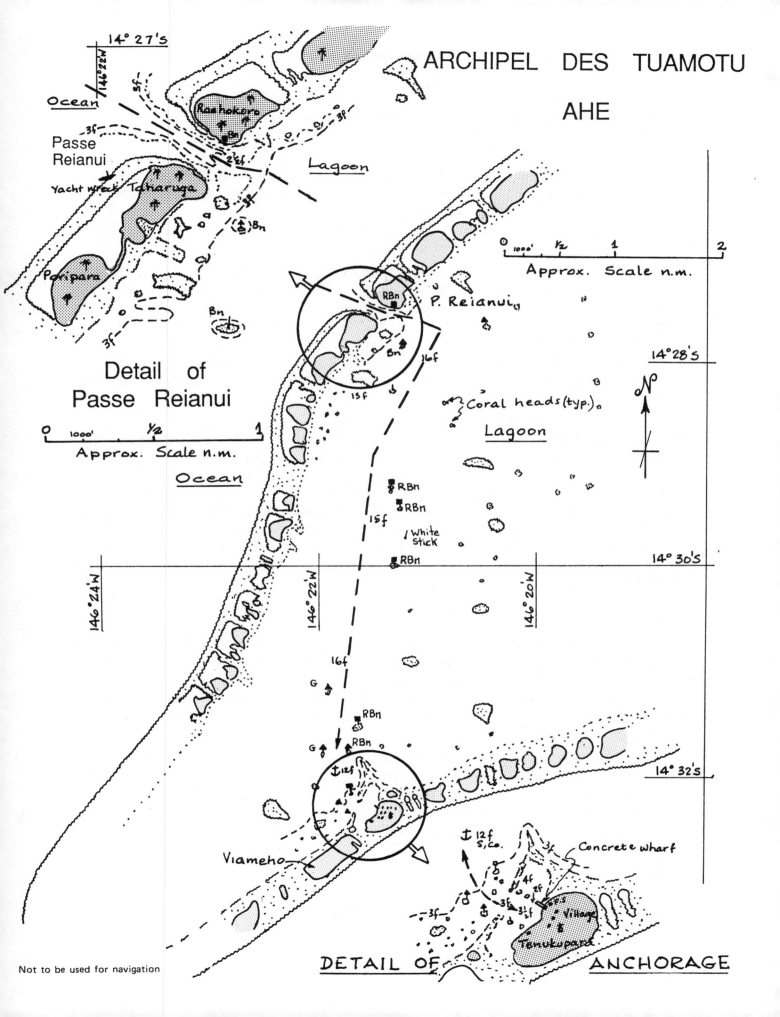

ARCHIPEL DES TUAMOTU
AHE

14° 27'S

146° 22'W

Ocean

3f

Passe Reianui

3f

Raanakoga

3f

2½f

Lagoon

Yacht wreck Teharuga

Poripara

(Δ)Bn

Bn

3f

RBn

P. Reianui

Bn

16f

15f

Detail of Passe Reianui

0   1000'   ½   1

Approx. Scale n.m.

Ocean

0   1000'   ½   1   2

Approx. Scale n.m.

14°28'S

Coral heads (typ.)

Lagoon

N

RBn

RBn

White Stick

15f

RBn

14° 30'S

146° 24'W

146° 22'W

146° 20'W

16f

G

RBn

G

RBn

16f

12f

Viameho

12f S, Co.

Concrete wharf

3f

4f

2f

3f   3½f

6f S

Village

3f

Tenukupara

14° 32'S

Not to be used for navigation

DETAIL OF   ANCHORAGE

ILES DU ROI GEORGES (Takaroa, Takapoto and Tikei)

TAKAROA

This is the northernmost atoll of the group and is often used as a landfall for the Tuamotu. It is easily identified from the north by the large skeletal wreck of the iron sailing ship *County of Roxburgh* rusting on the beach about 4 miles northeast of the pass. At least three other smaller wrecks lie around the island, two on the same beach as the *Roxburgh* and another on the other side of the atoll. Takaroa is lined with palm trees on all sides.

Passe Teavaroa is on the southwest side about 4 miles from the south point of the atoll. Three pairs of beacons, red on the north, black on the south, delineate the pass. It is about 75m (250') wide, rimmed with coral on both sides and a strong current can set out from the pass. The village of Teavaroa and the red-roofed Mormon church on the north side of the pass help to confirm the location. A 60m (200') stone wharf projects from the end of Teavaroa motu into and along the pass. Moorage at the wharf requires large fenders and 23m (75') of mooring lines or temporary anchorage can be taken off the reef on the north side of the pass, out of the current, in about 10 fathoms.

A large sign has been erected prohibiting entry to the lagoon due to pearl farming. Occasionally cruisers tied to the dock are invited to visit the pearl farms within the lagoon. After obtaining permission the vessel is then guided across the lagoon, taking care to avoid coral patches and the numerous ropes and buoys of the pearl farms. Entry into the lagoon involves a turn to port followed by a sharp turn to starboard to avoid the bar at the inner (lagoon) end of the pass. This should be done only at slack water or on the early ebb for ebb currents in the pass reach 9 knots. The sharp bend and strong currents limit vessels entering to 18m (60') in length, 3m (9') draft maximum. Most set an anchor in the channel and stern-tie to the wharf, and leave the wharf with assistance from the current. During heavy winds vessels have been pinned to the wharf by the current for as much as three days.

TAKAPOTO

This coral atoll lies about 5 miles southwest of the south end of Takaroa. It is about 10 miles long and well rimmed with islets and palm trees. Although it has no entry pass, there are villages ashore. The population of the island is about 800 and it has an airport and telephone service. At one time it was one of the richest pearl oyster atolls of the archipelago; pearl farming is once again a major occupation. The lack of a pass causes a higher level of calcium to accumulate in the lagoon, an advantage for pearl farming.

In calm conditions landing can be made at the wharf off the village of Fakatopatere which is easily identified by the red clock tower of the church. It is situated about .5 mile northwest of the south point of the atoll. Two miles to the north is the village of Okukina where a vessel can anchor off the reef and tie up to it. The south point of the reef is marked by a pyramid. The *Aranui* drops off cargo monthly, and tourists are ferried to the island for a few hours.

TIKEI

Located about 140 miles ESE of Takapoto is the two-mile long treed, coral island of Tikei. The island has a small village where landing at the small wharf is reputed to be difficult.

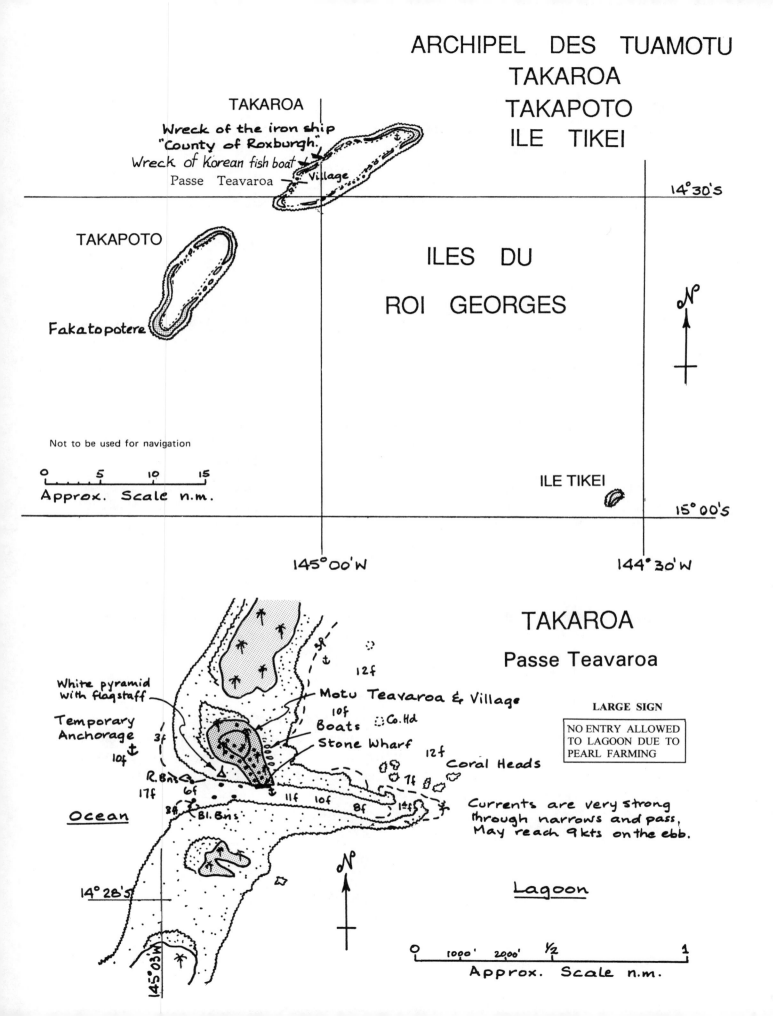

ARCHIPEL DES TUAMOTU
TAKAROA
TAKAPOTO
ILE TIKEI

TAKAROA

Wreck of the iron ship
"County of Roxburgh."
Wreck of Korean fish boat
Passe Teavaroa — Village

14°30'S

TAKAPOTO

ILES DU
ROI GEORGES

Fakatopotere

N

Not to be used for navigation

0   5   10   15
Approx. Scale n.m.

ILE TIKEI

15°00'S

145°00'W

144°30'W

TAKAROA
Passe Teavaroa

3f
12f

White pyramid
with flagstaff

Motu Teavaroa & Village

LARGE SIGN

NO ENTRY ALLOWED
TO LAGOON DUE TO
PEARL FARMING

Temporary
Anchorage

10f
Boats
Co. Hd
Stone Wharf

3f

10f

12f
Coral Heads

R. Bns
17f
6f
11f 10f
8f
14f
8f 7f 8

Ocean
8f
Bl. Bns

Currents are very strong
through narrows and pass,
May reach 9 kts on the ebb.

N

14°28'S

Lagoon

145°03'W

0   1000'   2000'   ½   1
Approx. Scale n.m.

MATAHIVA

This is the westernmost atoll of the Tuamotu Archipelago. Located 22 miles WNW of Tikehau, a deep channel separates the two atolls. It measures about 5 miles from east to west and 3 miles from north to south and has a dense covering of coconut palms. At its northwestern end is a small boat passage, marked by a little obelisk on the south side. Southwest of the boat passage is the village of Pahua with a population of about 200. Nearby is an airport. Anchorage is not possible off this atoll.

TIKEHAU

This populated, oval atoll is often used as a passage check-point to by-pass the Tuamotu chain. The many palm-covered islands and motus around its perimeter make it clearly visible; a sand bar occupies the center of the lagoon. Sharks abound in the lagoon which is a bird sanctuary. Little Eden is a religious center located on an atoll on the eastern side of the lagoon.

Passe de Tuheiava is at the western end of the atoll. A draft of up to 3m (19') can be carried over the bar, but the tidal stream can be very strong and can make entry difficult. The pass is marked by two red and white columnar range markers aligned at 127°. When waiting for improved conditions in the pass, anchor on a bank about 137m (450') north of the entrance in about 16m (8 -10 fathoms), provided the weather is suitable. When the tide permits, the pass can be traversed easily, the southwestern side of the channel having slightly deeper water.

The closest anchorage is off the small village on the north side of the entrance in depths of about 6m (3 - 4 fathoms). It is somewhat confined by the patches of coral which limit swinging space but can accommodate 4 or 5 vessels. Buoys mark the channel leading to a second anchorage off the village of Tuherahera which is at the SW extremity of the atoll. The passage is well marked but careful conning is necessary to avoid coral heads scattered along the way. In calm weather it may be possible to tie alongside the concrete wharf. This friendly village of 350 inhabitants has three stores, a bakery and several small pensions. It has been reported that another buoyed channel branches off the main entrance channel and leads eastward about 3 miles to Motu Aua where a hotel and the religious center of Little Eden are located. Weekly air service links the atoll to Papeete.

ILE MAKATEA

This small, 108m (360') high, coral island is about 44 miles south of Tikehau The coast is composed mainly of coral cliffs raised above sea level, known as makatea. The island was once mined for phosphate, but mining activity has ceased and port facilities are not maintained. There are mooring buoys at the west end of the island, but no protected anchorage. Since landing can be very difficult this island can be bypassed.

Booby

ARCHIPEL DES TUAMOTU
TIKEHAU
MATAHIVA

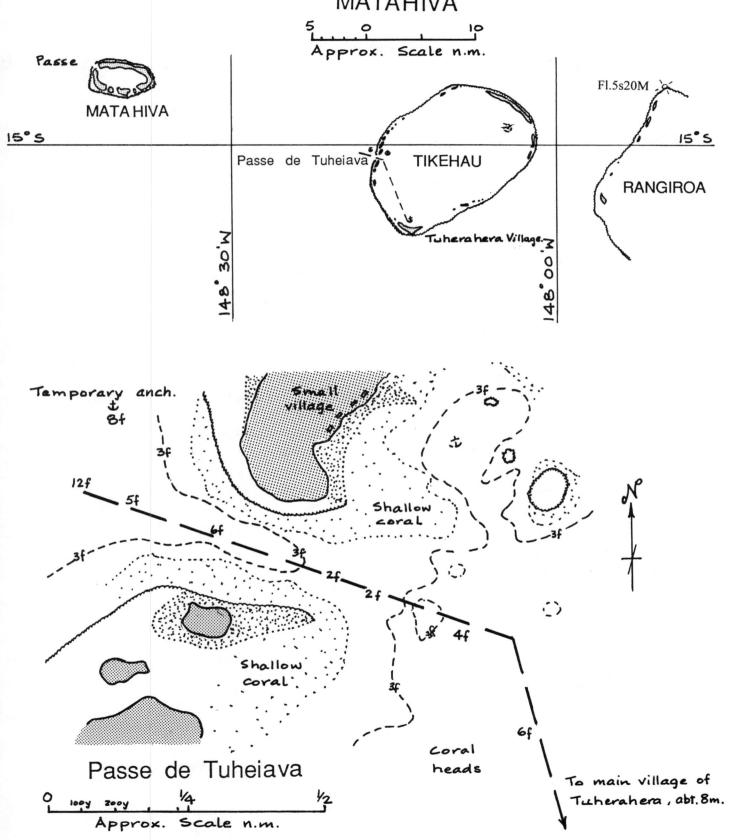

5   0   10

Approx. Scale n.m.

Passe

MATAHIVA

15° S

Passe de Tuheiava   TIKEHAU

Fl.5s20M

15° S

RANGIROA

148° 30' W

148° 00' W

Tuherahera Village.

Temporary anch.
⚓
8f

Small village

3f

⚓

12f

5f

3f

Shallow coral

3f

6f

3f

2f

3f

2f

N

Shallow coral

2f

3f   4f

3f

Coral heads

3f

6f

Passe de Tuheiava

To main village of
Tuherahera, abt. 8m.

0   100y   200y   ¼   ½

Approx. Scale n.m.

Not to be used for navigation

RANGIROA

This is an important landfall for vessels making a transit of the Tuamotu and is the largest atoll, having a circumference of about 100 miles. Located about 8 miles east of Tikehau, it is 40 miles long and 17 miles wide at its widest point. The ring is formed by some 240 motus or islets separated by about 130 channels called "hoas," most being very shallow. It is the second largest atoll in the world. The only deep water passes, Passe Avatoru and Passe Tiputa, are on the north side, and a village of the same name is near each pass. It is a **Port of Entry** with the gendarmerie office located south of Kia Ora Village Hotel. The total population is almost 2,000. Black pearl farming is a major operation in the lagoon. Care must be taken to avoid underwater lines associated with pearl farming.

When a strong outgoing current meets an easterly wind and ocean current at either of the two passes, steep, short seas and swells occur. These seas favor the western side of the passes and sometimes roll through the entrance and into the lagoon and are dangerous to a small vessel attempting to enter. In addition, a slick may sometimes extend beyond the breaking seas, giving a false sense of security. The tidal currents are so strong that eddies and rips can be found on the inside when the flood is in force. It is best to enter at or near slack water or during quiet sea conditions with a favorable current (provided rips are small). If it is necessary to await slack water, an emergency anchorage (difficult to find and usable only in easterly winds), is on a sand patch outside the reef about 1 mile south of the SW end of Rangiroa, in the lee of a small motu.

Passe Avatoru is about 8 miles east of the northwestern point of the atoll. Good landmarks are the large village on the eastern side and the conspicuous spire and red roof of the white church. The control tower and other buildings at the airport are visible from offshore. A small, wooded motu, Motu Kaveo, lies in the center of the channel at the inner end of the pass, dividing it in two.   Two white range markers lead into the pass. Swells and rips can be seen on the west side where the bar reduces depths to 3m (10') and an A-frame hut is visible among the palms and casuarina trees. The east side is the normal route, passing a red post beacon on a spit. Once past this red beacon, follow the deep blue water around the point to anchorage within the lagoon. Avoid the pale blue water with brown coral ribs along the shore.

Before reaching the anchorage pass a small boat basin, too shallow for yachts. A concrete wharf, intended for use by trading schooners, is at the lagoon end of the pass. Yachts cannot tie to the wharf for long. When strong trade winds are blowing across the lagoon, fore and aft anchors may be set ahead of the wharf at the side of the pass. However, the anchorages in the lagoon are both safe and attractive. The most popular anchorage is off Kia Ora Village Hotel which affords protection in east to southeast winds. A bank, post office, gas station and several grocery store are located in the village of Avatoru. An interesting tour of the pearl farm can be arranged at the Hotel and black pearls can be purchased directly from the pearl farm showroom.

The lagoon is safe to cross, as it is deep in most areas and the coral heads are generally visible. Trading vessels and yachts travel from Avatoru across to the anchorage at Tiputa and often leave by that pass. In good conditions you can sail across the lagoon to visit motus on the other side. The Isle of Birds (Ile des Oiseaux) in the middle of the lagoon, is a nesting ground for fairy and sooty terns and frigate birds. At the southwestern corner is the "Blue Lagoon," a pretty, small atoll within the larger one which is visited by tourists from the hotel.

Breakers near the entrance to Passe Avatoru, Rangiroa Atoll in the Tuamotus   *Charles Wood*

The entrance to Passe Tiputa, Rangiroa Atoll in the Tuamotus   *Charles Wood*

Sea level view of a coral reef   *Charles Wood*

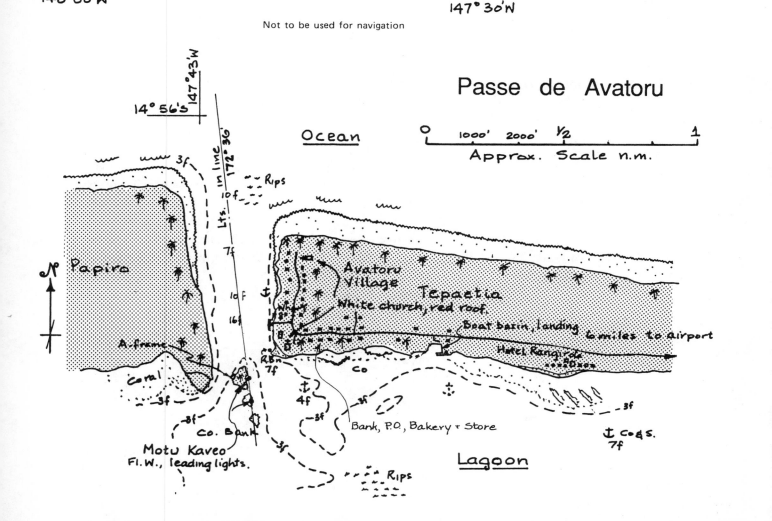

ARCHIPEL DES TUAMOTU
RANGIROA

Fl.5s20M
Avatika

Passe de Avatoru

Aero Bn, airport.

Passe de Tiputa

SEE DETAIL
NEXT PAGE

15°00'S

Paio
(Ile des Oiseaux)

Blue Lagoon
atollon

RANGIROA

15°10'S

Ex. Snorkeling

Vahituri

Fenuaroa

15°20'S

Otepipi

148°00'W

147°30'W

```
0        5        10        15
Approx. Scale n.m.
```

Not to be used for navigation

Passe de Avatoru

147°43'W

14°56'S

Ocean

```
0   1000'  2000'  ½              1
Approx. Scale n.m.
```

172°36

Lts. in line

3f

Rips

10f

7f

Papiro

10f

Avatoru
Village

Tepaetia

N

16f

White church, red roof

Boat basin, landing   6 miles to airport

A-frame

R.Bn

Hotel Rangiroa
20x0

Coral

Co

7f

3f

3f

4f

3f

Co. Bank

3f

Bank, P.O., Bakery & Store

Co&S.
7f

Motu Kaveo
Fl.W., leading lights.

Rips

Lagoon

RANGIROA Continued....

Passe Tiputa is a wide, clear pass and is the main entrance to the lagoon. A good landmark on the corner of the reef on the eastern side of the entrance is a tall, white concrete tower which is readily visible. The inner end of the pass is divided into two channels by Motu Fara, a sandy coral cay with a light structure. Behind this is a taller post with a green flashing light which provides a leading line through the pass. Buoys on each side of the channel and one on the southeastern side of Motu Fara define the entrance. The deep blue of safe water is clearly seen as the vessel passes around Motu Fara. Shoals on the east side of the anchorage are marked by a buoy.

At the tip of the land on the western side of the pass is a concrete wharf and behind it is a concrete block warehouse with a green roof. A good anchorage is off the old village in the bight west of the pass, level with the warehouse. Keep clear of any light blue water and brown coral patches. When leaving, you may tie to the wharf while waiting for slack water in the pass.

A luxury hotel, the Kia Ora Village, is along the shore nearby. It is a great place to go for a drink or a superb, but expensive dinner. Nearby are three scuba dive operators and for a modest fee you can join one of their dives in the pass, complete with divemaster and chase boat. Bicycles can be rented at the hotel; a pleasant way to visit the village of Avatoru, about 6 miles distant. The village of Tiputa is about a mile across the pass where local bakeries produce excellent bread.

An interesting snorkeling experience is to drift snorkel down straight passes such as those found here. The safest time to do this is on an incoming tide, near slack water when the water is relatively smooth, and easy pick-ups can be made. Using an inflatable or a dinghy that can be boarded by a swimmer without tipping, snorkelers enter the water about one-third of the way up the pass and drift down with the current. They should keep together and watch that the current does not take them close to coral motus where collisions are best avoided. Be sure to agree on a location for pick-up.

The eastern side of Passe Tiputa is prettier for drift snorkeling, as it has coral and many fish along the side of Motu Fara. The west side has coral in addition to a deeper, darker zone where sharks can be seen. A variety of coral can be seen and a myriad of tropical fish such as parrot, yellow butterflies, Napoleon and majestic angel fish. The sharks are so accustomed to being fed by crew on the glass-bottom boats from the hotel that they congregate where the boats anchor and wait patiently for the fish hand-out to begin. In Passe Avatoru, the eastern channel is prettier than the western one for snorkeling.

Reef Blacktip Shark
Carcharhinus melanopterus

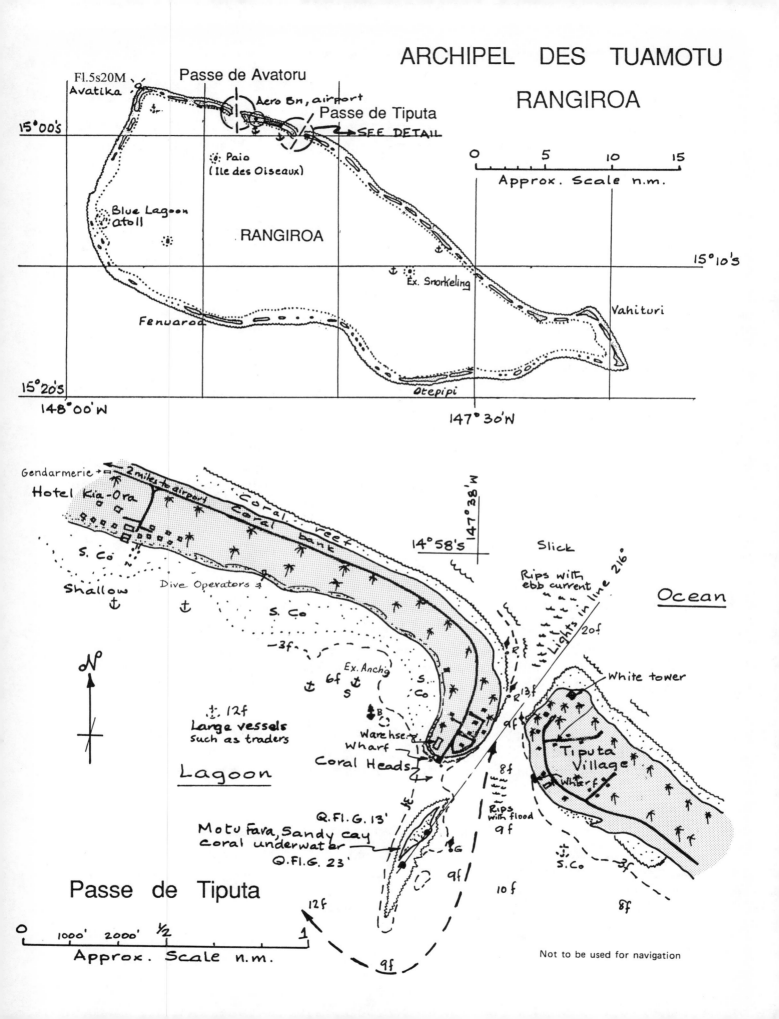

ARCHIPEL DES TUAMOTU
RANGIROA

Fl.5s20M
Avatika

Passe de Avatoru

Aero Bn, airport

Passe de Tiputa

→ SEE DETAIL

15°00'S

Paio
(Ile des Oiseaux)

RANGIROA

Blue Lagoon
atoll

15°10'S

Ex. Snorkeling

Vahituri

Fenuaroa

15°20'S

Otepipi

148°00'W

147°30'W

0   5   10   15
Approx. Scale n.m.

Gendarmerie →

Hotel Kia-Ora

2 miles to airport

Coral reef

Coral bank

14°58'S   147°38'W

Slick

Rips with ebb current

Ocean

S. Co

Shallow

Dive Operators

S. Co

—3f—

Ex. Anch'g

6f

S. Co

12f
Large vessels
such as traders

Warehse.

Wharf

Coral Heads

Lagoon

Lights in line 216°

20f

White tower

13f

9f

Tiputa
Village

Wharf

8f

Rips
with flood

9f

S. Co

3f

Q.Fl.G. 13'

Motu Fara, Sandy cay
coral underwater

Q.Fl.G. 23'

G

9f

10f

8f

Passe de Tiputa

12f

9f

0   1000'   2000'   ½   1
Approx. Scale n.m.

Not to be used for navigation

GROUPE DES ILES PALLISER

This group is made up of three atolls, Arutua, Kaukura, and Apataki. They are east and southeast of Rangiroa and southwest of the northernmost islands of Manihi, Ahe, Takaroa, and Takapoto.

ARUTUA

Arutua is located about 20 miles east of the southern part of Rangiroa. This wide channel forms one of the preferred routes for passage through the Tuamotu, especially if the vessel has made a landfall on Takaroa and is heading for Tahiti. An airport is northeast of the village.

When approached from the northeast, enroute from the Marquises, the palm-treed islets along the north and east sides help to make the atoll visible. But if your approach is from the south, the atoll is extremely dangerous since its southern sides are mostly bare, with the reef awash. Consequently, the reef is hidden by waves and spray until critically near, and thus passage in the vicinity is particularly hazardous at night.

Passe Porofai, the only pass into the lagoon, is near the south end of the eastern side. The village of Rautini is on the northern side of the pass and can be recognized from offshore by its flagstaff. This is a difficult pass to traverse and is only used by small vessels. The inner end of the pass is partially blocked by coral heads, forming three channels. Entry may be made by using either the center or southern channel. Anchorage may be taken off the village of Rautini within the pass as shown on the sketch. Entry to the lagoon is possible, but should be done only at slack water when the shallow bar is quiet and a route can be threaded between the coral heads.

KAUKURA

South of Arutua is a 25-mile long, oval atoll, Kaukura. Similar to Arutua, it has many islets on the northern and eastern sides and few on the southern side, making it dangerous to approach from this direction. However, during a hurricane many years ago, large coral blocks (some as much as 9m/30' high) were thrown onto the reef and they help to give it some visibility.

A pass into the lagoon is near the middle of the northern side near Motu Ura, which is recognizable by large clumps of palm trees. Tidal streams in the pass are very strong, setting eastward on the flood and westward on the ebb. The lagoon is shallow and filled with coral heads and shoals.

The village of Raitahiti is on the largest islet at the northwestern end of the atoll, making it the only permanently inhabited atoll in the area. The shallow boat passage north of the village near Motu Panao should not be transited. An airport is located on the northwestern part of the atoll.

ILE NIAU (Located in the general vicinity, but not one of the Groupe des Iles Palliser)

Located about 17 miles SW of Toau, this well wooded atoll has a village on the northeast side that is conspicuous from seaward. Strong currents in the vicinity set both east and west at various times.

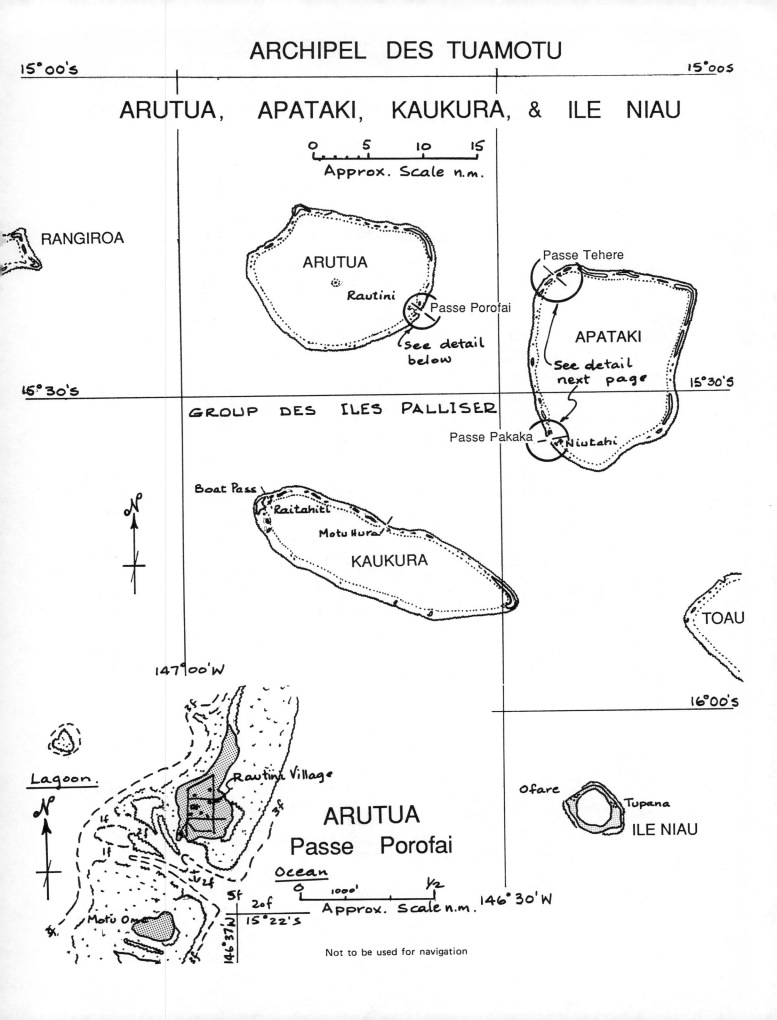

ARCHIPEL DES TUAMOTU

15°00'S

15°00'S

ARUTUA, APATAKI, KAUKURA, & ILE NIAU

0   5   10   15
Approx. Scale n.m.

RANGIROA

ARUTUA

Rautini

Passe Porofai

See detail below

Passe Tehere

APATAKI

See detail next page

Passe Pakaka — Niutahi

15°30'S

15°30'S

GROUP DES ILES PALLISER

N

Boat Pass

Raitahiti

Motu Hura

KAUKURA

TOAU

147°00'W

16°00'S

Lagoon.

N

Rautini Village

1f

2f

ARUTUA
Passe Porofai

Ofare

Tupana

ILE NIAU

3f

5f   2of

Motu Oma

146°37'2

15°22'S

Ocean

0   1000'   ½

Approx. Scale n.m.   146°30'W

Not to be used for navigation

GROUPE DES ILES PALLISER Continued......

APATAKI

This square-shaped atoll lies 10 miles east of Arutua and is 15 miles northwest of Toau. It is fairly well rimmed with wooded motus except for the southern side where the barrier reef is submerged. Strong currents on the southern side make travel along this coast dangerous. On the western side are two passes which give access to the lagoon. WARNING: fish poisoning occurs here.

Passe Pakaka is the southernmost pass, about 5 miles north of the southern end of the atoll. The pass is wide, deep and clear as far as the village of <u>Niutahi</u>, which is on Ile Niutahi, an islet on the south side of the pass. Lights on the village wharf provide a range line into the pass but if they are not seen in daylight a line can be taken on the flagstaff. Tie to the wharf or anchor in a niche in the western side of the reef, west of the wharf. This small anchorage is out of the current in well sheltered though shoaling water.

Entrance to the lagoon should be made only at slack water, in sunny conditions for good visibility to identify coral heads. Beyond Ile Niutahi the pass is divided by a reef and a bank forming three channels. When proceeding into the lagoon, steer down the center of the pass and take the middle channel. There are two current streams in the pass and they both change direction with the tide. The north side sets with the tide at about 4 knots, while the south side is a counter-current. The current increases in intensity to 5 or 6 knots in the narrow channels at the inner end of the pass. A few beacons mark some coral heads but don't expect them all to be marked.

Passe Tehere is at the northwestern tip of the atoll. When entering, line up the pass from at least .5 mile offshore to avoid the shoals located on both sides of the outer entrance. Shoals continue through the pass, reducing its width to about 122 m (400'). The pass is straight, short, fairly deep and clear. Currents of up to 4 knots run out of the pass. A black and white beacon marks a coral reef, covered 2'/.8m, located 1.5 miles ENE of the pass. Once inside the lagoon, anchorage can be found off the village of Rotoava following the route shown. It provides protection from north to easterly winds but is exposed to south / southeasterly winds.

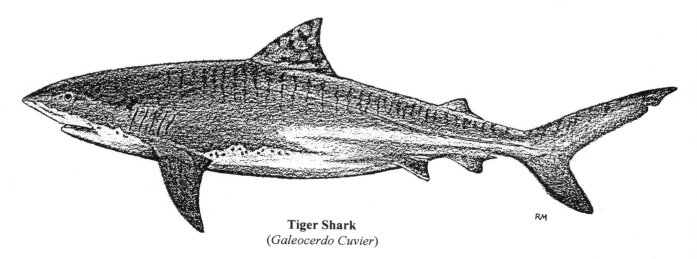

Tiger Shark
(*Galeocerdo Cuvier*)

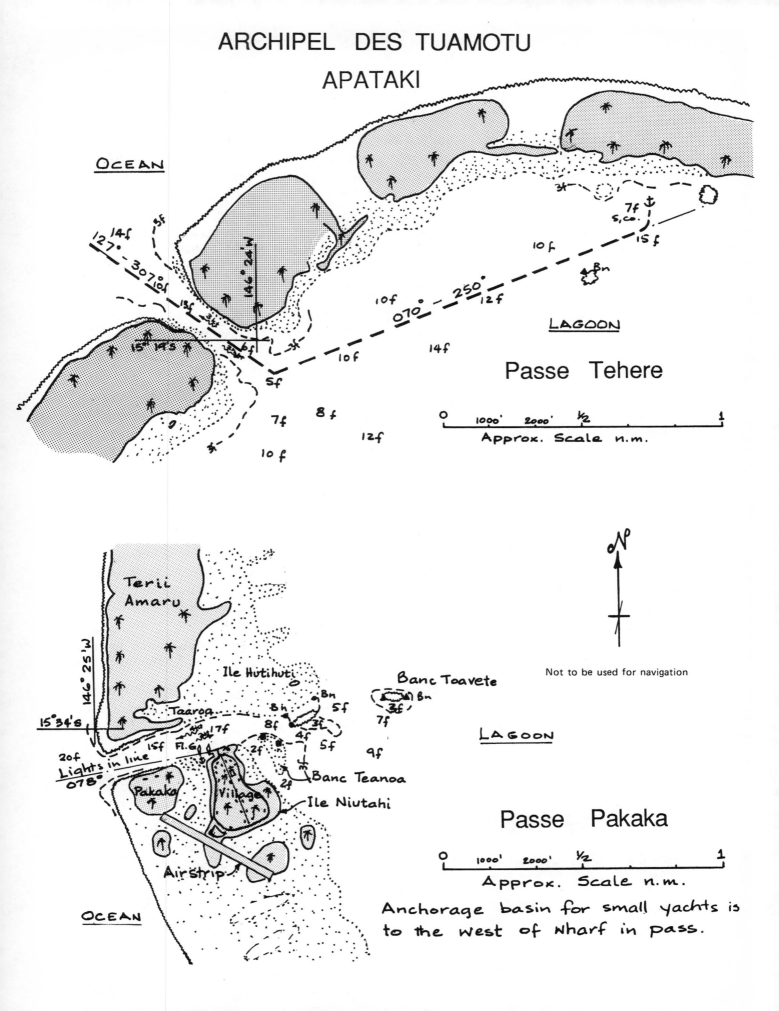

ARCHIPEL DES TUAMOTU
APATAKI

OCEAN

14f
5f
127° – 307°f
15f
3f
146° 24' W
15° 14'S
6f
5f
7f
8f
12f
10f

10f
070° – 250°
12f
10f
14f
5f

3f
7f
s,co.
15f
Bn

LAGOON

Passe Tehere

0   1000'   2000'   ½   1
Approx. Scale n.m.

Terii Amaru

146° 25' W

Ile Hutihuti

Banc Toavete
Bn
3f

Bn
5f
Bh
8f
3f
7f

Taaroa
15° 34'S
17f
4f
5f
9f

LAGOON

20f
Lights in line
078°
15f Fl.6.
2f
Banc Teanoa
2f

Pakaka
Village
Ile Niutahi

Air Strip

OCEAN

Passe Pakaka

0   1000'   2000'   ½   1
Approx. Scale n.m.

N

Not to be used for navigation

Anchorage basin for small yachts is to the west of Wharf in pass.

ARATIKA

A roughly triangular atoll, Aratika lies about 22 miles northeast of Toau on the northwestern side of Chenal de Fakarava. The north side is virtually one long island, low but well covered with palm trees. Smaller islets lie along the sides, but the entire southwestern side is bare and dangerous and the reefs are submerged. Many coral heads, visible and awash, are scattered throughout the lagoon. There are about 60 inhabitants on the atoll. An airstrip located near the southern end of the atoll provides a means of travel for guests from Tahiti who find accommodation in the small native hotel. WARNING: fish poisoning occurs here.

Both passes into the lagoon are challenging for an experienced cruiser and may be considered hazardous for a first-time sailor to the Tuamotu. Experience in other easier passes such as those at Manihi and Ahe give confidence and an understanding that prepares a skipper for the more demanding passes such as these. In addition, a less definitive means of identification makes passage via Chenal de Fakarava not as suitable as the route past Rangiroa when traversing the Tuamotu.

Passe Tamaketa is about 4.8km (3 miles) SSW of Pointe Turepuku, the northern extremity of the atoll. The pass is between two small islets on the reef, though the northern side is more reef than land. The opening is narrow, broadening out at the inner end where an inner reef splits the pass into two passages. The northern passage is the better one, but a bar of coral reduces depths to a scant 2m (7'), the other passage is even shallower. Not only may very strong currents be encountered in the pass but there are also several large coral heads in the lagoon just within the entrance.

Passe Fainukea is about 1 mile southwest of the northeastern corner of the atoll. It is harder to spot than Passe Tamaketa since it is bordered by reefs on both sides and no treed islands are near the pass. On the northern side is a partially exposed portion of the coral reef extending southwest from the island and continuing underwater. It is visible in the sunlight and care should be taken to identify it. Currents in the pass run at 5 - 6 knots and easterly winds create dangerous rollers, making it impassable. The pass has a least depth of 4.9m (16') but as it curves slightly and is bordered by underwater coral reefs, it should be traversed only in good conning conditions, preferably with the aid of a local guide.

Anchorage may be taken in an area roughly south of the thatched-roof hotel in the village of Paparara which is visible on the inside shore of the northern island. A spot clear of coral heads can be found that is large enough to allow swinging room.

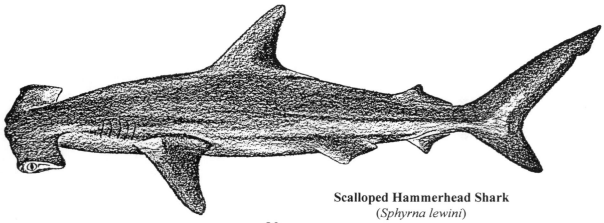

Scalloped Hammerhead Shark
(*Sphyrna lewini*)

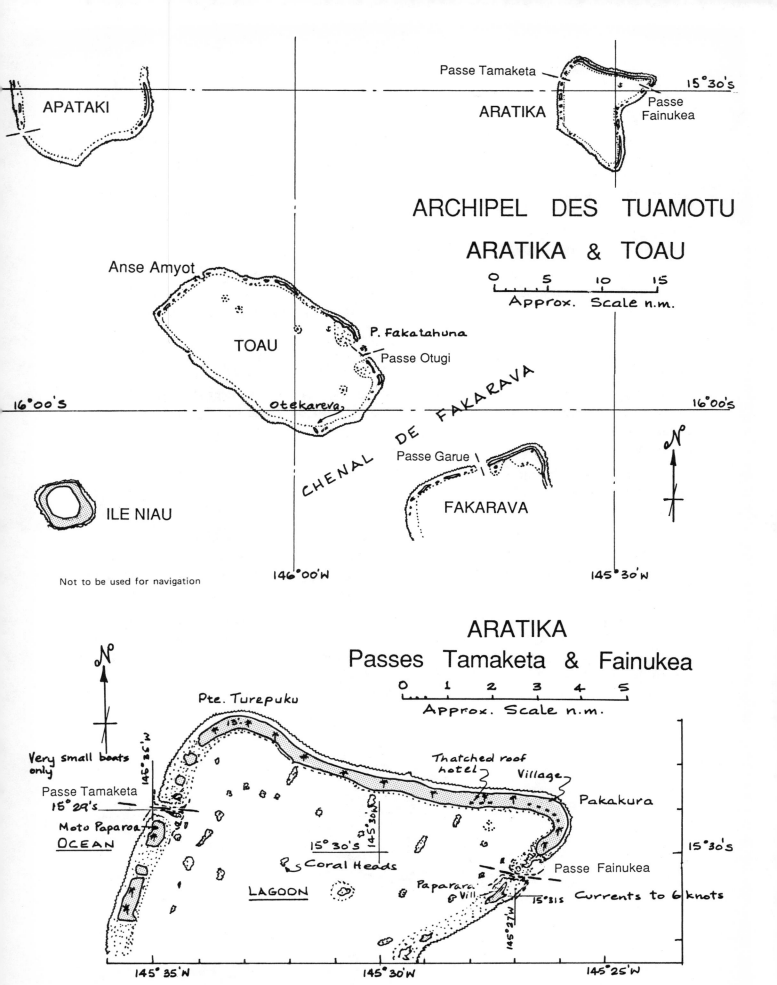

APATAKI

Passe Tamaketa

15°30'S

ARATIKA

Passe
Fainukea

ARCHIPEL DES TUAMOTU

ARATIKA & TOAU

Anse Amyot

P. Fakatahuna

TOAU

Passe Otugi

Otekareva

16°00'S   16°00'S

CHENAL DE FAKARAVA

Passe Garue

ILE NIAU

FAKARAVA

N

146°00'W   145°30'W

Not to be used for navigation

ARATIKA

Passes Tamaketa & Fainukea

0 1 2 3 4 5
Approx. Scale n.m.

N

Pte. Turepuku

Thatched roof
hotel

Village

Very small boats
only

Pakakura

Passe Tamaketa

15°29's

Moto Paparoa

OCEAN

15°30'S

Coral Heads

Passe Fainukea

LAGOON

Paparara
Vill.

15°31s   Currents to 6 knots

145°35'N   145°30'W   145°25'W

TOAU

Toau is a roughly rectangular atoll that lies between Apataki (15 miles to the NW) and Fakarava (8 miles to the SE). The atoll has many wooded islands along the northwest and northeast sides while the generally submerged reefs on the southern sides are dangerous. There are two passes close together on the northeast side and a small niche in the reef which can be used as an anchorage on the northwest side. The permanent population of the atoll is less than ten people. The villages on Toau are used by people from Fakarava when they harvest copra. WARNING: fish poisoning is reported here.

Passe Otugi is about 3.5 miles NNW of the eastern tip of the atoll. It is wide and clear of danger with depths of at least 4 fathoms. The out-going currents are so strong that eddies can be felt up to 2 miles outside the pass. A mid-channel course is best until the vessel is clear of the entrance.

Two anchorages are within the lagoon. The most convenient is about .5 mile south of the inner end of the pass in about 7 fathoms. This anchorage is some distance from the large area of coral heads and submerged coral reef within the lagoon. A masonry cistern, partially hidden by trees, is east of the anchorage. Alternatively, a route to the northwest for anchorage off the seasonally occupied settlement of <u>Maragai</u> can be taken through an area of coral heads by following the buoyed channel.

Passe Fakatahuna is less than a mile northwest of Passe Otugi and is separated from it by an island and section of reef. It is narrower than the other and thus effects of the current are felt to a greater degree. It is used primarily by small, local boats with local knowledge.

Anse Amyot is about 3 miles from the northern extremity of Toau, on the northwestern side. It is a slot in the reef which appears to be a pass, but which is really a cul-de-sac blocked by a coral bank across the inner side. Reefs and banks on each side reduce the entrance to less than 65m (200'); vessels with drafts of 4.5m (15') can anchor.

A shallow bank within the cove and extensions from the SW side reduce the useable part of the cove to anchorage in the northern part. Swinging room may be adequate for a small vessel, but most cruisers tie a line to the reef or palms to keep from swinging. Though the current is very strong, a yacht can lie here comfortably, as the spot is well sheltered from wind and swell. The family that lives here enjoys visits from cruisers and their extensive fish traps beyond the anchorage are interesting.

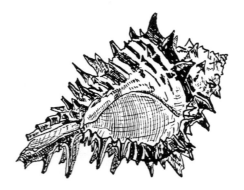

Black Murex
Muricanthus Nigritus (Phil.)

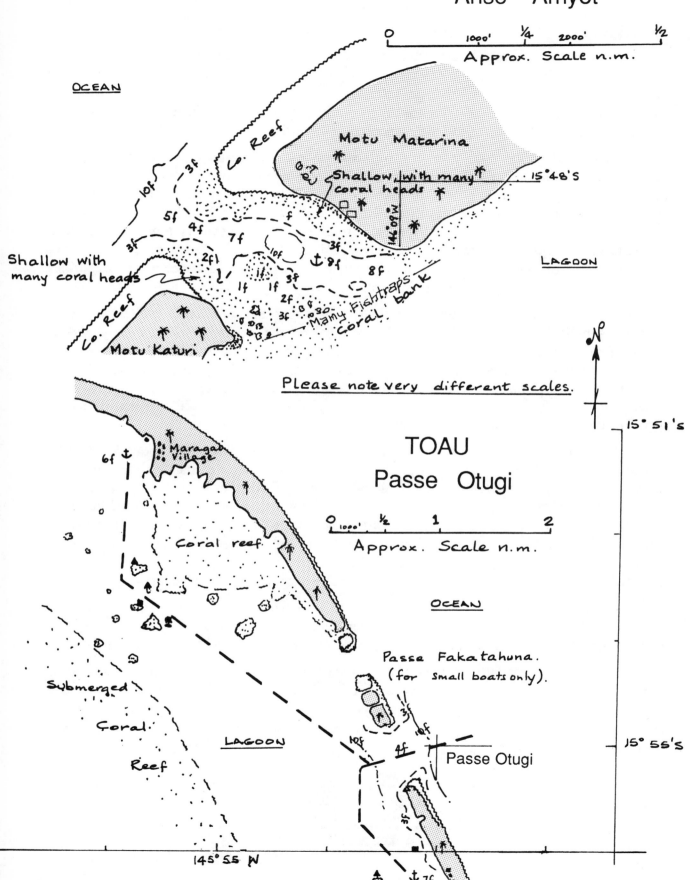

Not to be used for navigation

TOAU
Anse Amyot

OCEAN

0   1000'   ¼   2000'   ½

Approx. Scale n.m.

Co. Reef

Motu Matarina

Shallow with many coral heads

15°48'S

Shallow with many coral heads

Motu Katuri

Co. Reef

Many Fishtraps
Coral bank

LAGOON

Please note very different scales.

TOAU
Passe Otugi

N

15° 51'S

Maragai Village

Coral reef

0   1000'   ½   1   2

Approx. Scale n.m.

OCEAN

Passe Fakatahuna.
(for small boats only).

Submerged
Coral
Reef

LAGOON

Passe Otugi

15° 55'S

145° 55 W

FAKARAVA

This is the second largest Tuamotu atoll and is a 32-mile long by 15 mile wide rectangular shape lying roughly NW - SE. Fakarava is located 8 miles southeast of Toau and 10 miles northwest of Faaite. Chenal de Fakarava, which separates Fakarava from Toau, is a passage through the archipelago which is the most direct route from the Panama Canal to Tahiti. Currents are irregular and strong in the channel, usually setting westward.

Three sides of the atoll: northern, northeastern, and southeastern, have many islands and palm trees, particularly on the northeastern side. The southwestern side is low-lying and the few small islets along it are a mile or so in from the edge of the reef and give little warning of its presence. The tower in the NE part of the atoll, hidden by coconut palms from some directions, is 1.5 miles WNW of the village of Rotoava. Prominent landmarks in the town include a red-roofed residence and two churches. Three passes lead into the lagoon, the most important being Passe Garuae on the northern side. The atoll is visible by radar from a distance of about 15 miles. WARNING: fish poisoning occurs on this atoll.

Passe Garuae (Garue/Ngarue) is a wider pass than those normally encountered. The entrance is marked with a green buoy on the south side of the channel marking a reef and a red buoy marking the northern edge. The channel often appears forbidding because the outgoing stream, when strong, creates breakers across the entire entrance. Flood currents average 3 knots and ebb, 6 knots. Small vessels, especially auxiliary powered sailboats, must wait for slack water or enter with a favorable flow. However, the width of the pass allows vessels having speeds of more than 8 knots to enter at any time.

After clearing the entrance, give a safe berth to Pufana Reef which lies about .75 of a mile east of the inner end of the pass; it is marked by a beacon. After clearing this reef, two other drying coral reefs (Togamaitu-i-tai and Togamaitu-i-uta) marked by beacons, are about 2.5 miles along the route shown on the sketch. When approaching the anchorage they should be left to starboard and the vessel aimed for the flagstaff at the village. Anchorage is generally taken off the pier and flagstaff in about 6 to 10 fathoms, sand and coral. Although it is still deep closer in, the bottom has more coral and does not provide comparable holding. The anchorage is well sheltered except from southerly winds which may raise a sea across this large lagoon.

A cement dock at the village can be used as a landing. It is the largest village on Fakarava and has a store, post office, some tourist bungalows and very old cemetery. The store has a variety of packaged food and miscellaneous items. There are weekly flights to Papeete.

Another anchorage is southwest of the entrance at Passe Garue. It is on the lagoon side of Point Teheko (the northwestern extremity of the atoll), off a small island with a hut and palm trees. To reach this anchorage, good light and conning are needed to avoid shoals and to find the clear area which is located within a small group of reefs. This anchorage is lovelier, though more exposed to winds and surge.

Regular Cone
Conus regularis (Sow.)

84

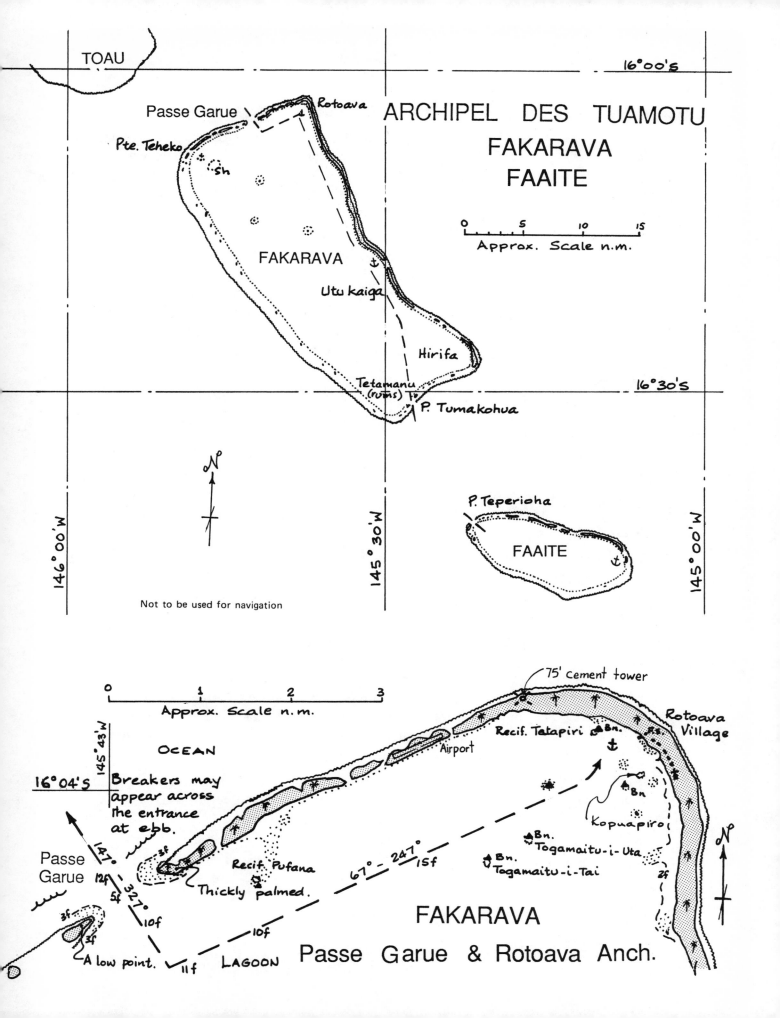

TOAU

Passe Garue Rotoava

Pte. Teheko

Sh

ARCHIPEL DES TUAMOTU
FAKARAVA
FAAITE

16°00'S

0   5   10   15
Approx. Scale n.m.

FAKARAVA

Utu kaiga

Hirifa

Tetamanu
(ruins)

P. Tumakohua

16°30'S

146°00'W

145°30'W

145°00'W

P. Teperioha

FAAITE

Not to be used for navigation

0   1   2   3
Approx. Scale n.m.

75' cement tower

OCEAN

Recif. Tatapiri Bn.

Rotoava
Village

145°43'W

16°04'S Breakers may
appear across
the entrance
at ebb.

Airport

Bn.

147°

3f

Passe
Garue

12f

5f

327°

10f

Recif Pufana

Thickly palmed.

67° - 247°

15f

Kopuapiro

Bn.
Togamaitu-i-Uta

Bn.
Togamaitu-i-Tai

2f

3f

3f

10f

10f

FAKARAVA

A low point.

11f LAGOON

Passe Garue & Rotoava Anch.

FAKARAVA Continued.....

Passe Tumakohua (South Pass) is about 2 miles northeast of the southern end of Fakarava. It is easily identified by a group of four islands, each well covered with palms. Counting from the west, the entrance to the pass is between the third and fourth islands. Though deep enough for most cruising vessels, the pass is more complicated than Passe Garue and careful conning is essential. It is advisable to enter at or near slack water, which lasts 30 to 45 minutes. Vessels having drafts of up to 3.5m (12') can be carried through the entrance.

The inner end of the pass is divided into two channels by a dark coral patch. The eastern channel is narrow, but feasible for shallow draft vessels. The western channel is broader, but appears blocked by the dark coral that makes it appear shallow, though it is deep enough for large vessels to use. Two families live in the village of Tetamanu which is now mostly in ruins. Anchorage may be taken close to the shore in 6 - 8 fathoms (11 - 14.5m) , sand and coral bottom. Approach the anchorage by passing north of the two banks which are almost awash.

Crossing the lagoon between the two villages or passes is dangerous during periods of poor visibility. A sharp lookout is essential to avoid coral heads scattered about. Anchorage may be taken about 12 miles north of the village, near the gap in the trees almost midway up the eastern side of the atoll.

FAAITE

Lying about 10 miles southeast of Fakarava, this atoll is only thinly covered with palms on its northern side. It is bare and low on its southern side, making it a dangerous atoll to approach, especially at night.

Passe Teperioha, the only pass on the atoll, is about .5 mile north of the western end of the atoll. A series of small islets lie on each side of the entrance, with the village of Hitiamaa on the south side. The town meeting hall, the largest building in the village is conspicuous from off the entrance.

The deep section of the entrance to the pass is about 120m (400') wide with a depth of about 4.5m (15'). At its inner end it is divided into two by a coral patch which forms a cul-de-sac on the northeastern side of the opening and a channel on the south having a depth of about 3.5m (12'). Since the southern channel is only 13m (45') wide the ebb current reaches velocities of 6 knots or more. The southern channel leads past the village wharf into the lagoon. Vessels can tie to the 18m (60') wharf which has depths to 2.7m (9') alongside, but the strong current and height of the wharf make this difficult.

The best anchorage is in the eastern end of the lagoon, and a passable one can be found about .25 mile south of the village in about 9m (5 fathoms), sand and coral. This anchorage is not protected from prevailing winds, although it is close to the village.

ARCHIPEL DES TUAMOTU

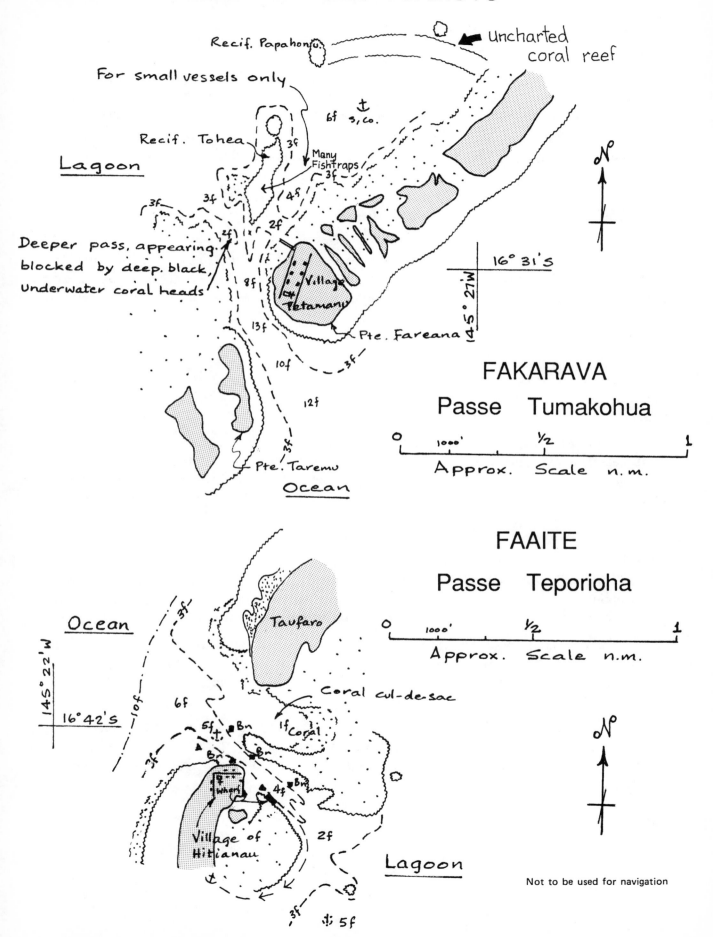

Recif. Papahonu

Uncharted coral reef

For small vessels only

6f s, co.

Recif. Tohea

3f

Many Fishtraps

3f

Lagoon

4f

3f   3f

2f

Deeper pass, appearing
blocked by deep black,
Underwater coral heads

2f

8f

Village Tetamanu

13f

Pte. Fareana

16° 31'S

145° 27'W

10f   3f

12f

3f

Pte. Taremu

Ocean

FAKARAVA

Passe   Tumakohua

0   1000'   ½   1

Approx.   Scale   n.m.

FAAITE

Passe   Teporioha

0   1000'   ½   1

Approx.   Scale   n.m.

Ocean

Taufaro

3f

Coral cul-de-sac

145° 22'W

16° 42'S

10f

6f

5f   Bn

1f Coral

Bn

Bn

Bn

4f   Bn

wharf

Village of
Hitianau

2f

Lagoon

3f   5f

Not to be used for navigation

KAUEHI

This green, low atoll is 18 miles southeast of Aratika and 24 miles northeast of Fakarava. It is well wooded except on the southwestern side which is bare and dangerous to approach. A prominent tower on the northern extremity of the atoll is a good landmark and the eastern edge is conspicuous.

Passe Arikitamiro is a deep, clear channel on the southwestern side of the atoll. Though the pass is about 460m (1,500') wide, the channel is about 300m (1,000') across. Entry should be made slightly south of the centerline, steering 045° true. Transit of the pass is best at or near slack tide. The current is so strong that eddies and overfalls are visible across the entrance at maximum outflow.

Coral heads are scattered in the lagoon, necessitating careful conning when looking for a spot to anchor. The small village of Tearavero lies across the lagoon on the northeastern side. Anchorage in sand and coral may be taken about .5 mile southwest of the wharf off the village. As swinging space may be restricted it may be necessary to set two anchors.

RARAKA

This circular atoll is about 11 miles southeast of Kauehi and 23 miles northwest of Katiu. The lagoon is surrounded by islands except on the southern side which is low, bare, and dangerous.

Passe Manureva provides a tricky entrance to the lagoon and can only be entered by small vessels using caution. Outgoing currents reach 6.5 knots. An islet and coral patch at the inner side of the entrance, combined with strong currents demand careful seamanship. A buoyed channel marks the route to anchorage off the village of Motutapu. Landing can be made by passing through a gap in the reef in front of the lodge with a mast.

TAIARO

This high, circular atoll, only 3 miles in diameter, lies slightly outside the main group, and is about 24 miles northeast of Raraka. It is completely encircled by an island which is well covered with palm trees. The island is visible on radar from a distance of 15 miles.

There is no entry to the lagoon, but landing can be accomplished off a group of huts on the western side. Here, small vessels can make fast to the reef when the winds are east to southeasterly. Another landing is near the village on the southeastern corner, but this area is affected by the swell.

W. A. Robinson of *Svaap* and *Varua* fame leased the island and it was his home during his efforts to investigate elephantiasis which was once prevalent in the South Pacific. His book, *Deep Water and Shoal* remains a classic in the annals of early circumnavigation in a small yacht.

ARCHIPEL DES TUAMOTU
KAUEHI, RARAKA & TAIARO

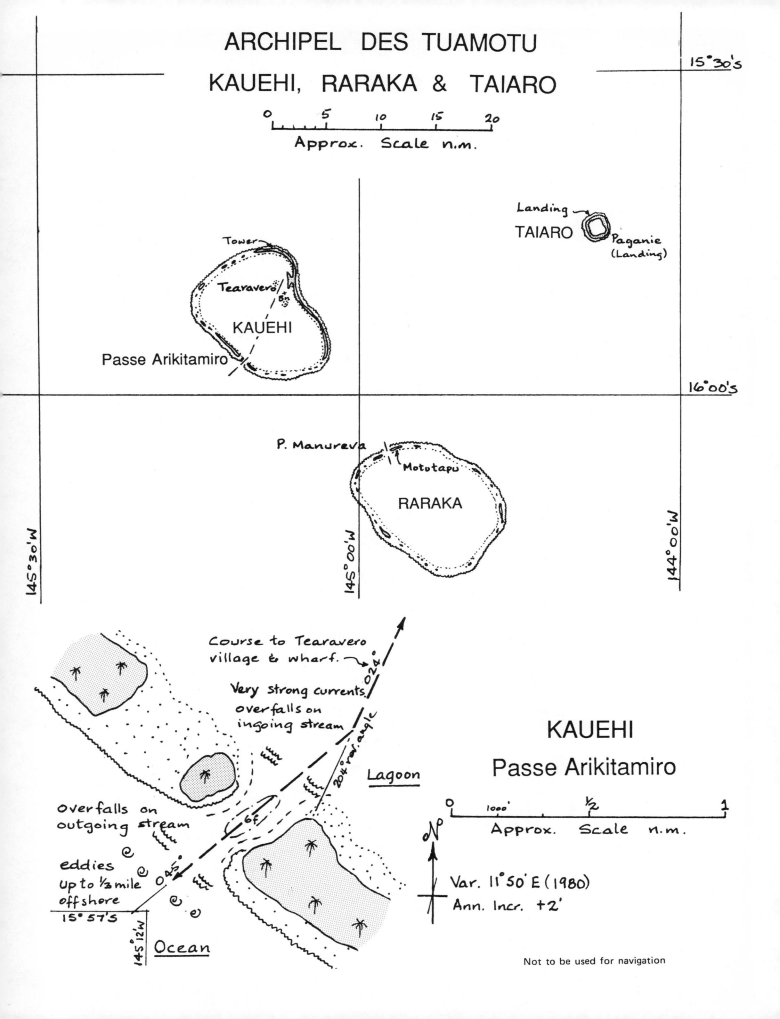

Approx. Scale n.m.

0 5 10 15 20

15°30'S

TAIARO

Landing

Paganie
(Landing)

Tower

Tearavero

KAUEHI

Passe Arikitamiro

16°00'S

P. Manureva

Motutapu

RARAKA

145°30'W

145°00'W

144°00'W

Course to Tearavero
village & wharf.

Very strong currents.
overfalls on
ingoing stream

024°

204° rel. angle

Lagoon

6f

045°

Overfalls on
outgoing stream

eddies
up to ⅓ mile
offshore

15°57'S

145°12'W

Ocean

KAUEHI
Passe Arikitamiro

0 1000' ½ 1

Approx. Scale n.m.

N

Var. 11°50' E (1980)
Ann. Incr. +2'

Not to be used for navigation

ANAA (Chain Island)

This atoll is the southern outpost of the northern group of Tuamotu atolls and it is about 35 miles SSW of Faaite. The 19-mile long atoll is partially rimmed by islands within the encircling reef. About 425 people reside in the five villages located here. The atoll is linked to Papeete with weekly air service. Several guesthouses have accommodation for tourists. Fishing and copra production provide a livelihood for the inhabitants.

There is no pass into the lagoon but anchorage may be taken on the northeastern side of the island, abreast of the village of <u>Tuuhora.</u> The village cannot be seen from offshore, but two sheds and a road lead to it. A current sets toward the reef, making it advisable to have an anchor watch aboard. Poultry, fish and lobster are sometimes available in the village. There is a radio station and airstrip on the island and it is a regular stop for inter-island freighters out of Papeete.

The island has several unique claims to fame. In 1906 a tidal wave devastated the atoll, leaving 100 people dead. Cyclones have devastated the villages on numerous occasions, the latest in 1982-83, and this may have been the basis for Nordoff and Hall's book, *Hurricane.* The men of the island have a well-known and highly respected reputation as sailors and make excellent crew when they can be persuaded to sign on with a vessel. Lastly, the island creates a curious mirage effect whereby the atoll projects on the clouds a beautiful greenish reflection visible from a great distance.

Coconut Palms
Food, drink, medicine, cloth & shelter

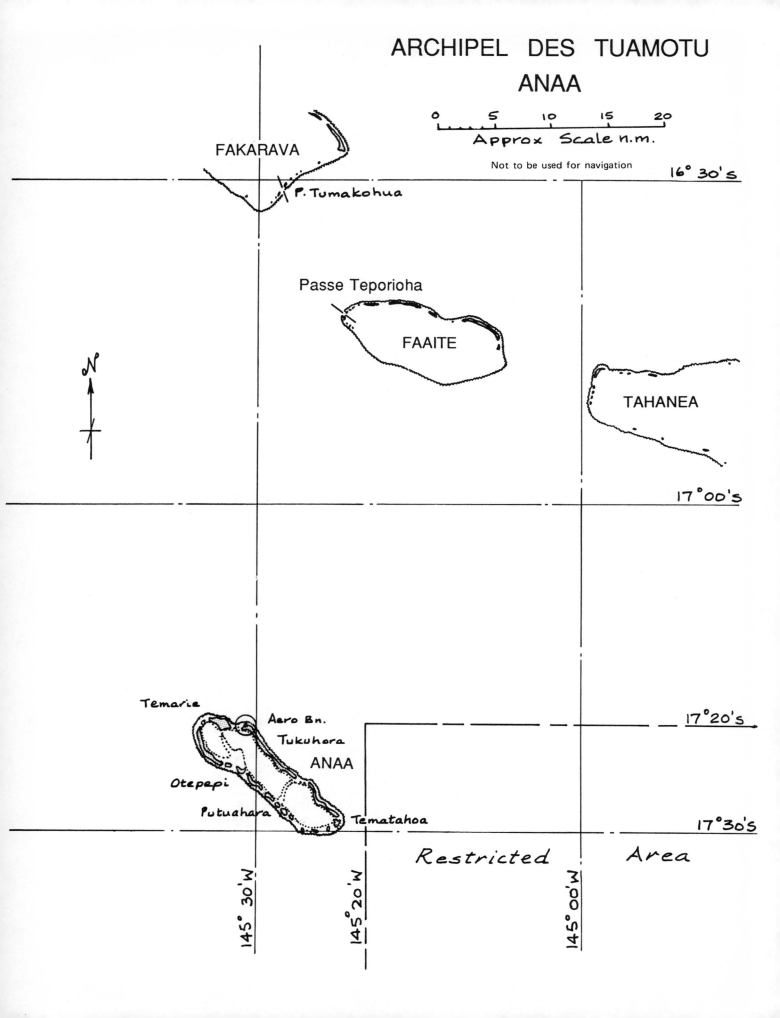

ARCHIPEL DES TUAMOTU
ANAA

0   5   10   15   20
Approx Scale n.m.

Not to be used for navigation

16° 30'S

FAKARAVA

P. Tumakohua

Passe Teporioha

FAAITE

TAHANEA

N

17°00'S

Temarie

Aero Bn.
Tukuhora

ANAA

17°20'S

Otepepi

Putuahara

Tematahoa

17°30'S

Restricted   Area

145° 30'W

145° 20'W

145° 00'W

KATIU

The atolls forming a group which includes Katiu are not well known since they lie far from the routes normally taken through the archipelago. Other better known atolls, Makemo and Hao, are east of this group near an old sailing ship route through the Tuamotu.

Katiu is a low atoll, covered with brushwood, located about 23 miles ESE of Raraka and 16 miles west of Makemo. Similar to most atolls, the northern sides are well rimmed with islets and palm trees, while the southern sides are poorly defined and consequently are dangerous to approach. There are about 250 inhabitants on the atoll, most of whom are occupied with pearl farming.

Passe Pakata is on the northeastern side, about 4 miles southeast of the northern extremity. It is identifiable by the clear gap between the palm trees, and, as the distance closes, by the flagstaff at the village of <u>Hitianau,</u> which is on the northwestern side of the entrance. The edge of the reef on the eastern side of the entrance is marked by two red spar beacons. This is a narrow pass which demands careful and precise attention to the vessel's position. Two black and white striped range markers/beacons are within the lagoon, south of the flagstaff. Best depths in the entrance are found by keeping these beacons in line, bearing 193° 30' true. Because of the difficulty of entering the lagoon, most vessels anchor within the pass, off the wharf in 13m (7 fathoms), near the western side. Currents through the pass can attain a velocity of 6 knots.

Coral reefs and underwater heads block much of the inner part of the pass except for a narrow navigable passage which follows a southeasterly direction. This narrow route is between the coral bank on the inner side of the main reef and a small, isolated reef marked by a white spar beacon. After traversing the 30m (100') wide opening, vessels entering the lagoon must then avoid the inner banks of coral heads. Pass clear of the 5.5m (3-fathom) line before turning west toward an anchorage which is southwest of the village of Hitianau

Passe Okarare is near the westernmost extremity of the atoll; it is only used by small local vessels.

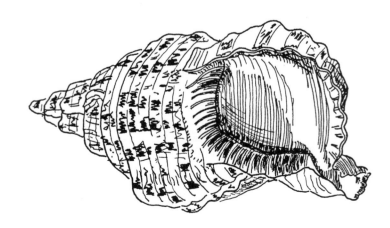

Pacific Triton
Charonia tritonis Linne

92

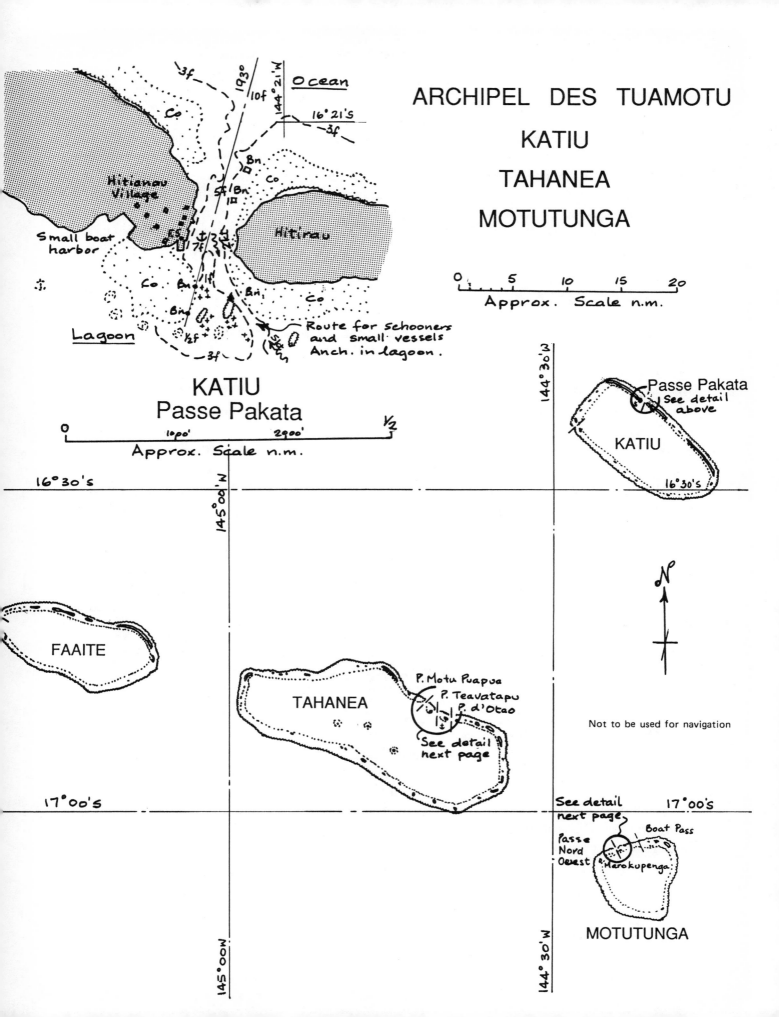

ARCHIPEL DES TUAMOTU
KATIU
TAHANEA
MOTUTUNGA

Ocean

144°21'W

16°21'S

3f

193°

10f

3f

Co

Co

Bn

Hitianau Village

Bn

Bn

Small boat harbor

Hitirau

Co

Bn

Co

Bn

Co

Lagoon

½f

3f

Route for Schooners and small vessels Anch. in lagoon.

KATIU
Passe Pakata

0   1000'   2900'   ½
Approx. Scale n.m.

Approx. Scale n.m.

0   5   10   15   20

16°30'S

145°00'N

16°30'S

144°30'3

Passe Pakata
See detail above

KATIU

16°30'S

N

Not to be used for navigation

FAAITE

P. Motu Puapua
P. Teavatapu
P. d'Otao

TAHANEA

See detail next page

17°00'S

See detail next page

17°00'S

Boat Pass

Passe Nord Ouest

Marokupenga

MOTUTUNGA

145°00'W

144°30'W

TAHANEA

This rectangular atoll is 7 miles southeast of Faaite. It is roughly 25 miles long and has islands distributed fairly well around its perimeter, those on the north side are large and well covered with palms. Three adjacent passes on the northeast side lead into the lagoon. Many coral reefs, visible and awash, are scattered in the lagoon, but in good visibility a vessel can find deep water routes between them. Anchorage here is exposed to southwesterly winds. An atoll within the lagoon is one of the few places where the endangered Tuamotu sandpiper survives for it is one of the only atolls where there are no rats. It is estimated that there are less than 100 of these rare birds in existence.

Passe d'Otao (Otaho Pass) is about 5 miles from the eastern end of the atoll. It is the narrowest of the passes and is generally preferred for leaving the lagoon rather than for entry. The village of d'Otao is on the eastern side of the pass, but two large coral heads block this side except for a narrow passage used only by local boats. The straighter, western passage, which has a least depth of 5.5m (3 fathoms), can be used by yachts. Although there are several houses, a church, and a cistern in the village of d'Otao, the island is uninhabited except during copra harvesting.

Passe Teavatapu (Passe Manino) is a deep (11m/6 fathoms), wide (300m/ 328yds.) entrance to the lagoon and is the normal passage of choice. It lies about 2 miles northwest of Passe d'Otao. The width and depth of the pass permit the swell to come well past the opening; this has given it a poor name. But there is no difficulty in using it if care is taken and transit is made when seas are not high. A course down the center of the pass gives a vessel plenty of room for maneuvering. There is a westerly drift during ebb tide which must be considered by the helmsman.

Good anchorage can be taken to the east or west of this pass. The western anchorage is in the bight formed by Teuakiri Islet and a coral reef. The eastern anchorage, off the village of Kari Karina, is reached by passing between the island and Mauru Nahi Nahi reef. Avoid coral patches.

Passe Motu Puapua, the westernmost pass, is one mile north of Passe Teavatapu. It is 9m (4.5 fathoms) deep, and about 200m (650') wide. A reef on the west side of the pass, Motu Taunoa, is covered by 1.5 fathoms (3m) and must be avoided.

MOTUTUNGA

This almost circular atoll lies 10 miles ESE of Tahanea and 34 miles south of Katiu. It is very low and has several treed islets on its northern side. One mile east of the northwestern end is Passe Nord-Ouest (Passe Motu Tuga), which is actually a cul-de-sac since an underwater reef blocks off the inner end of the opening. On the island to the east of the opening is a village with a wooden wharf in disrepair where vessels may tie, gaining good protection and surprisingly little effect from the current. A cistern is on each side of the pass.

A small boat passage into the lagoon is about 2 miles ENE of Passe Nord-Ouest, but it is not useable by yachts though local boats use it when the village is inhabited during the copra collecting period.

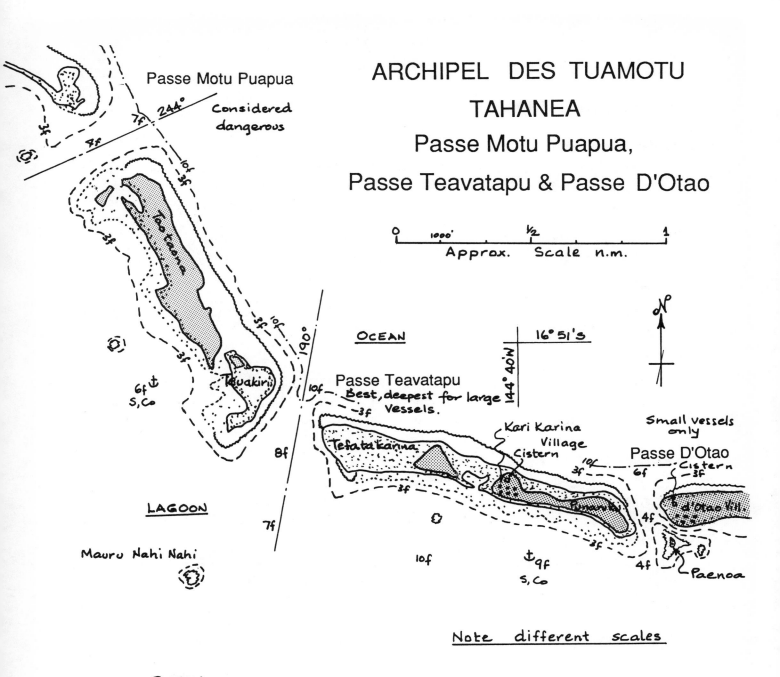

ARCHIPEL DES TUAMOTU
TAHANEA
Passe Motu Puapua,
Passe Teavatapu & Passe D'Otao

Passe Motu Puapua

Considered dangerous

244°

7f

3f

3f

9f

3f

10f
3f

Too taena

3f

10f

190°

6f
S,Co

Tevakiri

3f
10f

3f

0
1000'
½
1

Approx. Scale n.m.

OCEAN

16°51'S

144°40'W

Passe Teavatapu
Best, deepest for large vessels.

Kari Karina
Village
Cistern

Small vessels only

Passe D'Otao
Cistern
3f

10f

3f

6f

d'Otao Vil.

10f

8f

Tefatakarina

Punaoa

4f

LAGOON

7f

3f

3f

4f

Paenoa

Mauru Nahi Nahi

10f

9f
S,Co

Note different scales

OCEAN

MOTUTUNGA
Passe Nord-Ouest

Passe Nord-Ouest

3f
2f
3f

Cistern

Village
Mararokupenga

3f

N

Cistern

Whanga

7f

0
1000'
2000'
½

Approx. Scale n.m.

Cul de sac

3f

17°04'S

144°24'W

LAGOON

Not to be used for navigation

GROUPE RAEVSKI and TAENGA

GROUPE RAEVSKI

This group is made up of three small, uninhabited atolls: Hiti, Tepoto, and Tuanake. They lie to the southeast of Katiu, about 9 miles of channel separating Tuanake from Katiu. All three of the atolls are bare on the south side and heavily wooded on the north side.

HITI

This atoll is three miles in diameter and does not have a pass into the lagoon.

TUANAKE

This atoll is four miles in diameter. Though not practicable for cruising vessels, a pass on the south side of the atoll is used by small local boats.

TEPOTO

This is the smallest and southernmost atoll of the group and a cairn is situated near its eastern extremity. A pass, subject to strong tidal currents, is located on the NE side of the atoll. It is used only by small, local boats which tie to the small, wooden wharf in the pass.

TAENGA (Holt Island)

This atoll is about 19 miles northeast of Makemo and is less than half its size. As with many other atolls, it is rather bare on the southern side where the reef is submerged. Few vessels visit this atoll because of the consistently high speed of the permanently outflowing current from the lagoon. It has a population of fewer than 50 people.

Passe Tiritepakau is the only pass into the lagoon and it lies about 3 miles WNW of the southwest end of the atoll. It is about 45m (150') wide and 550m (1,800') long before it opens into the lagoon and is divided by a drying coral bank. The pass is about 14m (8 fathoms) deep until near Tarioi, where it shoals to less than 5.5m (3 fathoms). The shoal continues as far as the village of <u>Fenuaparea</u> which is on the south side of the bank. Sufficient swell comes over the submerged south side of the atoll to create an almost continuous outflowing stream in the pass, often reaching 10 knots. The village wharf is out of the strongest current and it is possible to moor here by setting a bow anchor toward the lagoon, in addition to tieing to the wharf.

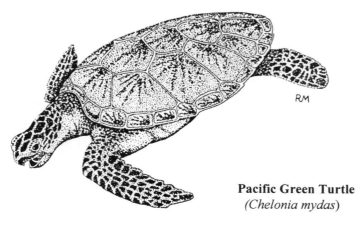

Pacific Green Turtle
(Chelonia mydas)

96

ARCHIPEL DES TUAMOTU
MAKEMO
GROUPE RAEVSKI

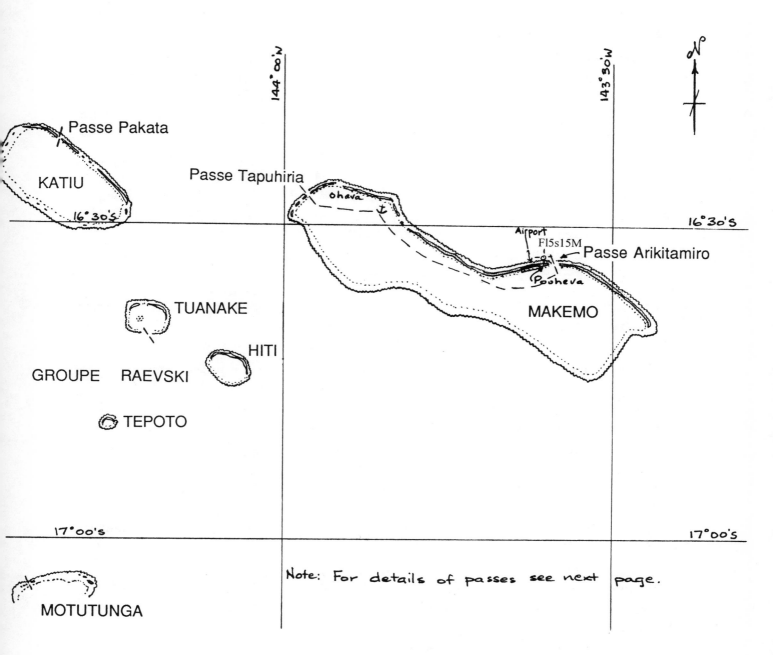

Approx. Scale n.m.

Passe Pakata

KATIU

16° 30'S

Passe Tapuhiria

ohava

144° 00'W

143° 30'W

16° 30'S

Airport
Fl5s15M

Passe Arikitamiro

Pooheva

MAKEMO

TUANAKE

HITI

GROUPE   RAEVSKI

TEPOTO

17°00'S

17°00'S

Note: For details of passes see next page.

MOTUTUNGA

Not to be used for navigation

MAKEMO

This elongated atoll is about 40 miles long and 10 miles wide at its widest point. It lies 16 miles west of Katiu. The northern side of the atoll has several long islands which are well treed with palms, but the southern side is bare and low, making approach from the south very dangerous. There are two passes leading into the lagoon, Passe Arikitamiro and Passe Tapuhira. The lagoon accumulates enough water from swells over the southern reef to cause very strong outgoing currents in both passes. Many shoals and coral heads, both visible and awash, are in the lagoon, but in good sunlight they can be easily seen.

Passe Arikitamiro is on the northeastern side of Makemo, about 10 miles from the eastern end. It is about 75m (245') wide and has a least depth of 11m (6 fathoms). It is easily recognized by a lighthouse north of the village, a break in the wooded reef and by the flagstaff at the village of Pouheva on the western side of the pass. At the inner end of the pass a coral reef, Rikiriki and a coral shoal, Ekoedo, divide the channel into three.

The seaward side of the pass is about 100m (109 yds.) and 10 fathoms (20m) deep, decreasing to 7 fathoms (38m) at the lagoon side. Enter at slack tide, aligning the rangelights at 147° True. The seaward rangemarker is at the north end of Ekoeko Nord Reef and the westernmost on Ekoeko Sud Reef. When the bearing of the light at Pouheva reads 270° T, steer 157 T to pass between Ekoeko reef on the east and Rikiriki reef to the west. This reef is marked by tree buoys, two of which are lit. In this passage beware of strong currents which can cause the vessel to swerve from the course. When transiting the pass, large vessels use the center channel before turning toward the anchorage. Small vessels can use any of the passages, though the side channels are narrower and need more care to negotiate. Entry is best at or near slack water since the outgoing current can reach 8 or 9 knots. It is possible to sail between the two passes inside the lagoon in good light. A careful lookout is needed to identify the few scattered coral patches.

The village of Pouheva (Puheva) is located on the western side of the pass. The population is less than 300 and is served by weekly air service to Papeete. The village has a huge cathedral as well as a dispensary and several small stores. Fresh produce and fuel are not available. The harvest of copra is the only source of income.

Passe Tapuhiria (Vahinatika Pass), at the northwestern end of the atoll, is 80m (85 yds.) wide and a least depth of 10 fathoms (20m). Within the pass two detached reefs divide the pass into three channels. Beacons mark the passage between Rikiriki Ruga Reef on the east and Rikiriki Raro Reef on the west. A visible shoal lies to the east of the entrance and vessels waiting for slack water or improved conditions for entry, can anchor on this shoal. Similar to Passe Arikitamiro, the outgoing stream can reach a velocity of 8 or 9 knots.

Transit of the pass is straightforward and it is well marked. The closest anchorage to the pass is south of Turuki in about 13m (7 fathoms). Another excellent anchorage is about 8 miles from the pass inside the curve of the northeast coast, in 4.5m (2.5 fathoms), sand. The village of d'Ohava, at the northwestern end of the atoll, is inhabited only during the copra harvesting season. Conning is needed when traveling the lagoon to avoid the coral heads scattered about.

ARCHIPEL DES TUAMOTU
MAKEMO

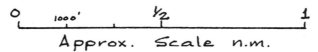

0   1000'   ½   1

Approx. Scale n.m.

Not to be used for navigation

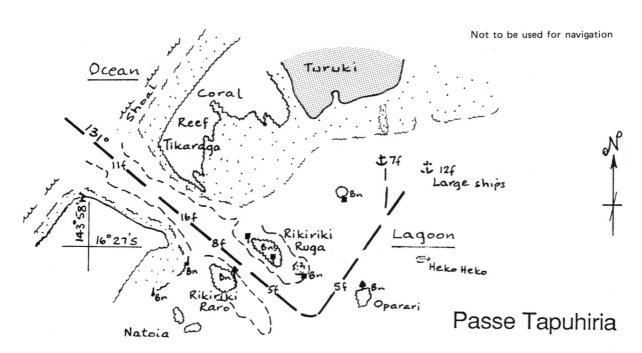

Ocean

Turuki

Coral

Reef

Tikaraga

Shoal

13'°

11f

16f

143°58'W

16°27'S

8f

Bn

Rikiriki Ruga

Bn

Bn

5f

5f

Bn

Bn

Rikiriki Raro

Natoia

7f

12f
Large ships

Bn

Lagoon

Heko Heko

Bn
Oparari

Passe Tapuhiria

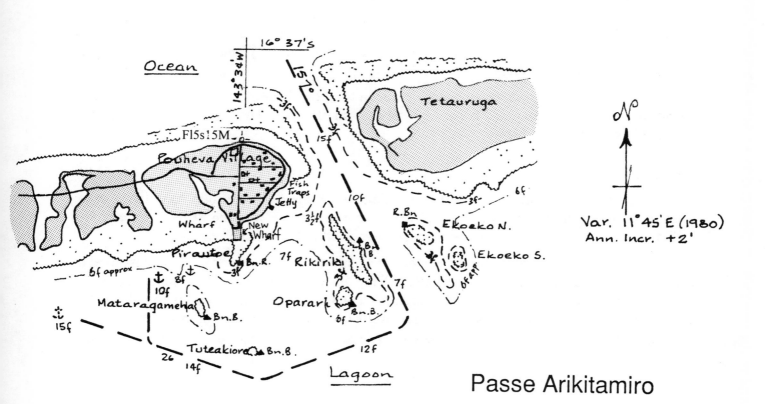

16° 37'S

Ocean

143°34'W

15'°

Tetauruga

Fl5s15M

Pouheva Village

Fish Traps

Jetty

Wharf

New Wharf

Pirautoe

Bn.R.

6f approx

8f

10f

15f

Matarasameha

Bn.B.

Tuteakiora

Bn.B.

2c   14f

10f

7f   Rikiriki

Oparari

Bn.B.

6f

12f

Lagoon

15f

R.Bn.

Ekoeko N.

Ekoeko S.

6f app

7f

6f

3f

Passe Arikitamiro

Var. 11°45'E (1980)
Ann. Incr. +2'

RAROIA and TAKUME

RAROIA

Raroia lies about 49 miles NE of Makemo and 5 miles southwest of Takume. With its partner atoll, Takume, it is the northeasterly spur to the line of the Tuamotu chain, in a very similar manner to the Manihi-Ahe and Takaroa-Takapoto groups. Further to the northeast are Napuka, Pukapuka, Fangatau and Fakahina, which are not included in this guide, as they are not generally visited by yachtsmen.

The northern and western sides of Raroia have much vegetation and the southwestern point is covered with brushwood. The westerly running current sets on to the eastern side of the atoll which is sparsely wooded and very dangerous to approach. Thor Heyerdahl's craft, *Kon-Tiki*, grounded on the eastern side of Raroia, ending his adventurous voyage. The approximate location of their landing, south of an old wooden wreck, is shown on the sketch.

Passe Garue/Ngarue (North Pass) is the only pass into the lagoon and it lies about midway down the western side. It is wide and clearly indicated by the open water between two heavily treed parts of the atoll. The pass is deep, except as described below, and fair sized vessels use it safely. Tidal streams and currents can reach 8 knots and slack water is usually of short duration.

The route through the pass favors the northern side where a channel about 120m (400') wide has a least depth of 7m (4 - 5 fathoms). A sand bank extends from the south side of the opening for about for 300m (1,000') and a lesser bank reaches southwest from the north side. Once through the pass, there are many coral heads visible and awash, several with beacons marking the passage to the village. Anchorage may be taken off the village jetty at Ngarumoava in 7m (4 to 5 fathoms), sand and coral bottom. The jetty has depths of only about .5m (2') alongside. A small boat harbor lies beyond the old coral jetty, but the depths may not accommodate yachts of average draft.

The village of Ngarumoava is almost hidden behind a mass of coconut palms on the long island southwest of the pass, and is not easily seen from offshore. The population is less than 50 and supplies are not available

TAKUME

This atoll lies 5 miles northeast of Raroia and the channel separating them has a strong westerly current and is often turbulent. The atoll is wooded except in the SE where the broken reef is partially submerged. Pearl farming and copra are the island's mainstay.

It does not have a pass into the lagoon for yachts and larger vessels. A boat pass used by the islanders is near the north end of the atoll. The village of Temania is at the southwest end of the atoll, a flagstaff and an obelisk can be seen from offshore. Landing can be done here, but the current and trade winds cause heavy seas and swells that run through the gap between the atolls, making landing difficult at best. It is unsafe for a vessel to remain near this coral reef.

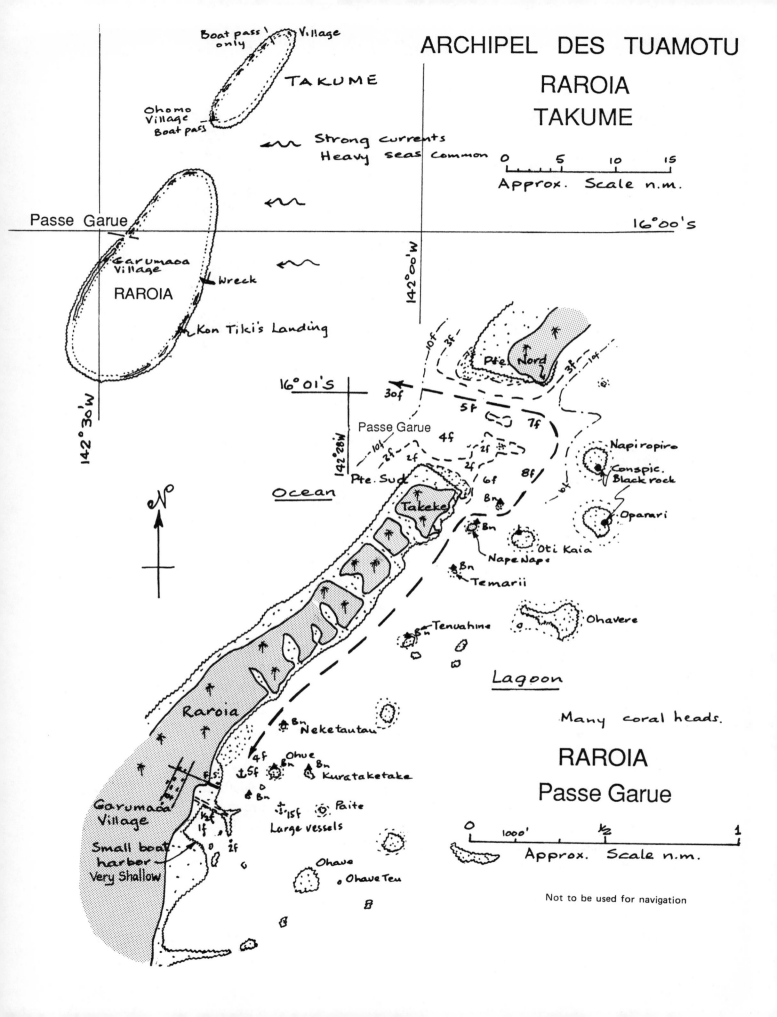

ILES GAMBIER (Mangareva Islands)

Located at the southeastern end of the Tuamotu is a group of about ten volcanically formed islands and numerous small islets within a barrier reef. The large islands of Mangareva, Taravai, Aukena and Akamaru are of volcanic origin, the reef and motus are of coral. The surrounding reef is roughly a square set on its diagonal in a north-south direction. The northern end is partially visible and partly awash, but it is submerged on the southern sides. Three passes lead over sunken portions of the reef into the lagoon. On approach, especially from the north, the pointed peaks of Mont Duff (441m/1,447') and Mont Mokoto (425m/ 1,394') are good landmarks. The total population is about 700. The channels and dangers are well marked with navigational aids. Use French charts 6418, 6463 and 6464 when cruising here.

Passe de l'Ouest is on the northwestern side about 4.4km (2.75 miles) southwest of Motu Tenoko. It is easily identified by the gap between Iles Mangareva and Taravai, at the reef by Motu Tenoko, and the surf breaking over Banc de Tokorua. The sketch shows the proper line leading through the pass and the successive ranges as a vessel turns past Pointe Teonekura into the Rade de Tikitea on the eastern side of Mangareva. The bar between the two islands has shallow spots, limiting entry to vessels with a maximum draft of 3.9m (13'). Another shallow spot is at Seuil d'Aukena where the route crosses a submerged reef between two buoys. When the village of <u>Rikitea</u> is clearly visible and the beacons near the wharf bear 298°T, the vessel can be taken through the coral heads into a well protected anchorage with good holding in 11 fathoms, gray mud.

The village of Rikitea is the largest on these islands and the local administrator and gendarme reside here. Entry formalities should be followed as this is a **Port of Entry.** Water and some fresh produce can be obtained and occasionally some fuel. Bread is available as the island has monthly air connections to Tahiti. The islanders have numerous pearl farms in the lagoon, many of which are marked by floats.

Passe du Sud-Ouest is an easy, straight-forward pass to transit. It joins the northwest route near the island.

Passe du Sud-Est is another easy entrance, well suited to sailing vessels because of the prevailing wind. The islet of Makapu acts as a milestone along the route, and when past it a direct course can be laid for the range leading across Seuil d'Aukena to Rikitea. Travel across the lagoon should be done with care since coral heads are in the vicinity of all routes.

The record of Honore Laval, a Jesuit priest, who came here in 1834 is shameful and unfortunately, typical. After converting and dominating Maputeoa, the last king, Laval ruled the island as a despot. He set stringent rules, and forced the people to erect coral stone churches, convents and other buildings. In the process, he caused the death of over 5,000 people, eliminated the will of the people to survive and destroyed an entire culture. The cathedral and ruins of archways and other buildings stand as monuments to his egomania, yet the inscription on the statue donated by France reads, "His memory is blessed in these islands." Today, only a few pure blood Mangarevans remain.

Approaching from the northwest   102

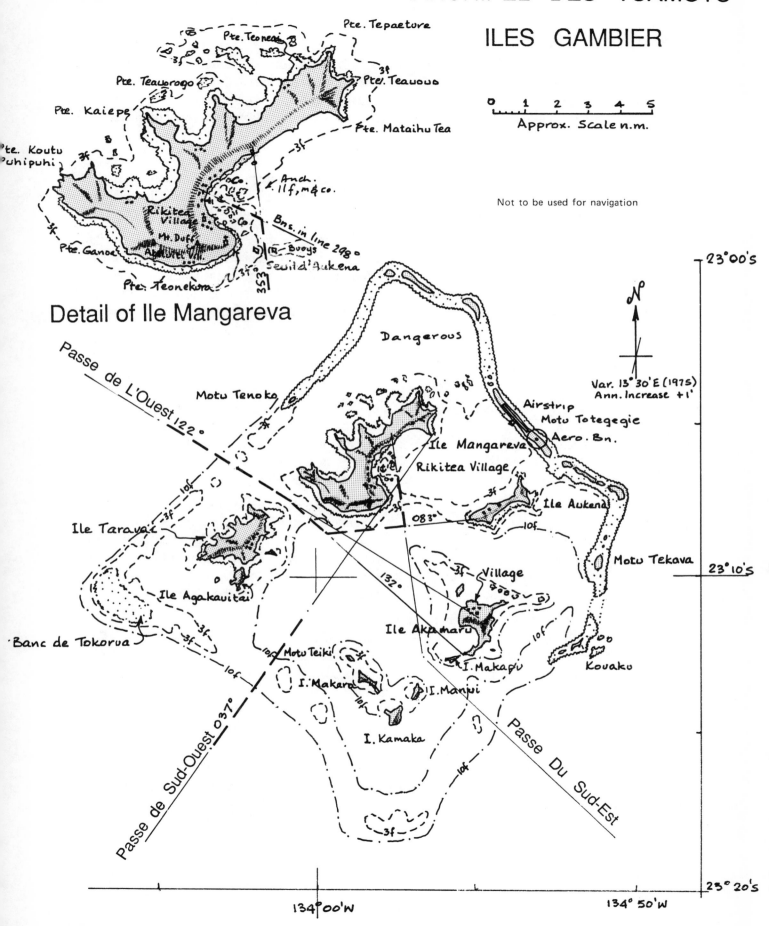

ARCHIPEL DES TUAMOTU
ILES GAMBIER

Pte. Tepaetore
Pte. Teoneai
Pte. Teauorogo
Pte. Teauoua
Pte. Kaiepe
Pte. Koutu Puhipuhi
Pte. Mataihu Tea
Anch. 11f, m & co.
Rikitea Village
Bns. in line 298°
Mt. Duff
Buoys
Pte. Ganoe
Seuil d'Aukena
Pte. Teonekura

Detail of Ile Mangareva

0 1 2 3 4 5
Approx. Scale n.m.

Not to be used for navigation

23°00'S

Var. 13°30'E (1975)
Ann. Increase +1'

Dangerous

Passe de L'Ouest 122°

Motu Tenoko

Airstrip
Motu Totegegie
Aero. Bn.

Ile Mangareva
Rikitea Village

Ile Aukena

Ile Taravai

083°

Motu Tekava

23°10'S

132°

Ile Agakauitai

Village

Banc de Tokorua

Ile Akamaru

Kouaku

Motu Teiki
I. Makapu
I. Makaroa
I. Manui

Passe de Sud-Ouest 037°

I. Kamaka

Passe Du Sud-Est

23°20'S

134°00'W   134°50'W

PITCAIRN ISLAND

Pitcairn Island lies about 330 miles southwest of Iles Gambier and about 860 miles west of Ile Rapa. In the general area is a group of small, widely scattered, uninhabited islands that includes Ducie, Henderson and Oeno. Of volcanic origin, Pitcairn is high, rising to about 300m (1,000') and most of the coast is composed of steep cliffs. The soil is fertile and luxuriant vegetation covers the island.

Pitcairn is a British dependency. The inhabitants are mostly descendants of mutineers of the *Bounty* and Tahitians who accompanied them into exile. The remains of the *Bounty* lie in 8m (25') of water in Bounty Bay where she was driven ashore and set afire by Fletcher Christian. The main settlement of Adamstown was named after John Adams, the last mutineer to die.

Bounty Bay is an open bay on the northeastern coast, about .5 mile northwest of St. Paul's Point, the easternmost point. From offshore, the roof of a boathouse near the water and one or two bright tin roofs of the houses above, help to identify the anchorage and main landing place. Large vessels anchor about .5 mile offshore with St. Paul's Point visible past Adams Rock. Yachts and small vessels can anchor a little closer, in about 11-14m (6 to 8 fathoms), sand bottom with rocky patches. Holding is good in the sandy areas, but an anchor watch aboard is advisable because of possible wind shifts. For extra security, two anchors are advised. If the wind shifts to northerly quadrants neither Tedside nor Bounty Bay are safe anchorages and vessels may have to heave to for several days while waiting for better weather.

During easterly or southerly winds anchorage may be taken on the northwestern coast at Tedside. The anchorage is deep 13-18m (7 to 10 fathoms), sand and coral and landing ashore is possible. A trail leads to Adamstown. Neither Tedside nor Bounty Bay can be used if the wind shifts to the northern quadrants. Another anchorage is in Down Rope Bight on the southeastern coast, but this is seldom used by yachts as landing ashore is impossible.

Landing ashore may be very difficult and should not be attempted in rough conditions. When visiting Bounty Bay it is best to contact the islanders who maintain a radio watch on VHF Ch 16 and have them take you ashore in their own surf boat–trips cost $10 NZ. Landing here can be a spectacular feat, for at the last minute as the boat rushes in, it must be swung hard to port around a stone wall and run up a concrete ramp built out from the boathouse. An inflatable tender is satisfactory for landing in moderate conditions. A steep pathway leads to the plateau above.

The islanders are exceedingly hospitable and will often sell their surplus fruit and vegetables to visitors. A small co-op store has a limited selection of canned, frozen and dried foods. Except during periods of drought, drinking water may be available from a tap at the boat shed in Bounty Bay. Diesel and gasoline are not available to cruisers as the island's supplies are purchased with difficulty and considerable expense from passing ships. Visas are not required for brief visits, but those wishing to stay ashore for an extended period must obtain permission from the Island Council and pay a $150 landing fee. Entry fees are approximately $11US per person.

Letters mailed from Pitcairn Island may take up to five months to reach their destination. The beautiful Pitcairn stamps with hand-canceled postmarks are rare and become valuable with time. Wood carvings, finely crafted baskets and printed T-shirts make good souvenirs.

PITCAIRN ISLAND

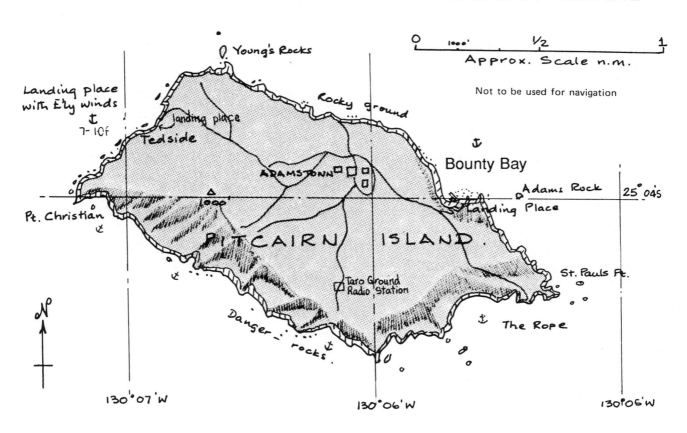

Young's Rocks

Landing place
with E'ly winds
7-10f

Tedside

landing place

Rocky ground

ADAMSTOWN

Bounty Bay

Adams Rock   25° 04S

Landing Place

Pt. Christian

PITCAIRN ISLAND

St. Pauls Pt.

Taro Ground
Radio Station

The Rope

Danger rocks

130°07'W   130°06'W   130°05'W

N

0   1000'   ½   1
Approx. Scale n.m.

Not to be used for navigation

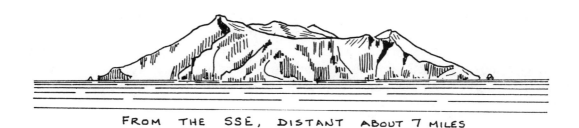

FROM THE SSE, DISTANT ABOUT 7 MILES

Not to be used for navigation

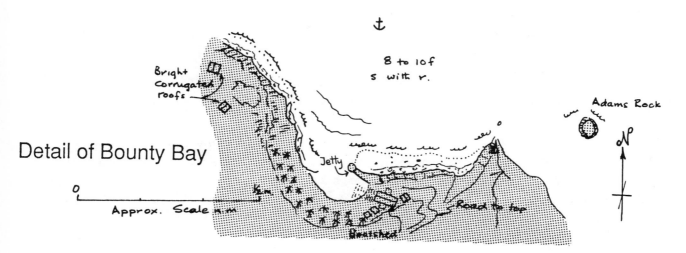

8 to 10f
s with r.

Bright
Corrugated
roofs

Adams Rock

Detail of Bounty Bay

Jetty

N

0
Approx. Scale n.m.

Road to top

Boatshed

ISLA DE PASCUA (EASTER ISLAND)

Famous for its huge stone statues, this is the easternmost outpost of Polynesia. Truly isolated, it is 1,400 miles west of Pitcairn Island, 2,260 miles from Tahiti, and over 1,900 miles from Valparaiso, Chile. Easter Island is a Chilean Possession though the governor is a Rapanui (locally-born Polynesian). Spanish is the official language although 70% of the population is of Polynesian descent and speak Pascuan (a Polynesian dialect) when speaking among themselves. Weekly flights connect the island to Papeete and Santiago, Chile.

It is a volcanically formed island having several extinct volcanoes as high points. Cerro Terevaka at 425m (1,400') is the highest and nearby is the crater of Volcan Rano Aroi; when seen from a distance they appear to be two islands. The shores are predominantly rocky and steep-to with no sheltered anchorages. Most of the bays are open, although there are a few coves with sandy beaches. The main village and **Port of Entry** is <u>Rada Hanga Roa</u> which is visible from offshore. The roadstead is encumbered with rocky patches and foul ground. Approach should be made on the ranges as indicated. It is best to anchor outside the 6-fathom line to be clear of the rocky ground, although it is possible with extreme care to move slightly closer to the pier.

The Port Captain, an officer of the Chilean Navy, monitors VHF Ch 16 and may attempt to contact entering vessels. He and the officers from Health, Agriculture and Immigration, board arriving yachts that anchor off <u>Hanga Roa</u>. A call on VHF Ch 16 to "Hanga Roa Port Control" will contact the Port Captain and the launch will come out. Several boats have been damaged by the over enthusiastic islanders who give officials a ride to the yachts in their large, rough and unwieldy fishing skiffs, so have fenders and fender boards ready. The officials process tourist cards and clearances on board. At present, entry and exit fees and visas are not required for brief visits.

In the summer months (October to April) when the southeast trades blow, Hanga Roa is a reasonable anchorage. During northerly gales the vessel should move to Rada Vinapu on the south coast. During the winter months or when westerly winds are blowing reasonable anchorage may be taken on the north coast at Anakena Cove which is identified by a white sand beach at its head. It is protected from all but northerly winds and landing through the surf is usually possible on the beach where a dinghy dock is located. La Perousa Bay offers more protection from swell during westerly winds than tieing to the Armada mooring buoy.

This commercial harbor is used by motorized barges unloading supply ships from Chile every six months. Hanga Piko is sheltered in all but westerly winds, when it becomes an extremely dangerous trap. Vessels drawing less than 2m (6') may obtain permission from the Port Captain to tie up inside Hanga Piko Harbor where the yacht will be in the middle of the harbor with lines ashore in four directions. This is at the discretion of the Port Captain who often allows only one yacht at a time in Hanga Piko Harbor. Weather forecasts are available from the Armada on VHF Ch 16. At the first forecast of a westerly wind yachts inside Hanga Piko should either put to sea or shift to another anchorage after obtaining permission from the Port Captain. Water is sold at the Hanga Roa landing or inside Hanga Piko harbor; diesel and kerosene are available at a service station near the airport.

The Armada may direct yachts to anchor next to the Armada buoy which is nearly in line with the day mark beacons. Do not anchor if you feel conditions are too rough in Hanga Roa no matter what the Armada says. Vinapu may be safer, but landing can be difficult at the broken down oil tanker wharf.

EASTER ISLAND
(ISLA DE PASCUA)

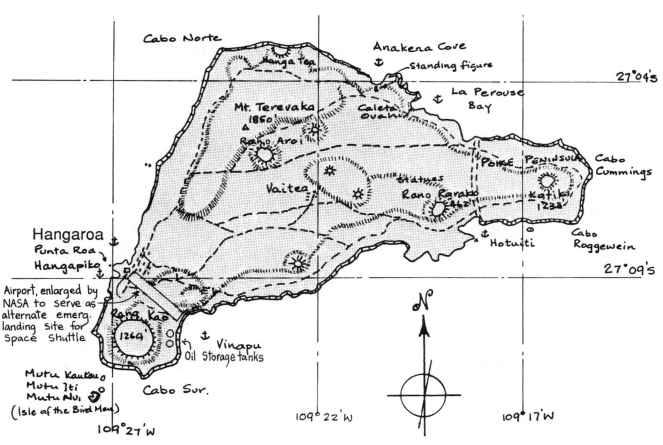

Approx. Scale n.m.

Not to be used for navigation

Maritime Authority - Rules for Visiting Yachts

1. Do not enter Hanga Piko Bay without permission from the Port Captain.
2. Fly the Chilean courtesy flag at all times.
3. Visitors must have permission of the Maritime Authority before boarding a yacht.
4. Do not leave the vessel unattended
5. Before moving to another bay <u>for any reason</u>, obtain permission from the Port Captain
6. The anchor light must be kept on at night
7. Do not dispose of trash, oil or fuel in the sea.
8. Allow a minimum of 4 hours to request clearance to sail from the island.

Hangaroa Anchorage

Approx. Scale n.m.

ILES DE LA SOCIETE - SOCIETY ISLANDS

These islands come to mind at the mention of the South Seas for they are part of every cruising sailor's dreams. Although still beautiful, the multitude of tourists arriving by sea and air and the facilities developed to cater to them have caused some areas to lose their natural charm.

The islands extend over 400 miles in a WNW direction and are divided into two sections for administrative purposes. The Iles du Vent (Windward Isles) are the southeastern group and include Meetia, Tahiti, Moorea, Tetiaroa, and Maiao (Tubuai Manu). The Iles Sous le Vent (Leeward Isles) are the northwestern group and include Huahine, Raiatea, Tahaa, Bora-Bora, Maupiti, Tupai, Maupihaa, Manuae and Moto One.

With the exception of Tetiaroa and the smaller western islands, all of the islands are high, volcanically formed and surrounded by coral reefs. Coral formations that are detached from the island leaving a passage with sufficient water for a vessel to travel are known as fringing reefs. The islands are the worn remnants of once tall volcanoes that now show jagged towers and various other shapes. The largest of the south seas islands, they enjoy an ideal climate. This made them the favored base for all the major explorers of the Pacific, beginning with the Polynesians.

Though probably seen by Quiros in 1606, it was not until the late 1700's that Tahiti became important on the evolving charts of the Pacific. In 1767, Wallis in the frigate *Dolphin,* anchored in Matavai Bay during the first recorded visit. In 1768 Bougainville visited the islands briefly and stayed at Hitiaa. But it was Captain Cook's many weeks in Tahiti, observing the transit of the planet Venus in 1769 that brought the island to the full notice of the Western world. Though Cook was an ideal observer and one unusually concerned with the effects of his visits, it was the many less scrupulous people who came after him, including the missionaries, who radically changed this culture. In 1880 these islands were taken under French protection, and by 1888 were made part of the French nation. Discussions are ongoing regarding independence, and in 1977 the territory was granted Interne Autonomie, or self-government. The full effect of the ECU has been delayed until 2002 and there are concerns regarding the long-term changes that will occur when/if it is fully implemented. France controls defense and to an ever decreasing degree, immigration.

The islands lie within the southeast trade wind belt, with winds from the southeast to east predominating. The trades are strongest in the winter months of July to September. Gales are infrequent, though at times a series of cyclones can be experienced as in late 1982 and early 1983. Except in showers, visibility is very good. In the vicinity of high islands the winds are altered and affected in various ways; land and sea breezes have greater force, and in the lee of the islands there may be calms and variable winds.

The currents follow the direction of the wind, except near the coasts. With the dominating easterly wind driving it, the current runs west at about 10 to 15 miles per day.

NOTE: The Uniform System of Buoyage (Red Left Returning) with some special additions, is used in French Polynesia. See Appendix I and explanatory notes.

ILES DE LA SOCIETE

Not to be used for navigation

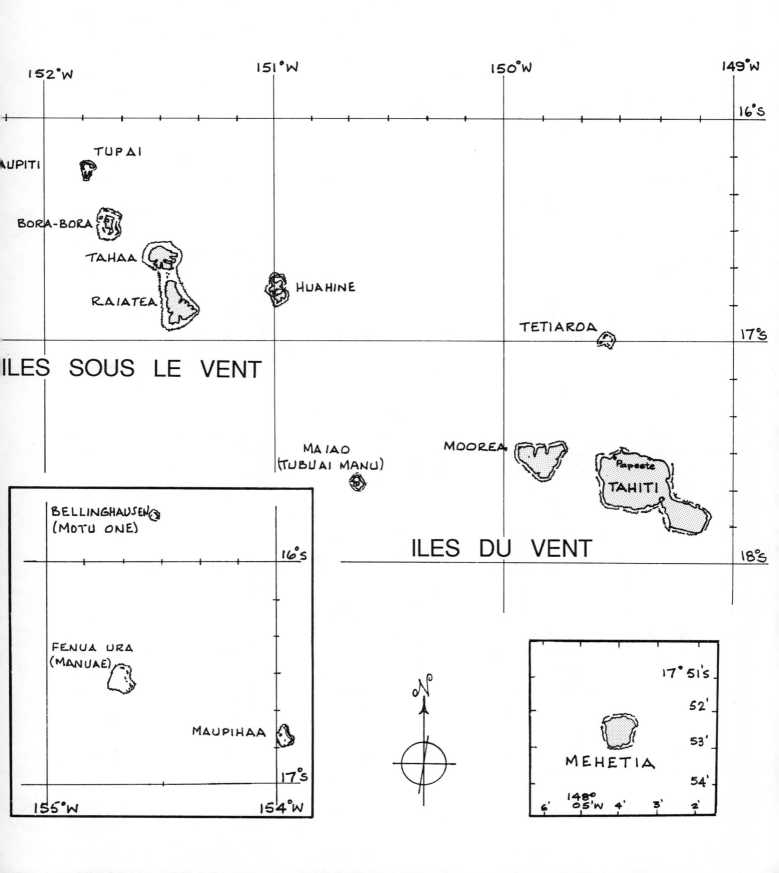

ILE TAHITI

Tahiti is the largest island and easternmost of the group, with the exception of little Meetia, which lies some 60 miles further east. The hourglass shape is due to the double volcano that once formed the island. The larger, almost circular section in the northwestern part is called Tahiti Nui; the oval-shaped smaller section is Tahiti Iti or the Taiarapu Peninsula. The neck joining them is the Isthmus of Taravao. Both parts of the island are broken into high, spectacular, sharp peaks, those on Tahiti Nui rising to Orohena at 2,238m (7,340'), on Tairapu to Pic Ronia at 1,323m (4,340').

A strip of coastal plain surrounds the peaks. It is larger on the western side where most of the people live. The mountain peaks are often obscured by clouds or mist but when visibility is good they can be seen from a great distance. The valleys between them are striking because of their depth and size, and together with the peaks are used as guides to the passes through the coral barrier reefs. Since most skippers using this guide will be making their landfall enroute from the Tuamotu or the Marquises, the key feature is Pointe Venus, which should be identified before closing the coast. Note: The second paragraph on page 102 gives a description of Pointe Venus.

The entire island is surrounded by a coral barrier reef varying from half a mile to two miles off the coast, and in two areas it is a submerged shoal. There are many passes allowing entry or exit through the reef. Several good anchorages are behind the reef, Papeete on the northwestern side and Port du Phaeton on the south. Passage behind the reef and between the passes is possible at many places, and in a detailed section which follows, information on these passes and anchorages is given.

The main port and administrative center for French Polynesia is at Papeete. It is the largest city in French Polynesia and a steady population drift to it from the other islands has been continuous for many years. It is a gathering place for yachts cruising the South Pacific, but there is much more to Tahiti than Papeete and it shouldn't be missed. Details of the entry and harbor are given on the following page.

A cruise around the island is not often undertaken by most skippers, who seem content to lie in Papeete. Yet such a cruise will show the island in a very different perspective to the adventurous sailor, one that is perhaps truer to the Tahiti of old than what is seen in the bustling city of Papeete. It is a little wetter and windier on the south and east coasts; anchorages are deep but uncrowded and the views of Tairapu Peninsula are worth the trip.

Several passes through the reef are suitable for use and though sketches are drawn of their approaches, a running log of openings and passes should be kept as a backup if clouds obscure the peaks. Most passages behind the reef are well marked by beacons and those near Papeete are lit. Nevertheless, it is best to travel on days with good visibility and to use visual methods navigation when behind the barrier reef.

ILES DE LA SOCIETE
ILE TAHITI

Approx. Scale n.m.

Not to be used for navigation

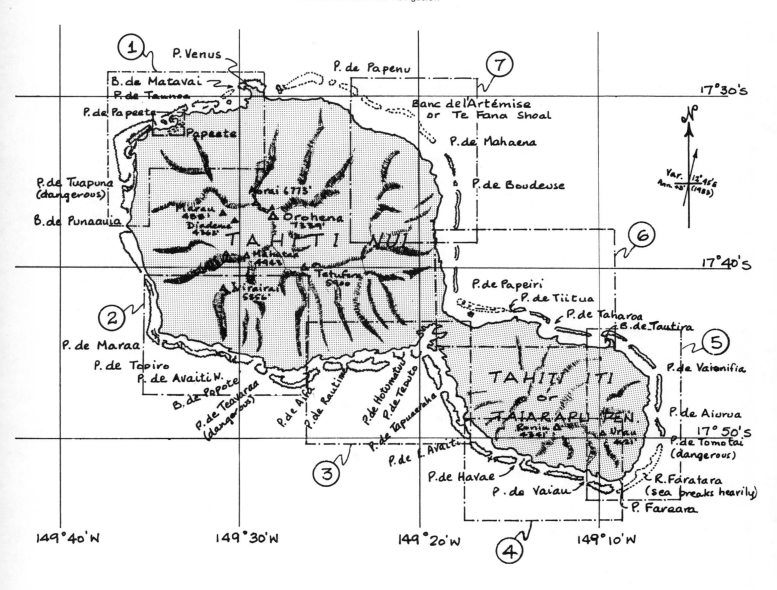

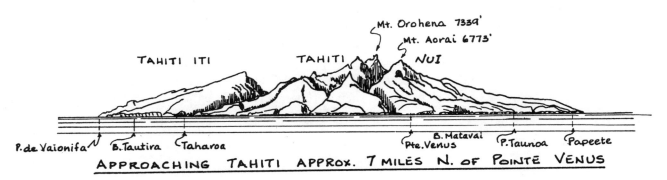

APPROACHING TAHITI APPROX. 7 MILES N. OF POINTE VENUS

PAPEETE

Papeete is the most sheltered harbor in Tahiti. It is on the northwestern coast, about 5 miles west of Pointe Venus (the northern extremity of the island). **Passe de Papeete** is the opening in the barrier reef into the harbor. Though it appears quite wide, the actual dredged opening (capable of accommodating large cruise ships) is about 60m (200') wide between the buoys. There is no difficulty for any small, capable vessel entering in good weather, even though currents of up to 5 knots run out of the pass. A heavy northerly swell can cause breakers across the pass and at such times it is best to await calmer seas. Outside the pass the westerly current generally runs at about one knot. Before entering the pass contact Port Control on VHF Ch 12 or SSB 2638Khz. All vessels must fly the yellow quarantine ("Q") flag when entering the port.

From a distance, the deep cleft of Vallee Fautauna helps identify the approach to the entrance and the sketch shows the view of the harbor when closer in. The Protestant Church on the waterfront toward the west is a prominent feature when approaching the pass and the city of Papeete extends along the shore for a considerable distance. At one time, pilots were compulsory for all vessels, but most yachts enter without one. Once the pass is seen and the buoys are visible an entry can be made on leading lights or marks, on white pylons with red bands on a bearing of 149°. Once through the pass, the yachts along the Quai are seen, and there are leading lights and a range leading to them.

The Harbormaster (Port Directeur) controls all yachts within the port and all around Tahiti. The harbor is divided according to the purposes of the vessels that use it. The important section for yachts is the **Quai Bir-Hakeim**; the dockmaster monitors VHF Ch 12. Moor bow or stern-to with an anchor out in the stream. The concrete-faced Quai has bollards to tie to and sometimes a plank to form a gangway for going ashore. Since most spaces are taken up by local boats it may be necessary to anchor off the beach in sand, tying two long stern lines ashore. A good spot is off the little park with a statue of Charles de Gaulle. Neighboring boats are usually helpful in getting newcomers settled and in passing on needed advice.

After the boat has been moored, entry procedures include a visit to Customs (Douane) immigration and the port captain, all conveniently located a short walk from the quay. An attempt to speak French is usually rewarded by a helpful response. Be prepared by having crew lists, passports and finances in place for posting the required bond. Take on fuel, water and basic provisions early in your stay to be prepared for the next leg of your journey. Duty free fuel is available in Papeete after obtaining port clearance and a form signed by Customs. It is available only from the Mobil pontoon next to the Moorea ferries, by truck from Shell or from the Total station at Marina Taina.

All services of a large city are found here such as stores, open-air markets, banks and marine repair services such as welding, refrigeration, engine repair and rigging shops, etc. Papeete is a busy, expensive city to visit, and although some shopkeepers speak limited English, it is wise to keep a French/English phrase book handy. Three museums, accessible by "Le Truck" or walking, that will broaden your appreciation of Polynesia and are well worth visiting: Museum of Tahiti and her Islands, the Pearl Museum and the Gauguin Museum. Within close reach of Papeete is the northwestern coastal section where anchorages some distance from the crowded downtown zone are located. They are described on the following page.

When checking in with port authorities ask for the free booklet entitled, *Yacht Guide - Papeete Tahiti.* It is full of useful information such as repair services, medical resources, emergency telephone numbers, etc.

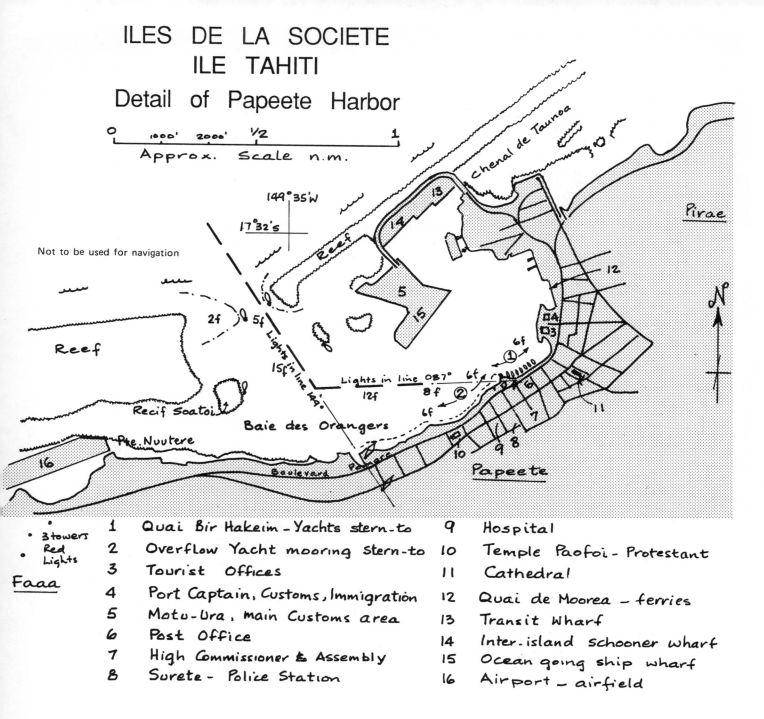

ILES DE LA SOCIETE
ILE TAHITI
Detail of Papeete Harbor

Approx. Scale n.m.

Not to be used for navigation

149°35'W
17°32'S

Reef

Chenal de Taunoa

Pirae

Recif Soatoi
Pte. Nuutere
Baie des Orangers
Boulevard
Papeete

Faaa
• 3 towers Red Lights

1	Quai Bir Hakeim – Yachts stern-to	9	Hospital
2	Overflow Yacht mooring stern-to	10	Temple Paofoi – Protestant
3	Tourist Offices	11	Cathedral
4	Port Captain, Customs, Immigration	12	Quai de Moorea – ferries
5	Motu-Ura, main Customs area	13	Transit Wharf
6	Post Office	14	Inter. island schooner wharf
7	High Commissioner & Assembly	15	Ocean going ship wharf
8	Surete – Police Station	16	Airport – airfield

Vallee Fautaua, deeply cut

Pte. Venus
Baie Matavai
Passe Papeete
Airport
Cathedral Prot. Church

ILE TAHITI FROM NE, ABT. 1MILE, APPROACHING PAPEETE

ILE TAHITI - NORTHWEST COAST (Pointe Venus to Pointe Nuuroa)

Beginning at Pointe Venus, the guide proceeds in an a counter-clockwise direction around the coast of Tahiti. A small part of the coast is not detailed because it is too exposed and does not have suitable anchorages.

Pointe Venus is a long, low point easily identified by the 28m (92') lighthouse at the tip and a radio pylon about .5 mile to the south. The coral reef, awash, extends about 610m (2,000') on each side and seaward from the point In 1769 Captain Cook built a small fort on the point to observe the transit of Venus, thus giving the point its name.

Baie de Matavai, with its black sand beach, lies to the west of Pointe Venus. The fringing reef is submerged, but an opening with a depth of 9 fathoms is the entrance. Banc du Dolphin, on which there is a beacon, restricts the opening. This deep anchorage was used by Wallis, Cook and Bligh and is suited to sailing vessels of an earlier era, its attribute is historical interest.

Passe Taunoa is about 3 miles west of Pointe Venus, and leads into Taunoa and Papawa. It is a 275m (900') gap in the reef that is reduced by shoals on each side. An anchorage is in the basin but it is exposed to swell coming through the pass. A slightly less exposed anchorage is near the eastern reef, in black sand. **Chenal Taunoa** is a narrow passage leading to Papeete which is marked by beacons and used by local vessels.

From the western side of Papeete harbor **Chenal de Faaa** leads behind the reef and past the airport at Pointe Faaa, after which it turns southward towards Passe Taapuna. Chenal de Faaa is easily negotiated because it is marked by lighted pipe beacons and has a width of 60m (200'). The currents run northeasterly out of Chenal de Faaa and westerly from Taunoa, all into and then exiting from **Passe de Papeete**. Two anchorages that are comfortable alternatives to Papeete are along this passage; "Le Truck" provides quick transportation to downtown Papeete. The Port Authority has moorings for rent west of Maeva Beach Hotel; .25 mile to the south is Continent, the largest supermarket in Papeete.   Tahiti Aquatique at the hotel has a dinghy dock, showers, and laundry service available for yachts on a weekly basis. Marina Lotus is south of Continent and is the easiest place in Polynesia to take on fuel and water.   It may be possible to leave your boat inside the marina if you need to fly home, although it isn't considered by local sailors to be "hurricane proof."

Passe Taapuna is about 1.5 miles south of the above anchorages. Although it is marked "dangerous" in the Pilot, it is suitable for auxiliary powered yachts. The pass is 90m (300') wide between the reefs awash although it is actually narrower because of shoals on each side. Vessels should favor the northern side since the shoal on the south side is only 1.8m (6') deep. The outgoing current can be strong, and if the swell is high, the pass will be white with breakers and transit should not be attempted. Such a high swell is evidenced by large breakers and spume, seen as you travel behind the fringing reef.

Frigate Bird

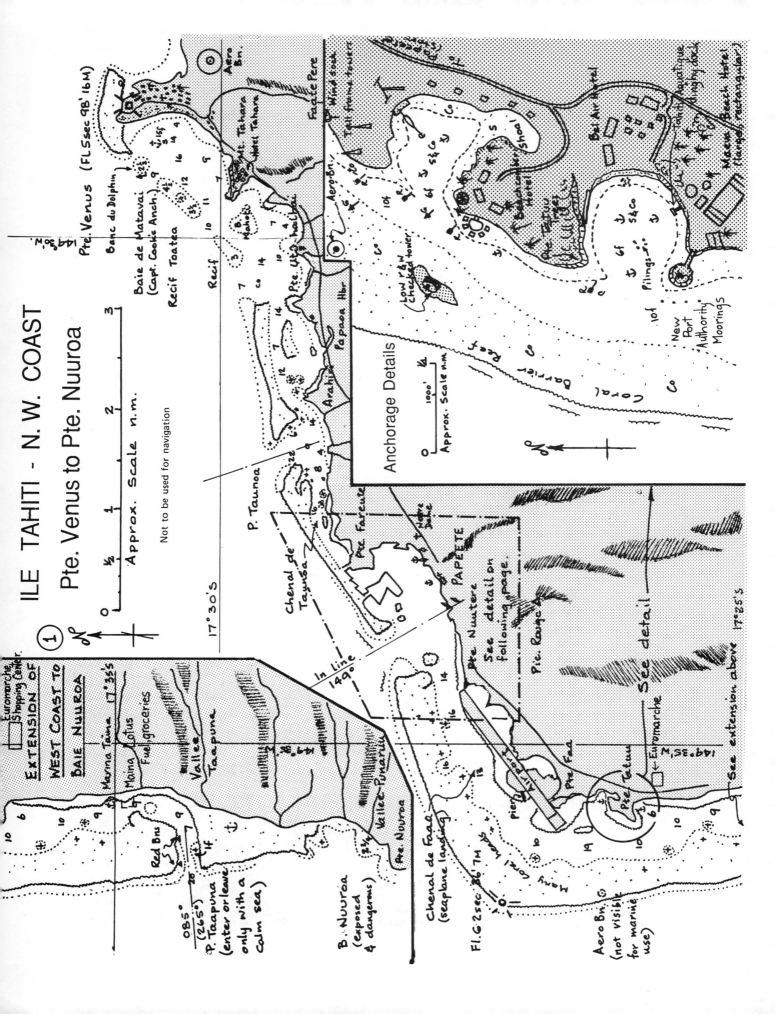

ILE TAHITI - N.W. COAST
Pte. Venus to Pte. Nuuroa

① Approx. Scale n.m.
0   ½   1   2   3

Not to be used for navigation

17°30'S

Pte. Venus (FL 5 sec 98' 16M)

149°30'W

Banc du Dolphin

Baie de Matavai (Capt. Cook's Anch.)

Recif Toatea

Recif

B. Mahaiea

Pte. Uta-hati

Papeoa Hbr.

Arahiti

P. Taunoa

Chenal de Taunoa

Pte. Fareute

In line 149°

Anchorage Details

Aero Bn.

Wind Sock
Tel. phone towers

Fasse Pere

Mt. Tahara
West Tahara

Low R&W Checked tower

Coral Barrier Reef

New Port Authority Moorings

Beachcomber Hotel Shoal

Tahiti Aquatique Supply dock

Maeva Beach Hotel (turned rectangular)

Pilings

Approx. Scale n.m.
0   1000'   ¼

PAPEETE

Pte. Nuutere
See detail on following page

Pte. Rouge

See detail
See extension above 17°25'S

149°35'W

Euromarche Shopping Center

EXTENSION OF WEST COAST TO BAIE NUUROA

Mayma Taune   17°35'S

Moina Lotus
Fuel, groceries

Vallee Taapuna

Vallee Punaruu

Ave. Nuuroa

085° (265°)
P. Taapuna (enter or leave only with a calm sea)

Red Bns.

B. Nuuroa (Exposed & dangerous)

Chenal de Faaa (seaplane landing)

Fl.G 2 sec 36'7M

Pierre

Pte. Faaa

Pte. Tataa

← Euromarche

Aero Bn. ① (not visible for marine use)

Many coral

Chenal de Faaa

ILE TAHITI - SOUTHWEST COAST (Pointe Maraa to Pointe Mahaitea)

Between Pointe Nuuroa and Paea, the coral reef approaches the coast, making Baie Nuuroa so exposed that it should be bypassed. The immense gorge of Vallee de Punaruu extends into the mountains and is a good landmark. Large private estates prohibit public access to this part of the coast. The barrier reef returns at Pointe Nuuroa and off the low point of Pointe Maraa it widens to about .75 mile. The coast then turns eastward.

Passe de Maraa is the westernmost of two passes at the point, separated by a steep hill. It provides entrance to a small bay at the point. Shallow spits extend from both sides of the channel, but beacons mark the navigable water and the clear pass can be easily entered along the centerline. The current sets westerly across the pass and should be taken into account. When southwesterly winter swells cause breaking seas across the entrance it should not be used. Within the pass, anchorage may be taken off the small stream near the point or in front of the steep cliff.

Several basins are behind the reef in the next 3 miles. In good visibility it is possible to thread a route into these basins from the one at the point. The only usable passage for exiting the area is **Passe Maraa** as both Passe Topiro (Fr. name: Passe de Teavaiti), one mile to the east, and Passe West Avaiti (Fr. name: Passe Toapiro), apparent openings in the reef, are shallow and have coral heads which make them unusable except for small local craft.

The remainder of the coastal reef in this section has no useful passes, though they will be described so that a running check on position can be kept. As the peaks which are often used to define a line through the passes are sometimes obscured, such a running check acts as a navigating backup. The reef is broken in some places, but in general it extends about 610m (2,000') from the shore.

Pointe Mahaitea is the highest and most clearly defined of the relatively low points along this coast and is marked by a white building to the north. To the south of the point is **Passe Teavaraa,** a gap in the reef about 275m (900') wide. Though it has a depth of 1.8m (2 fathoms), the swell and surge often cause breakers and lumpy seas, making it dangerous to cross.

* * * * *

NOTE: In this and in sections to follow, the apparently wide passes are reduced in actual width to a narrower navigable area. The breakers that occur across the shallows usually mark the edge of the deep portion of a pass. In a few cases the spits are sufficiently deep that breakers do not occur and so no warning is given. Passes should be entered carefully, especially those slanted toward the coastline, but in most cases a centerline route clears the dangers.

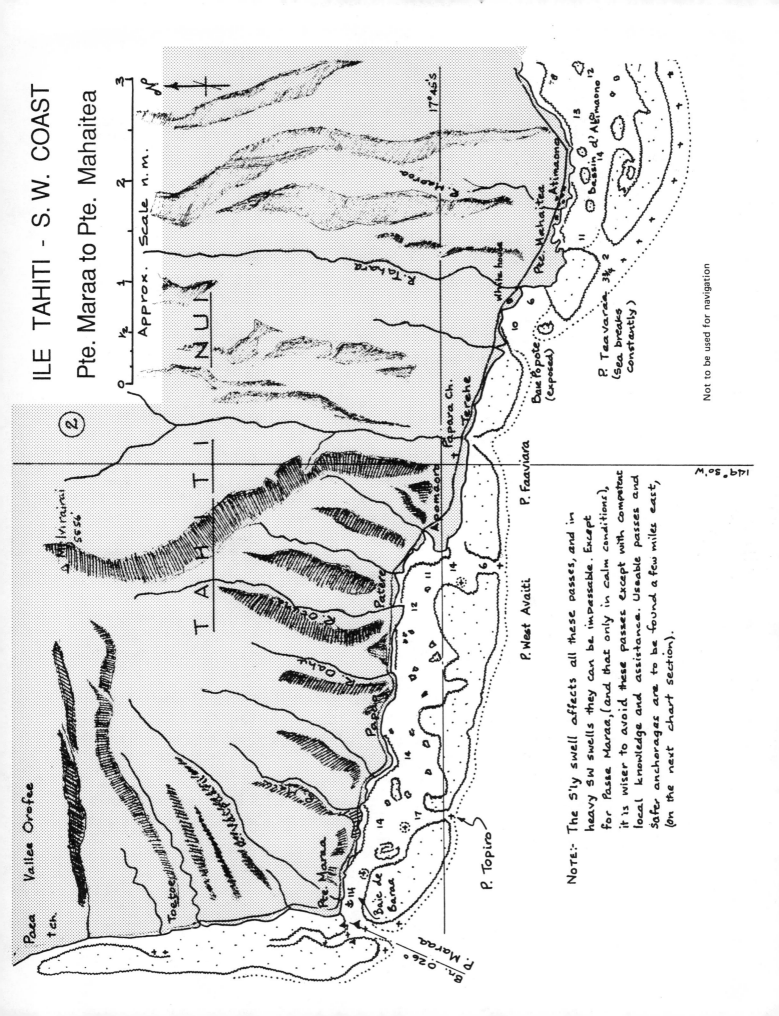

ILE TAHITI - S.W. COAST

Pte. Maraa to Pte. Mahaitea

②

NOTE:- The S'ly swell affects all these passes, and in
heavy SW swells they can be impassable. Except
for Passe Maraa, (and that only in calm conditions,)
it is wiser to avoid these passes except with competent
local knowledge and assistance. Useable passes and
safer anchorages are to be found a few miles east,
(on the next chart section).

Not to be used for navigation

ILE TAHITI - SOUTH COAST (Passe Aifa to Pointe Patoa)

Beyond Passe Teavaraa the reef bulges out to extend almost 1.5 miles offshore. Behind the reef is a good natural basin, but to enter it you must weather the bulge to reach Passe Aifa which is about 2 miles to the east.

Passe Aifa has an apparent width of 305m (1,000') but is reduced by shoals on both sides to a usable passage 90m (300') wide. The first wooded islet to appear along the coast, Ile Mapeti, is on the reef on the eastern side of the pass; a small cay is on the western side. Between them are three small reefs awash which leave sufficient room for passage.

The pass is entered on a bearing of 317° aiming at the small sandy cay and cutting close to the eastern side of the reef. When the south side of Ile Mapeti bears about 040° the vessel must turn northward to pass the three small reefs to port, and a shallow 5.5m (3-fathom) patch ahead to starboard. The pass leads directly into Baie d'Aifa, then westward into Baie d'Atimaono which is behind the bulge of the reef. It can be used in good weather, and anchorage may be taken in the lagoon in 15 - 18m (8 - 10 fathoms).

Passe Rautirare is a deep, clear pass leading directly into Bassin de Papeuriri. It is about 275m (900') wide and thus in strong winds it does not provide as much shelter as other less ideal passes. Ilot Pururu stands on the eastern reef well back of the breakers and it provides the best anchorage in good holding, black sand.

Chenal d'Otiaroa is a beacon-marked, 45m (150') wide channel leading from Bassin de Papeuriri to spacious Port d'Ataiti. Following the easy passage, anchorage may be taken southeast of the village in 14.5 to 18m (8 to 10 fathoms). Port d'Ataiti is connected to Bassin Papeari. on the east by beacon-marked, 45m (150') wide Chenal Motuaini. This basin is also accessible via Passe de Temarauri. which is 3 miles east of Pointe Rautirare. Though the eastern side has shoals and reefs, it can be traversed during good visibility.

Passe de Hotumatuu is about 1 mile east of Pointe do Temarauri and it leads into the cul-de-sac of Port de Paul. Anchorage is available for small vessels off the restaurant on Pointe Taunoa which is tucked in the niche behind the reef to the west. A small wharf is nearby, but patches of coral which have to be avoided to reach the anchorage also prevent a vessel from mooring to the dock.

Passe de Teputo (Teputa) is one of the entrances leading to Port du Phaeton. Within the opening a large reef (Banc Matuu) divides the pass into two: Passe de Matuu on the west (encumbered by reefs) and Passe de Teputo (deep and clear) which continues along the eastern side. Beacons mark the channel leading to Port du Phaeton, where very good anchorage may be taken at the head of the inlet.

Passe Tapuaeraha is 3 miles south of Passe de Teputa and leads into Bassin de Tapuaeraha and north to Port du Phaeton or south through Mouillage de Vairo where a naval base is located, to an exit at **Passe East Avaiti (P. Teavaiti).**

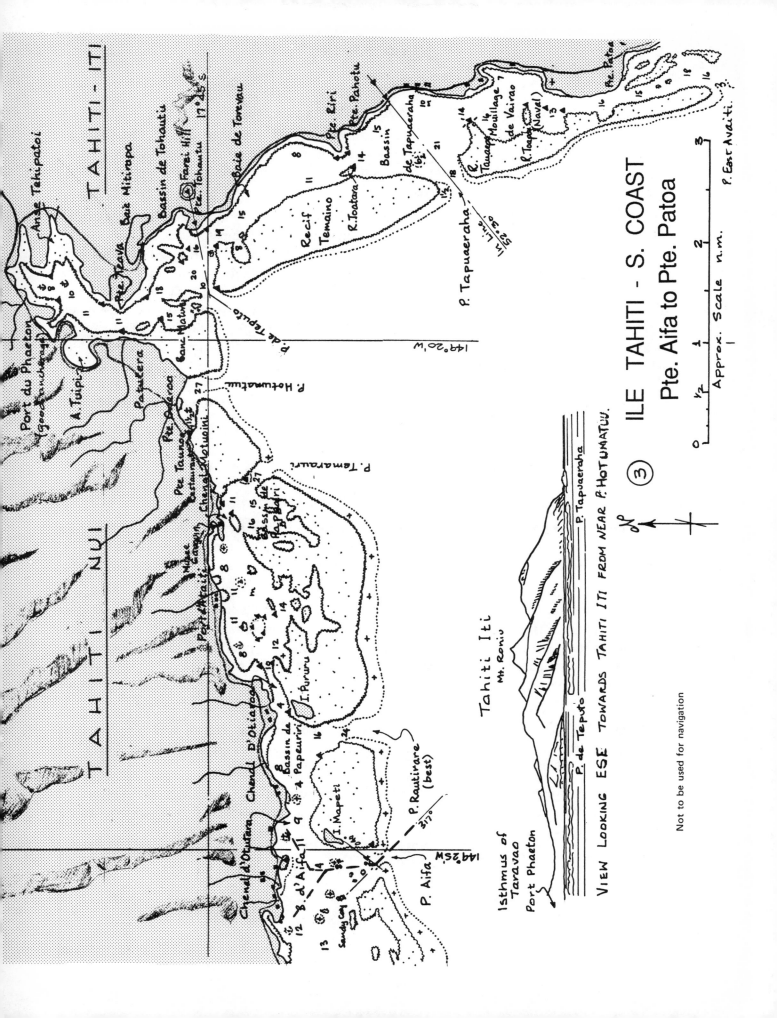

③ ILE TAHITI - S. COAST
Pte. Aifa to Pte. Patoa

Approx. Scale n.m.

0   ½   1   2   3

Not to be used for navigation

VIEW LOOKING ESE TOWARDS TAHITI ITI FROM NEAR P. HOTUMATU.

Tahiti Iti
Mt. Roniu

Isthmus of Taravao
Port Phaeton

P. de Tepito   P. Tapuaeraha

ILE TAHITI - SOUTH COAST (Pointe Patoa to Pointa Fareara)

This section of the coast forms the southwestern and southern side of the Taiarapu Peninsula or Tahiti Iti. The land is scored into peaks and valleys making a fantastic skyline and rising to a high plateau at the center of the island. The barrier reef continues around the shore with several usable passes leading to anchorages.

East Avaiti Pass (Passe Teavaiti) is about 1 mile south of Pointe Patoa, and it provides access to Mouillage (Anchorage) de Vairo and Bassin Teahupoo. The pass is 150m (500') wide, with least depths of 3.6m (12'). In good weather it is usable by small craft but dangerous seas rise across the bar during strong winds. Approach to the pass is made by steering 065° toward the massive bulk of Mont Tarania (820m/2,680') until close-to when the pass can be seen. When within a mile of the pass the alignment can be corrected to a bearing of 060° on the flat-topped Mont Araope (275m/899') which is near the coast. Anchorage in 18m (10 fathoms) can be found in a basin formed by the projection of a reef, Banc Toa Maere, which projects about 600m (2,000') southwest of Pointe Arahuku. Alternatively, slightly more open anchorage is available in Bassin Teahupoo, about .5 mile northwest of Pointe Arahuku, close to the coast, sand and coral bottom. Passe Avaino (Passe Teavaino), 1.5 miles to the east is a foul bar with coral heads.

Passe Havae is about 1.5 miles beyond Passe Avaino and is the best of this group. It is straight, deep and clear except for the narrowing of the apparent width of 365m (1,200') to 180m (600') by submerged reefs on each side of the opening. A bearing of 30° on Mont Vaipuu (760m/2,500'), with the cleft summit of Mont Te Hau (390m/1,273'), leads through the pass. Many yachts use the pass to leave the lagoon traveling from Port du Phaeton.

The coral reef extends from Pointe Fara Mahora, curves eastward and opens at Passe de Puuotohe. The eastern side of the reef extends underwater, reducing the passage to 45m (150'). Coral heads within the pass make it dangerous and one that should be avoided since a better pass is nearby.

Passe Vaiau has a good, 180m (600') wide entrance. A leading line into the pass is at 008° on the summit of Mont Faretua (975m/3,190'), a bulky mountain from which three arms extend toward the coast in the form of an "E". It is divided at the inner end into two channels by a reef awash. Either channel may be used, but the western side is preferable. Port de Vaiau is the basin within the reef where anchorage may be found in the cove formed by the coral reef below Pointe Maraetiria.

Passe Tutataroa is not a recommended passage because it is narrow and winding as it goes eastward from Port de Vaiau near underwater reefs and passes Pointe Vareara where the seas are often heavy due to a submerged offshore shoal, Faratara Reef.

The coast turns northeasterly around Pointe Fareara and this portion is called Cote de Pari. Give it a wide berth as the offshore reef is submerged and spectacular breakers are caused when there is a heavy swell.

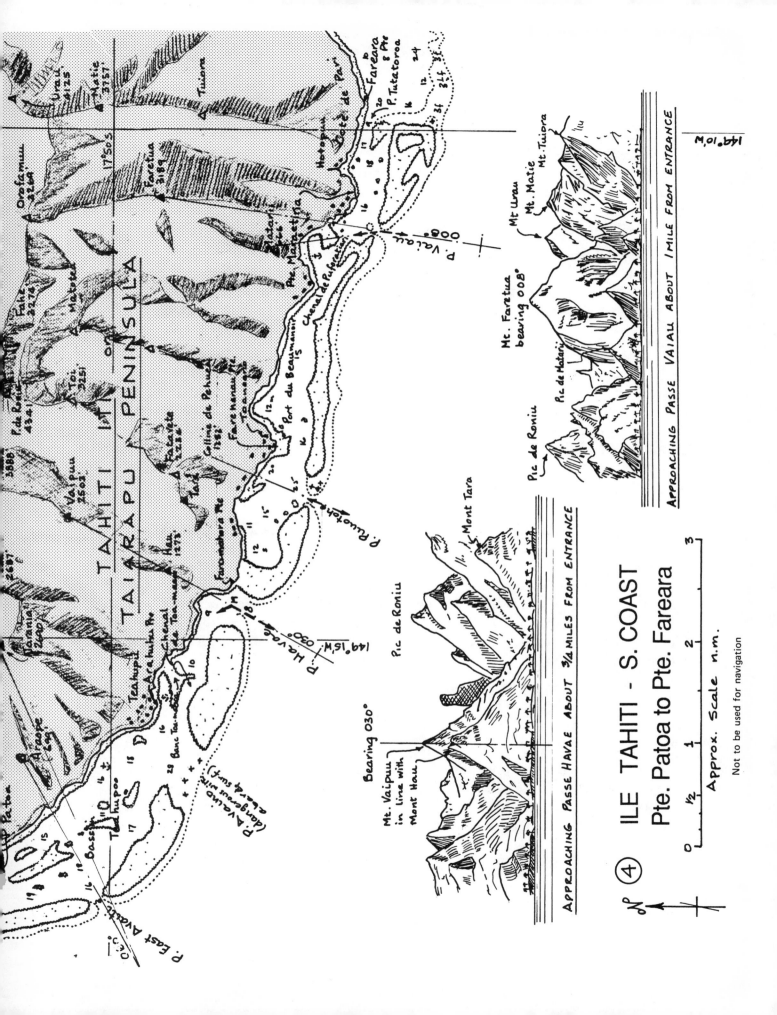

ILE TAHITI - S. COAST
Pte. Patoa to Pte. Fareara

N° ④

APPROACHING PASSE HAVAE ABOUT 3½ MILES FROM ENTRANCE

APPROACHING PASSE VAIAU ABOUT 1 MILE FROM ENTRANCE

Approx. Scale n.m.

Not to be used for navigation

ILE TAHITI - SOUTHEAST COAST (Pointe Fareara to Pointe Tautira)

From Pointe Fareara to Pointe Puha, about 3 miles up the coast, the Faratara Reef extends underwater about 4 miles out from the coast. It is submerged to depths varying from 3 to 23m (2 to 11 fathoms), and this leaves the coast unprotected. Small vessels must stand clear when sailing up the coast. Because there are no roads in this section until Pointe Tautira, the villages, anchorages, and island views are similar to the Tahiti of old, though the villagers are completely modernized and they speed along in outboard-powered outriggers.

Passe Tomotai, just beyond Pte. Puha, is between the north end of Faratara Reef and the recommencing visible barrier reef that continues up the coast. Ilots Tiere and Fennaino, both covered with palms and clearly visible from seaward, are north of the entrance and help to identify it. Cruisers are advised not to use this pass because of the many hazards near Faratara Reef.

Passe d'Aiurua, located I mile north of Pointe Tomotai, is a deep, 183m (600') wide pass with easy access to the lagoon behind the reef. A shallow, 3.5m (2-fathom) patch extends southward from the end of the northern reef and requires that the course through the pass be made a little south of the center-line. From seaward a bearing of 276° on the sharp pinnacle of Mont Teiche takes the vessel on this course. Anchorages are on each side of the pass in coves formed by coral projections extending from the land. The southern anchorage is more exposed, but prettier, and the islets, reefs and motus on the outer reef give some protection. More coral heads are exposed and awash behind the barrier reef, necessitating careful conning while traveling to Pointe Vaitoto if the vessel leaves from Passe Vaionifa.

Passe Vaionifa is about 3 miles north of Passe d'Aiurua and though reduced from its 185m (600') width by shallow spits on each side of the opening, it is an easy pass to transit. It should be approached on a bearing of 233,° taken on the highest peak of the group framed in the deep cut of Vallee de Vaitoto. A shallow patch, marked by a beacon, lies almost on the axis well within the pass and is easily avoided. Le Crabe, marked by a beacon, is a rocky patch awash about 150m (500') from the shore and 1 mile northwest of Pointe Vaionifa. Anchorage can be found either midway up <u>Bassin de Tautira</u>, or at the head near Pointe Tautira in about 25m (14 fathoms).

The opening in the reef about 1 mile from the head of the basin is not navigable as it is obstructed by coral heads. There isn't a passage between Pte. Tautira and the reef. In order to travel northward the vessel must exit from Passe Vaionifa, proceed around the reef, and enter Baie Tautira from the north.

Pointe Tautira is a low projection from the mountains that extends northward from the curve of the coastline. The barrier reef bends around the point to end on the west side. The bay is open to the north as there is a half-mile gap in the reef before it begins again. The town of <u>Tautira,</u> an important local center, is extends around the tip of the point.

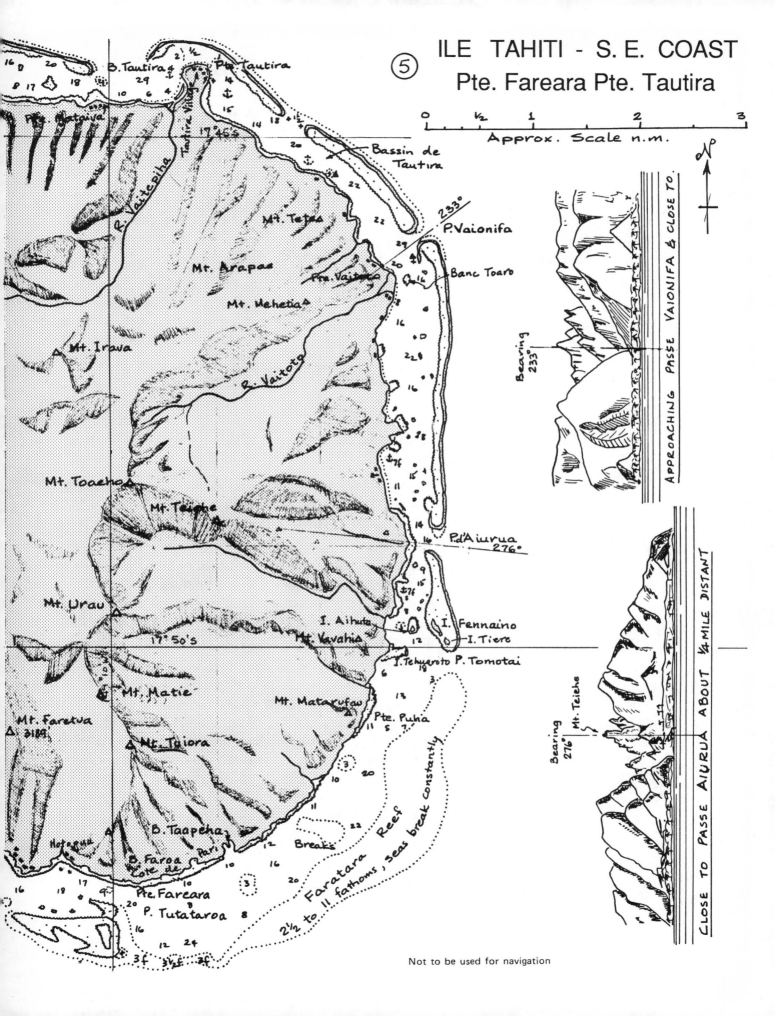

ILE TAHITI - S.E. COAST
Pte. Fareara Pte. Tautira

⑤

Approx. Scale n.m.

Not to be used for navigation

ILE TAHITI - EAST COAST (Pointe Tautira to Pointe Paritautia)

This portion includes 8 miles of the north coast of Tahiti Iti and the east coast of Tahiti Nui. The hills begin at the shoreline and numerous waterfalls are evident. Vallee Haavini is a spectacular cleft through which the peaks at the center of the island can be seen.

Baie de Tautira is within the curve of land along the point and behind the half-mile opening in the reef. It can be entered easily via **Passe Teafa** and anchorage found off the beach near the village, in l0 -18m (6 - 8 fathoms). Winds from the N to WNW make this a lee shore. The fine, black sand beach is one of the few large beaches in Tahiti.

Port de Pihaa is the basin enclosed by the barrier reef that begins west of the opening. It can be entered from either end and is marked by beacons, though a spit of land at the west end, Pte. Pihaa, almost reaches the reef. Several small exposed reefs within the basin can easily be avoided. Anchorage may be taken east of Pte. Pihaa in 25m (14 fathoms), sand and mud.

Passe Taharoa is the next gap in the reef and is about .5 mile wide. Banc Tuatua, a shoal covered .9m (3'), lies on the inside of the pass, dividing it in two. The eastern side is 180m (600') wide and some scattered reefs must be negotiated when turning to Port de Pihaa. The western side is clearer and turns almost directly past Pointe Faraari into the next basin, Port de Pueu. A submerged portion of the outer reef could be mistaken for a pass but it is blocked by coral heads and therefore cannot be used.

Passe de Tiitau is .5 mile west of the above false opening. It lies between the end of the barrier reef and a portion of the reef awash, Banc Toapu, which is almost 300m (1,000') across. Ranges on shore give a line through the pass but they are difficult to discern from seaward. There are no problems leaving via this pass.

Baie Taravao is between Pointe Tiitau and the northward turn of the coast. Almost the entire barrier reef in this area is submerged and becomes a series of shoals, except for a few motus. Breaking surf usually identifies the position of underwater reefs. Anchorage here is not recommended; although the holding is good in much of the bay, it is exposed to winds from the north to east and the swell crosses the reef unimpeded.

Passe Papeiri is between the western end of the sunken reef and the visible reef which angles northward. The town of Taravao in the low lying land between the two parts of Tahiti is a good landmark. A 10m (6-fathom) shoal. lies in the entrance. The most popular anchorage is off the village in Port de Vaitoare in good holding, mud and sand; another spot is closer to the offshore reef in slightly less depth. This area can also be entered from the north via **Passe de Faone**. The reef continues for a short distance north of Passe de Faone before the wide opening of Passe d'Utuofai exposes the coast.

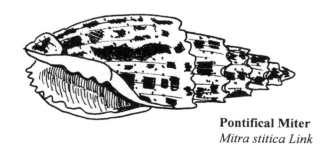

Pontifical Miter
Mitra stitica Link

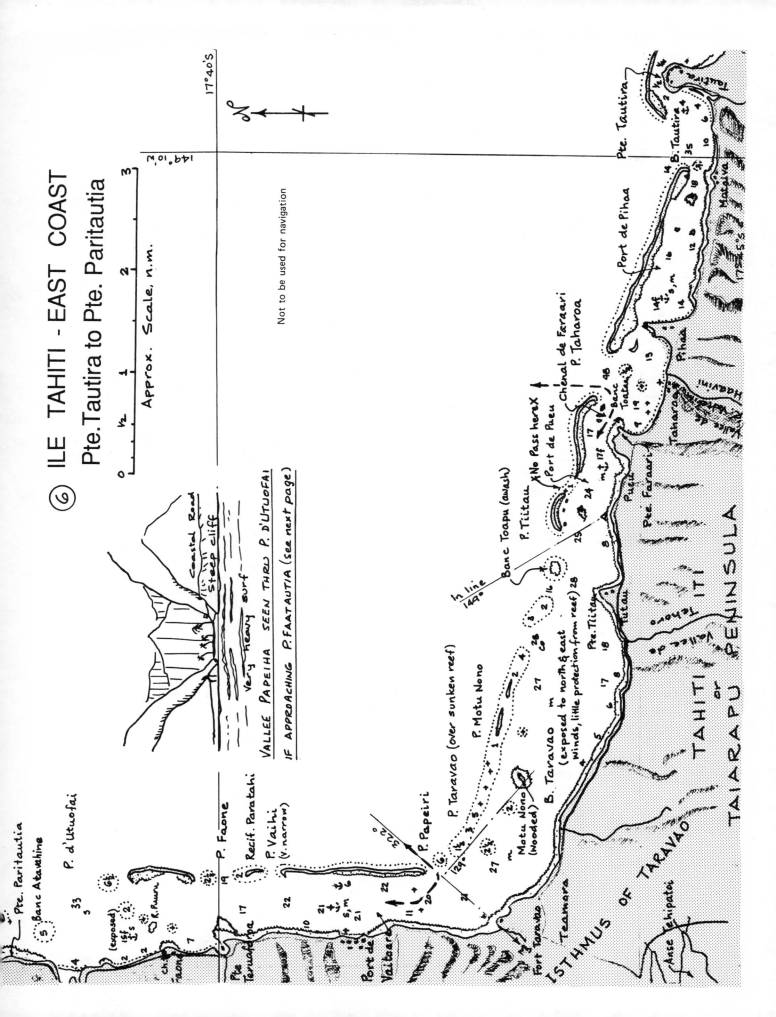

⑥ ILE TAHITI - EAST COAST
Pte.Tautira to Pte. Paritautia

Approx. Scale, n.m.

Not to be used for navigation

17°40'S

149°10'W

Coastal Road
steep cliff
Very heavy surf

VALLEE PAPEIHA SEEN THRU P. d'UTUOFAI
IF APPROACHING P.FAATAUTIA (see next page)

Pte. Paritautia
Banc Atauahine
P. d'Utuofai
(exposed)
Ch. Puunui
Pte Tanuofaga
Port de Vaitaare
Fort Teamara

P. Faone
Recif Paratahi
P. Vaihi (v. narrow)

P. Taravao (over sunken reef)
P. Papeiri
P. Motu Nono
Motu Nono (wooded)
B. Taravao (exposed to north & east winds, little protection from reef)
Pte. Tiitau

Banc Toapu (awash)
In line 149°
P. Tiitau
No Pass here X
Port de Pueu
Port de Pueu
Chenal de Faraari
P. Taharoa
Banc Toatai
Pte. Faraari
Puaa
Tiitau
Teahoro
Tahoro
Vallee de

ISTHMUS OF TARAVAO
TAHITI ITI or TAIARAPU PENINSULA
Anse Ehipatoa

Port de Pihaa
Pte. Tautira
B. Tautira
Mataiva
Pihaa
Taharoa
Haavini
Vallee de

17°55'S

ILE TAHITI - NORTHEAST COAST (Pointe Paritautia to Pointe de Rauraia)

Pointe Paritautia is an unobtrusive point on the land opposite the recommencing barrier reef at the north end of Passe d'Utofai. The steep cliffs and cleft of Vallee de Papeiha, which is south of the point are more evident as landmarks.

Behind the protection of the reef is a sheltered basin, Porte de Temato (Tamatoe), where good anchorage can be found. The basin is entered through **Passe de Faatautia**, staying within 90m (300') of the offshore reef when turning into the anchorage. The small detached reef on the western side should not be approached closely. Dinghies can land on a black sand beach on the southern side of Pointe d'Hitiaa The town of Hitiaa lies along the nearby coastal road. A small boat channel is around the coral reef projection at Hitiaa; its depth and suitability for yachts is unknown.

Passe de la Boudeuse is opposite the town of Hitiaa. It is wide although it has some dangerous covered rocks and coral heads on the northern side and vessels should keep close to the edge of the southern reef. Mouillage de Bougainville lies between the island shore and the offshore reef, which is partly submerged. Though this was Bougainville's anchorage it is not a well protected basin as wind and swell continue across the reef unabated.

The barrier reef is submerged for the entire 11 miles separating Pointe Mahaena and Pointe Venus. It becomes a chain of dangerous shoals, known as Banc de l'Artemise (locally called, Te Fana), lying from .75 to 2 miles offshore. These shoals do not provide protection from the prevailing wind and seas, and vessels passing this part of the coast should stand well offshore.

The coast angles northwesterly for the 4 miles between Hitiaa and Pointe Faaru before curving westward. Several deep valleys reach the shore with steep mountain ridges between. Near Pointe de Papenoo, about 9.5 miles from Hitiaa, the great cleft of Vallee of Papenoo extends well into the center of Tahiti. Between this valley and Pointe Venus, only 4 miles away, there are some sandy beaches along the low coast. They are broken by a rocky bluff at Tapahi which can be seen about 1.5 miles from Papenoo. The leper's hospital stands on this bluff and is visible from offshore.

The coast between Pointe de Papenoo and Pointe Venus should be given a wide berth because shoals extend about 600m (2,000') east of Pointe Venus and are 2 miles offshore at Pointe de Papenoo. A vessel coming from the south must stand well to the north (until all of the island of Moorea is open to view beyond Tahiti) before setting a course toward Pointe Venus and Papeete.

The cruise around Tahiti can be made in either direction, but since the western side has light and variable winds, it is easier to follow the pattern described. In this way, the fair, prevailing easterly winds and following seas will take one past the dangerous shoals on the eastern side.

Hebrew Cone *(Conus ebraeus Linne)*
Strigate Auger *(Terebra strigilata Sowerby)*

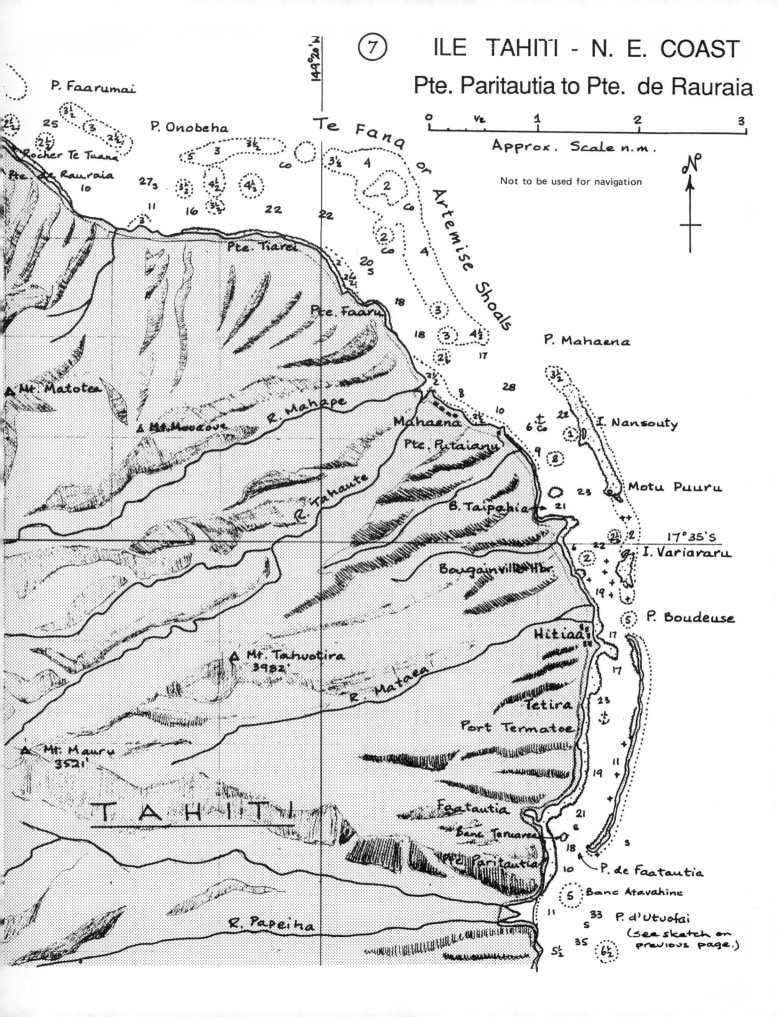

P. Faarumai

P. Onobeha

Te Fana or Artemise Shoals

0   ½   1   2   3
Approx. Scale n.m.

Not to be used for navigation

N°

25
2½
2½
Rocher Te Tuana
Pte. de Rauraia
10
27₃
11
16
22

3½
3
3
2½

5   3   3½
4½
4½
3½
3½

CO
3½ 4
2
CO
4
2
CO
2
CO

22
22
20₅
2₂
2½
18
3
18   3   4½
17
2½
2₄
2½
2
8
28
10

Pte. Tiarei
Pte. Faaru

△ Mt. Matotea
△ Mt. Moueoue
R. Mahape
R. Tahaute

Mahaena
Pte. Putaianu
B. Taipahia

P. Mahaena
3½
22
6 † CO
⚓ 1   I. Nansouty
9   2
23   Motu Puuru
21

6   22   2½   2
2   22
19

17°35'S
I. Variararu

P. Boudeuse
5

△ Mt. Tahuotira
3982'

R. Mataea

△ Mt. Maura
3521'

T A H I T I

Hitiaa   1½   17
17
23   ⚓
Tetira
Port Termatoe
11
19

Faatautia
Banc Temaree
Pte. Paritautia
18   6
P. de Faatautia
10

Banc Atavahine
5
11   33   P. d'Utuofai
5₅½   35   6½   (see sketch on
previous page.)

R. Papeiha

ILE MOOREA (Excluding Baie de Cook and Baie d'0punohu)

The usual approach to Moorea takes the swell at an angle and closes the coast near Pointe Faaupo, the easternmost point. As the fringing reef is steep-to and close to the coast, a yacht can sail fairly close to the edge of the reef in good conditions. Proceeding in an counter-clockwise direction around the island, the coast angles northwesterly for about 2 miles until turning south of westerly at Pointe Aroa, which is the northernmost part of Moorea and is marked by a light.

Passe Avaiti is a small pass used by local vessels and is a short distance west of Pointe Aroa. About 1.5 miles further is a slightly wider and usable pass, **Passe Irihonu**, which opens westward into a small lagoon. Anchorage may be taken in front of the Bali Hai Hotel, easily identified by its over-the-water bungalows. A small channel leads westward behind the reef to Baie de Cook, but since the easier entrance of Passe Avaroa is very close, this narrow channel should not be used.

A separate sketch and description is given for the two main bays of Moorea: Baie de Cook and Baie d'Opunohu. Beyond them the coast continues westward for about 2 miles to Passe Taotoi. (Passe Taotai). This entrance can be used in good weather, but it only leads into a long, narrow passage behind the two islets at the western end of Moorea. The channel shallows as it opens into a bay where Club Med is located. The bay and its approaches are shallow and beset with coral heads.

The western coast of Moorea runs southeasterly towards Haapiti and the southern tip of the island. Several hotels are behind the sandy beaches and though a beacon-marked channel runs in front of them, the channel is used mainly by fishing craft. About 6 miles along the curve of the reef from Passe Tautoi is Passe Taota, and a mile further, is Passe Avamotu. Both are narrow and lead into small lagoon cul-de-sacs. Husky rollers are usually seen at the entrance bars of these passes and they should not be entered.

Passe Matauvau is a mile beyond Passe Avamotu and it leads into an extensive lagoon behind the reef where the pretty village of Haapiti is located. During calm conditions this pass can be used but it can be rough and dangerous when a southwesterly swell is running. Passe Avarapa, about 2.5 miles further south, is a rough pass leading to a small lagoon; it can be ignored. The southernmost part of Moorea is a mile east of Pointe Avarapa, after which the coast begins to turn northeasterly toward Pointe Faaupo.

Passe de Teruaupu and Passe Tupapaurau both lead into a lagoon which borders the villages of Maatea and Afareaitu. Though rollers invade both entrances, Passe Tupapaurau is preferred since the turbulence is less pronounced. Anchorage can be taken near <u>Afareaitu</u>, the largest village in Moorea.

Three miles northeast of Passe Tupapaurau is **Passe Vaiere**, which can be rough but is usable for cruising vessels and anchorage is available. Several high-speed ferries and a cargoship use this pass when making frequent scheduled runs from Papeete to a wharf and port at the head of the bay. A new marina south of the ferry dock has room for about 20 yachts.

ILES DE LA SOCIETE
ILE MOOREA

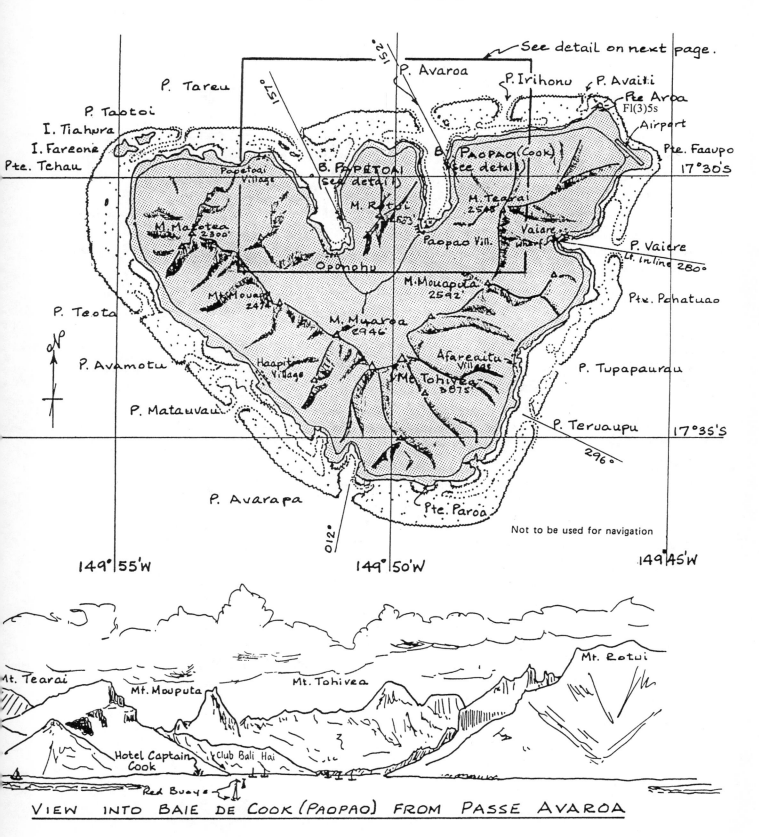

Approx. Scale n.m.

See detail on next page.

P. Avaroa
P. Irihonu   P. Avaiti
P. Tareu   Pte Aroa
                                              Fl(3)5s
P. Taotoi   Airport
I. Tiahura
I. Fareone   B. Paopao (Cook)
Pte. Tehau   B. Papetoai   (see detail)   Pte. Faaupo
                    Papetoai   (see detail)   17°30'S
                    Village
                              M. Rotoi   M. Tearai
                                                 2545
                    M. Mouatea   Vaiare
                    2300   Paopao Vill.   wharf
                                                          P. Vaiere
                         Oponohu   Mt. inline 2800°
                                    M. Mouaputa
P. Teota   2542
                    M. Moua   Pte. Pohatuao
                    2471   M. Muaroa
                           2946
P. Avamotu   P. Tupapaurau
              Haapiti   Afareaitu
              Village   Village
P. Matauvau   Mt. Tohivea
                             2875
                                         P. Teruaupu   17°35'S
                                              296°

P. Avarapa
                    Pte. Paroa
                                   Not to be used for navigation
              012°

149°55'W   149°50'W   149°45'W

VIEW INTO BAIE DE COOK (PAOPAO) FROM PASSE AVAROA

Mt. Tearai   Mt. Mouputa   Mt. Tohivea   Mt. Rotui

              Hotel Captain   Club Bali Hai
              Cook
                    Red Buoys

ILE MOOREA (Baie de Cook /Baie de Paopao and Baie d' Opunohu/Baie Papetoai)

Even more than Tahiti, these two bays have probably come to represent the sailor's idea of Polynesia because they have been photographed so often. The spectacular view of the peaks behind them is one of the reasons that Moorea is known as one of the most scenic islands in the world.

Baie de Cook is entered through the wide, well marked pass of **Passe Avaroa**. It is easy to negotiate as the wind and sea have little effect in the partial lee of the island's mountains. Once through the reef, the water's colors indicate the deep portions leading to anchorages on either side of the entrance behind the reef or to passage further into the bay.

On the east side of the entrance to the bay is the prominent Hotel Captain Cook dock. The most popular anchorages are off Club Bali Hai hotel which is midway along the eastern side, or at the head of the bay before the village and clear of the shallows. Numerous grocery stores, restaurants, a pharmacy, dive operators, and bike/scooter/car rental firms are located around the bay. Water is available south of Club Bali Hai Hotel at the concrete wharf of the fishing cooperative. The spire of Mont Mouaputa is at the end of the bay; a hole through it near the top resembles a patch of snow and can be seen from the north and northwest. Another hole-pierced mountain is on the eastern side of the bay.

Baie d'Opunohu is entered using **Passe Tareu** which is 2.5 miles west of Passe Avaroa. It is well marked, wide and clear but because it is slanted to the line of the reef it requires more caution to negotiate. A wreck, which resembles a pile of rocks, lies on the western side of the pass. The vessel should proceed well into the bay and clear extensions of the reef before turning to anchor. Pretty anchorages are on each side of the pass behind the reef. The anchorage on the east side is off a sandy beach below the bulk of Mont Rotui (the mountain between the bays. On the western side a channel leads to the village of Papetoai where anchorage may be taken in front of the octagonal church. A short distance beyond is a small boat basin used by local boats; its depth may not be adequate for large yachts. Water is available in the basin and grocery stores, small restaurants, and a post office are nearby.

Other anchorages are further up the bay, the first being the little cove at Orufara on the western side, where an anchor can be laid in the bay and stern line tied to the palms. Another popular spot is Robinson's Cove which is on the eastern side, a short distance past the white board structures that give a leading line through the pass. This famous anchorage is slightly more open; an old house in a lovely garden is on the point to the south which helps to form the cove. Anchorage may also be taken at the head of the bay, closer to the village, since a limited number of vessels can use the smaller coves.

The view behind the bay includes the massive bulk of Mont Tohieva and the spire of Mont Mouaroa, famous not only from sailing stories but also as the backdrop in the film version of *South Pacific*. There is an excellent view of both Opunohu and Cook Bays from "Belvedere," a lookout above Opunohu experimental farms. Two miles up the Opunohu valley is a collection of marae (temples) and other archeological sites.

The skyline of Moorea as seen from Papeete   *Charles Wood*

Welcoming the Bounty to Baie de Matavai, Tahiti with Moorea in the distance   *Charles Wood*

Baies de Cook and de Opumohu indent Moorea's coast   *Charles Wood*

Entering Passe Avaroa, Baie de Cook (Paopao), Moorea   *Charles Wood*

ILES DE LA SOCIETE
ILE MOOREA
Baies de Cook & D'Opunohu

0   1000'   ½   1   2
Approx. Scale n.m.

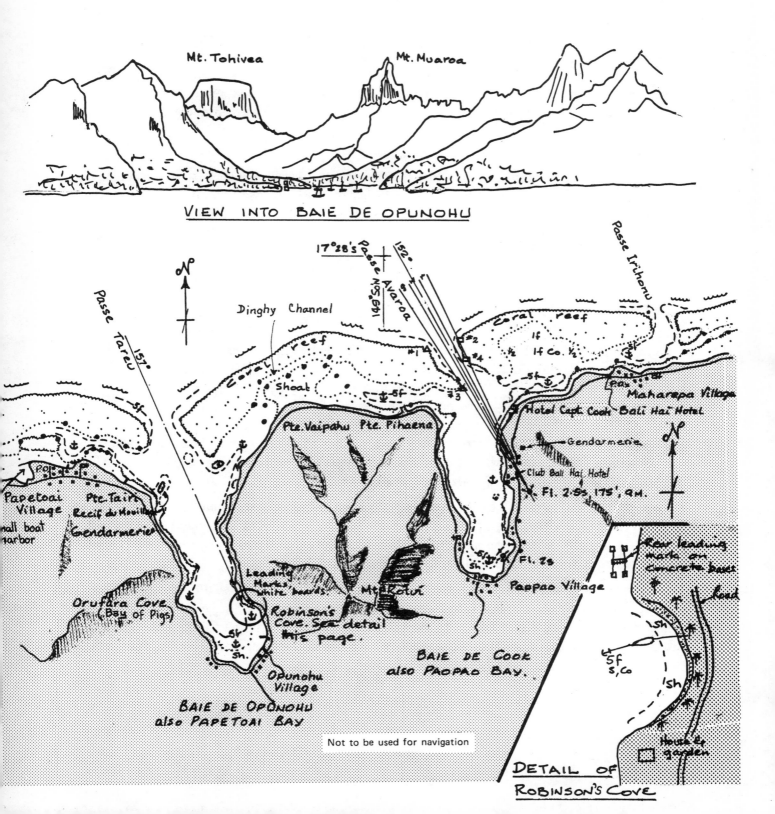

Mt. Tohivea   Mt. Muaroa

VIEW INTO BAIE DE OPUNOHU

Not to be used for navigation

DETAIL OF ROBINSON'S COVE

SMALLER ISLANDS of the ILES DU VENT

This group consists of the islands of Mehetia, Tetiaroa, and Maiao (Tubuai Manu). They are described for information only as they are not recommended for visits by yachts since they have neither entry to lagoons nor anchorages.

ILE MEHETIA

This high little island is 60 miles east of Tahiti, and is the easternmost of the Society Island Group. It is 180 miles south of Mataiva, the westernmost island of the Tuamotu. It is formed by a remarkable, peaked cone, Fareura 435m (1,427'), which descends in steep cliffs to the sea on all sides except the south. The island is usually uninhabited and going ashore is very difficult. It is a good sighting landmark to use when approaching Tahiti from the east.

ILE MAIAO (also known as TUBUAI MANU)

This is the westernmost island of the group and lies 40 miles west of Moorea. The fringing reef closely surrounds two interlocked islands that enclose shallow lagoons. At the center are two hills, the higher one reaching 134m (440'). The hills are visible from seaward before the island itself is clearly defined. A small cut in the reef in the southern end is sometimes used by local vessels for landing; an indifferent, deep, exposed anchorage is just offshore. Landing is hazardous on this inhabited island.

ILE TETIAROA

This is the only atoll of the Iles du Vent, and is composed of twelve islets enclosing a protected lagoon. It lies about 30 miles north of Tahiti, and should he kept in mind by navigators when laying a course to a destination point north of Pointe Venus on Tahiti. The southern tip of the island is marked by a light. Superb snorkeling and diving can be enjoyed in the 30m (100') depths of the lagoon. It is a very beautiful atoll having brilliant white beaches and is a nesting site for thousands of sea birds which congregate on Birds Island in the southern part of the lagoon. There is no entrance into the lagoon for other than very small boats; the wharf-like structure on the reef at the southwest corner is used by trading vessels. For permission to visit the atoll contact Hotel Tetiaroa, P.O. Box 2418, Papeete, Tahiti, Tel. (689) 42.63.02 or 42.63.03.

The island is owned by Marlon Brando who purchased it when he played Fletcher Christian in the 1966 version of "*Mutiny on the Bounty.*" In 1973 the island was opened to tourists who are flown in to the airstrip on Motu Onetahi; hotel development has been kept low key. Twice daily flights link the island to Papeete.

Historically, the island was a resort for Tahitian Chiefs and the Pomare royal family. Long ago the motu of Rimatuu where they resided was planted with royal 'tuu' trees. The female members of important families were sent there to 'fatten' and get fashionable lighter skin before their marriages. In 1904 the royal family gave the atoll a Canadian dentist who eventually put it on the market.

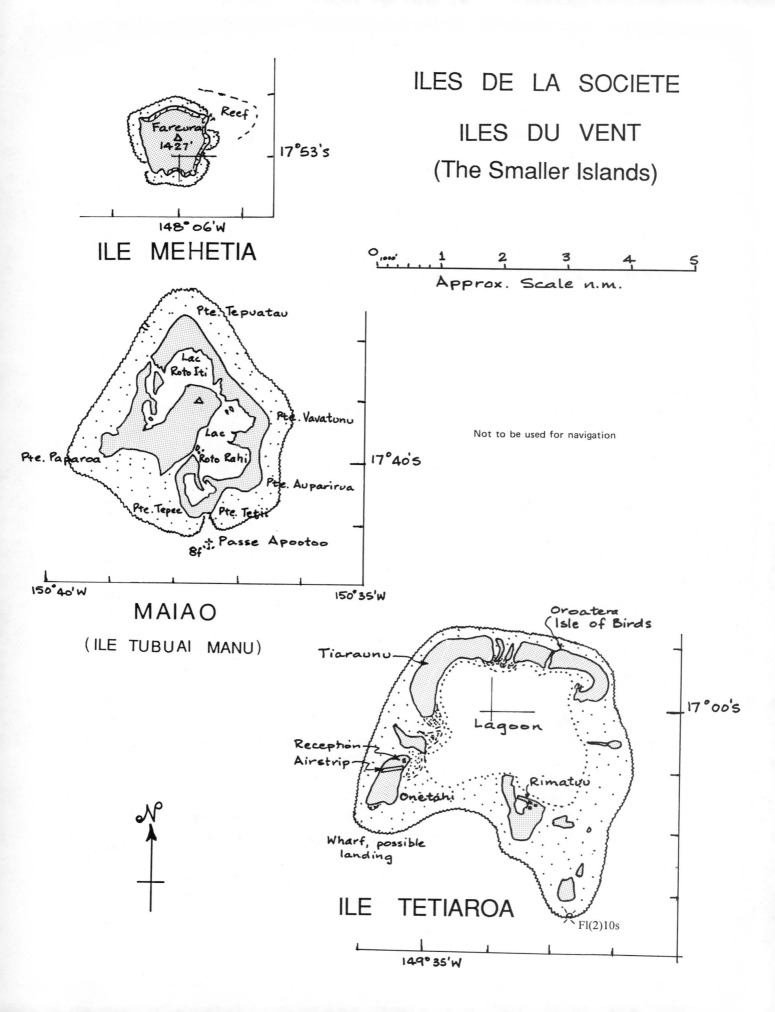

ILES DE LA SOCIETE

ILES DU VENT

(The Smaller Islands)

ILE MEHETIA

Reef

Fareurai
△
1427'

17°53's

148°06'W

0 1000' 1 2 3 4 5
Approx. Scale n.m.

Not to be used for navigation

MAIAO

(ILE TUBUAI MANU)

Pte. Tepuatau

Lac
Roto Iti

△

Pte. Vavatunu

Lac
Roto Rahi

Pte. Paparoa

17°40's

Pte. Auparirua

Pte. Tepee

Pte. Tetii

Passe Apootoo
8f

150°40'W

150°35'W

N

ILE TETIAROA

Oroatera
(Isle of Birds

Tiaraunu

Lagoon

17°00's

Reception
Airstrip

Rimatuu

Onetahi

Wharf, possible
landing

Fl(2)10s

149°35'W

ILE HUAHINE

Huahine is the closest of the leeward island group to Tahiti, lying 90 miles to the northwest. This group forms an ideal cruising area, combining both the rural quality of Huahine and Raiatea with the spectacular beauty of Bora-Bora. The passage from Tahiti should be arranged so the approach to Huahine is made in daylight. The safest method is to plan for landfall after sunrise by leaving Moorea just before dusk, keeping the boat speed down to about 5 knots, expecting the current to give a boost as the island is approached.

The land mass of Huahine is made up of two mountainous islands, Huahine Nui and Huahine Iti, connected by a narrow isthmus and bridge. The islands are enclosed by a common barrier reef that is close to the northern coast but extends as much as a mile offshore elsewhere. There are five passes through the reef, the four most useful to yachts are described below.

Passe Avamoa, on the northwest side, is the major pass to Huahine, easy to negotiate, and gives entry to the village of Fare. Its apparent width of 365m (1,200') is reduced to 120m (400') by shoals on each side. Buoys mark the deep water of the pass and ranges with lights give a line through the entrance. Port de Fare lies along the southeastern shore. A pier at the waterfront is used by trading vessels; yachts anchor southeast of it or off the Bali Hai Hotel, which is on the seaward side of the pier. This is not an all weather anchorage, and every year the combination of gusty winds and reversing tidal currents causes boats to drag ashore onto coral heads. It is necessary to check in with the gendarme, whose office is visible from the main wharf. Water is available from faucets southeast of the main commercial wharf. Check the clarity of the water before filling your tanks; following heavy rain it will be turbid from sediment.

Passe Avapeihi is 1 mile south of Passe Avamoa. Though slightly narrower than Passe Avamoa it is almost as easy to use. Range lights visible for 4 miles, bearing 094°, and green buoys, mark both the pass and a passage between the two passes behind the reef. Anchorage can be taken near the end of Baie Haavai though it is deep and narrow. Several good, but deep anchorage spots are also found in the basin of Port du Bourayne which is reached using the clear passage behind the barrier reef south of the passes. Use only the northern channel past Motu Vaiorea when entering; the southern entrance is wider but it is shallow. The sides of the channel are shown with red markers. The dinghy can be taken through well marked Passage Honoava.

Passe Farerea is deep and straight though the curve of the reef from Motu Topati toward the coast reduces the pass to a width of 91m (300'). It should be used only in good weather as strong trade winds can make the pass very difficult to negotiate. A bearing of 262°24" taken on the range on the north side of the entrance to Baie de Maroe leads through the pass. The passage is marked by beacons and the vessel should favor the northern side. The best anchorage is off the village of Maroe where landing can be done at the pier. Squalls can blow off the steep mountains around the bay. Use French Chart 6434 if anchoring other than at Fare or Haavai.

Passe Tiare is about 1.5 miles north of Passe Farerea. It is deep, narrow and should only be used in calm weather after being checked by dinghy. A small boat harbor dredged to a least depth of 1.8m (6') is in the bay's northeast corner; good anchorages are in the lee of Motu Vavaratea.

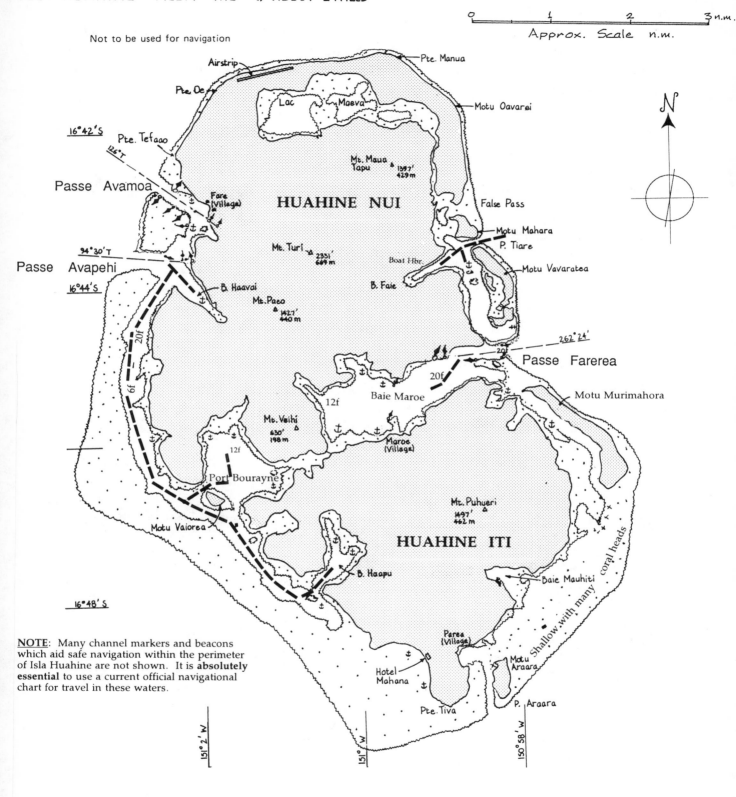

ILE HUAHINE FROM THE W, ABOUT 6 MILES

Mt. Tabu   Mt. Turi   Mt. Paeo   Fare   P. Avamoa

ILES DE LA SOCIETE
ILE HUAHINE

0   1   2   3 n.m.

Approx. Scale n.m.

Not to be used for navigation

N

Airstrip
Pte. Manua
Pte. Oe
Lac   Maeva
Motu Oavarei

16°42'S
Pte. Tefaao
126°T

Mt. Maua Tapu   1397' 429 m

Passe Avamoa

Fare (Village)
HUAHINE NUI

False Pass

Motu Mahara
P. Tiare

94°30'T

Mt. Turi   2351' 669 m
Boat Hbr.
Motu Vavaratea

Passe Avapehi
16°44'S

B. Haavai
B. Faie

Mt. Paeo   1427' 440 m

20f

262°24'
Passe Farerea
20f

6f

Baie Maroe
20f
Motu Murimahora

12f

Mt. Vaihi   650' 198 m

12f
Maroe (Village)

Mt. Puhueri   1497' 462 m

Port Bourayne
HUAHINE ITI

Motu Vaiorea

Baie Mauhiti

B. Haapu

Shallow with many coral heads

16°48'S

NOTE: Many channel markers and beacons which aid safe navigation within the perimeter of Isla Huahine are not shown. It is **absolutely essential** to use a current official navigational chart for travel in these waters.

Parea (Village)

Motu Araara

Hotel Mahana

151°2'W

151°W

Pte. Tiva

P. Araara

150°58'W

APPROACHING HUAHINE FROM TAHITI, i.e. FROM S.E.

ILE RAIATEA AND ILE TAHAA

Raiatea and Tahaa lie within the same coral reef, about 20 miles west of Ile Huahine. Both are mountainous with spurs radiating from central ranges to the coast forming an indented shoreline. Many maraes in Raiatea attest to the long period when it was the cultural and religious center of the Societies.

The surrounding barrier reef is awash in some places and submerged in others. Eight passes lead through the reef around Raiatea and two into Tahaa. Deep and navigable water between the reef and the islands makes it possible to travel entirely around Tahaa and about two-thirds of the way around Raiatea. Shoals and coral heads are scattered in the inner waters but the routes between them pose no difficulty if traveled in sunlight with a person aloft.

Passe Teavapiti is the normal entry for vessels from Huahine or Tahiti and can be used during all weather conditions. Approach it by heading toward the square-topped bulk of Mont Tapioi 305m (998') at the north end of Raiatea. As the pass is closed, align the leading lights and marks ashore on a bearing of 269° or if not visible, the depression between a pair of skyline peaks south of Mont Tapioi can be used. The opening in the reef has two channels separated by Ile Taoru. The southern channel is **Passe Teavarua**, the northern is Passe Teavapiti with a width of 185m (600'). On each side of the opening the reef is partly submerged, but its extent is clearly indicated by islets and surf. The north side of the pass should be favored (where the reef is steep-to) as any current in the pass is usually southerly.

Beacons mark the channel leading from Passe Teavapiti to Uturoa. The town is spread along the coast but the center is near Pointe du Roi Tomatoa. A concrete wharf used by freighters and ferries extends along the shore southeast of the point. A fuel dock suitable for stern-to mooring is next to the main Uturoa wharf and an excellent supermarket is next door. A municipal marina with a capacity of 50 boats is .25 miles north of the fuel dock and sometimes has room for cruisers. Good anchorage can be taken in the channel northeast or southeast of the wharf in 27-32m (15 to 18 fathoms), sand and mud. A pier at the northern end of the main wharf can be used as a dinghy dock. Two blocks from the wharf is a market with many shops and the famous "Cafe au Motu."

Passe Teavarua is the southern channel of Passe Teavapiti and it is used if the vessel's course turns southward behind the reef. The channel is marked by beacons but care is needed for it has many coral heads to avoid. The open bays along the coast at Vairahi, Averaiti and Averarahi provide safe anchorages. They are open to the trade winds but protected from the sea by the reef.

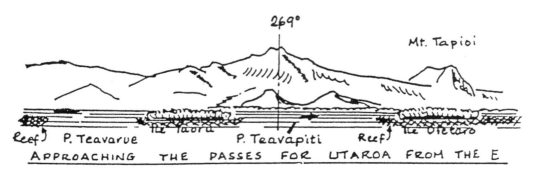

APPROACHING THE PASSES FOR UTAROA FROM THE E

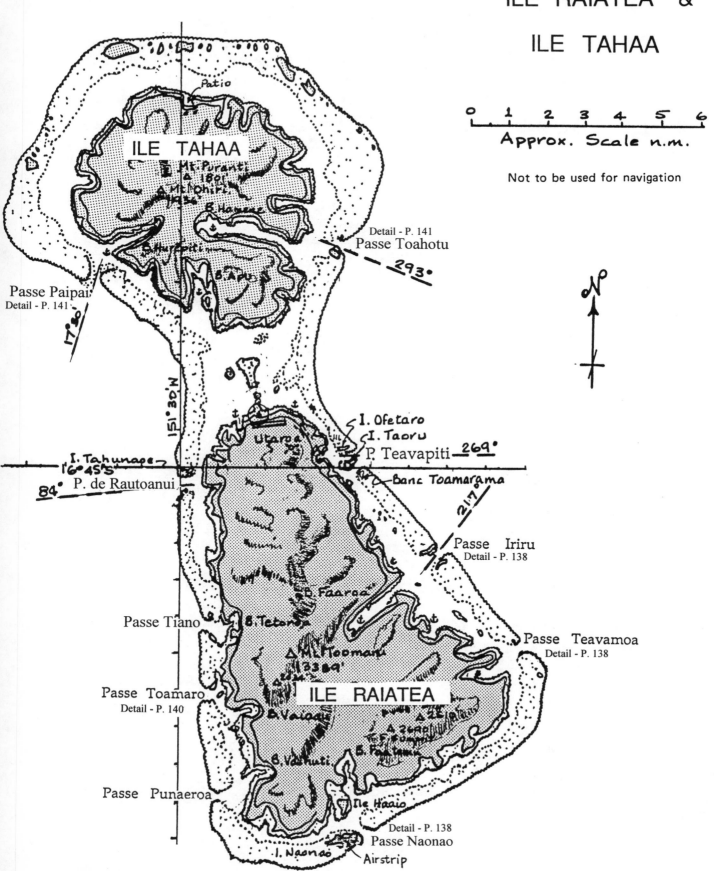

ILES DE LA SOCIETE
ILE RAIATEA &
ILE TAHAA

0 1 2 3 4 5 6
Approx. Scale n.m.

Not to be used for navigation

N

Patio

ILE TAHAA

Mt Puranti
1801
Mt Ohiri
1936

B. Hanene

S. Hurepiti

B. Apu

Detail - P. 141
Passe Toahotu
293°

Passe Paipai
Detail - P. 141
17°30

151° 30' N

Utaroa

I. Ofetaro
I. Taoru
P. Teavapiti 269°

I. Tahunape
16° 45' S
84° P. de Rautoanui

Banc Toamarama

217°

Passe Iriru
Detail - P. 138

B. Faaroa

Passe Tiano

B. Tetora

Passe Teavamoa
Detail - P. 138

Mt Tooman
1338'

ILE RAIATEA

Passe Toamaro
Detail - P. 140

B. Vaioaa

B. Faatemu

B. Vaihuti

Passe Punaeroa

Ile Haaio

Detail - P. 138
Passe Naonao

I. Naonao
Airstrip

Passe Iriru (Maire) is about 3 miles southeast of Passe Teavapiti and is clearly identifiable by the two islets on the coral reef bordering each side of the pass which is 150m(500') wide. An entry on a bearing of 217° taken on the sharp peak of Mont Maufenua (which lies to the south of Baie Faaroa) leads through the reef near the southern side where the sea is quieter. Good anchorage is available near the head of Baie Faaroa in 14 - 21m (8 to 12 fathoms), mud. An interesting dinghy trip is up the Aoppomau River at the head of the bay. The passage behind the reef between Passe Iriru and Passe Teavamoa can be traversed but careful conning is needed to avoid many shoals and coral heads.

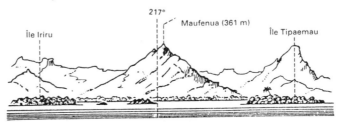

Raiatea. Passe Iriru.
Pacific Islands Pilot. Volume III - U.K.

Passe Teavamoa is deep, narrow, fairly short, and can be easily entered. Care is needed on entry to avoid the coastal reef that projects at the outer ends of the bay, especially from the south. The pass leads to a very nice anchorage in Baie Hotopuu, about midway up the bay in 15 fathoms, mud. A short walk to the northwest leads to Marae Taputaputea, the most important religious and historical site in Polynesia.

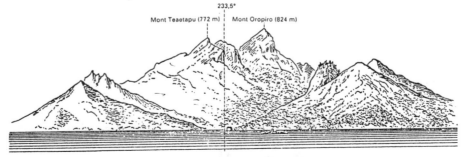

Raiatea. Passe Teavamoa.
Pacific Islands Pilot. Volume III - U.K.

Passe Naonao is about 91m (300') wide and a bar at the narrows causes the sea to break if a southerly swell is running, so it is not recommended in unsettled weather. There are attractive but deep anchorages in the lee of Iles Naonao and Haaio. A small store is in the village of Tautara.

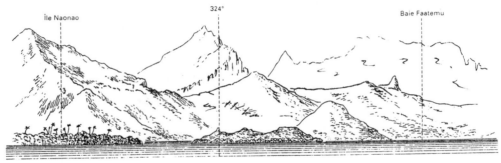

Raiatea. Passe Naonao.
Pacific Islands Pilot. Volume III - U.K.

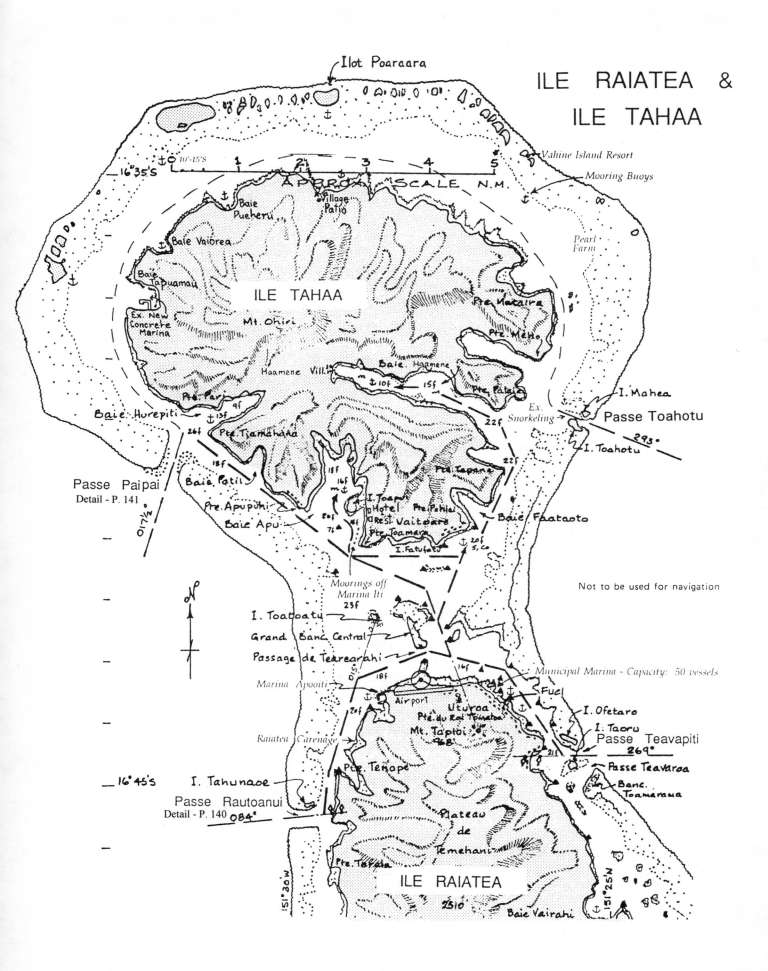

ILE RAIATEA &
ILE TAHAA

Ilot Poaraara

Vahine Island Resort

Mooring Buoys

16°35'S   10'-15'S   1   2   3   4   5

APPROX SCALE N.M.

Baie
Pueheru

Village
Patio

Pearl
Farm

Baie Vaiorea

Baie
Tapuamau

ILE TAHAA

Pte. Mataira

Ex. New
Concrete
Marina

Mt. Ohiri

Pte. Meho

Haamene Vill.

Baie Haamene

15f

Pte Par

9f

10f

Pte. Patai

Ex.
Snorkeling

I. Mahea

Passe Toahotu

Baie Horepiti

13f

Pte. Tiamahana

22f

I. Toahotu

295°

Passe Paipai
Detail - P. 141

26f

18f

18f

22f

017½

Baie Patil

16f

Pte Tapane

Pte. Apupuhi

20f

I. Toar
Hotel
Rest. Vaitoare
Pte. Toamaro

Pte. Patie

Baie Faataoto

Baie Apu

8f

7f

I. Fatufatu

20f
S, co

Not to be used for navigation

Moorings off
Marina Iti
23f

N

I. Toatoatu

Grand Banc Central

16f

Municipal Marina - Capacity: 50 vessels

Passage de Tearearahi

Marina Apooiti

18f

Fuel

20f

Airport

I. Ofetaro

Uturoa
Pte. du Roi Tamatoa
Mt. Taptoi
968'

I. Taoru
Passe Teavapiti
269°

Raiatea Carenage

21f

Passe Teavaroa

Pte. Tenape

Banc.
Toamarama

16°45'S   I. Tahunaoe

Passe Rautoanui
Detail - P. 140 084°

Plateau
de
Temehani

151°20'W

151°25'W

ILE RAIATEA

Pte. Tetooa

2510

Baie Vairahi

Passes Punaeroa, Toamaro, and Tiano are along the lower western side of the island. The first two can be used in good weather, but they lead to separate lagoon pockets not joined to the lagoon around Raiatea. In good weather with the sun overhead it is possible to sail inside the reef from Ile Naonao, around the southern end of Raiatea and exit at Passe Punaeroa or Passe Taomaro. Passe Tiano is not recommended.

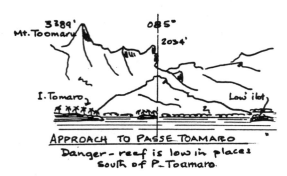

APPROACH TO PASSE TOAMARO
Danger - reef is low in places
South of P. Toamaro.

Passe Rautoanui is the main pass on the western side and is an all-weather entrance for the port of Uturoa. It is over 305m (1,000') wide and is easy to navigate with leading lights and marks. An equally wide passage to the north, marked by beacons, makes connections to Uturoa or Tahaa. Near the western end of the airport is Marina Apooiti where temporary moorage, fuel, water and ice are available. This is one of the best "hurricane holes" in the area. Anchorage outside the basin is also possible. Just to the south is Raiatea Carenage, a first-rate shipyard equipped with two travelifts and a marine railray. Services include long-term dry storage, painting, engine, sail, and equipment repairs.

Pointe Motutapu is the northernmost part of Raiatea and the coastal reef extends northward from it for about 610m (2,000'). The gap between this reef and Grand Banc Central (a large reef between Raiatea and Tahaa) is about 305m (1,000') wide. Marked on both sides by beacons, Passage de Tearearahi is deep and provides the shortest route across the lagoon as well as access to Tahaa's anchorages and passes via channels on both east and west sides of the Banc. **Passe Tohahotu**, on the eastern reef can he used in good weather to access Tahaa.

On the north coast of Tahaa is the main village of Patio where the bank, Gendarmerie, post office and largest shops on the island are located. An excellent anchorage is located 1.25 miles north of Patio (south of Ilot Poaraara) in 12m (6.5 fathoms), sand. On the southeastern coast near Baie Faataoto is the village of Vaitoare where anchorage may be taken or further to the north in Baie Haamene, near its head in 14 - 18m (8 to 10 fathoms). Another spot is at Baie Apu, on the SW coast behind Ile Toapui. A safe hurricane moorage is a marina in Baie Aapuamau on the NW coast where water, fuel and fresh bread are available.

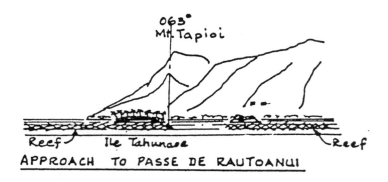

APPROACH TO PASSE DE RAUTOANUI

Breakers north of Passe Rautoanui clearly outline the barrier reef surrounding Iles Tahaa and Raiatea

Overlooking the Grand Banc Central with Tahaa beyond as seen from Raiatea   Margo Wood

The summit of Bora-Bora is hidden in the clouds as we approach from Raiatea   Margo Wood

The view across Bora-Bora's latgoon from the north with a motu in the middle distance   Charles Wood

Passe Paipai is located on the southwestern side of Tahaa and gives access to Hurepiti Bay, Apu Bay and Tahaa village. It is about 275m (300 yards) wide and about .5miles long. The entrance is marked with beacons and is deep and free of dangers except for a shoal extending about 185m (200 yds.) from the SE tip of the NW edge of the encircling reef. The shoal is marked by a heavy swell. Do not use this entrance in southerly weather when a very heavy swell sweeps the pass, making it dangerous. Currents in the pass are reported to be strong.

Good holding anchorage can be found about half-way into Hurepiti Bay just beyond the reef extending from a small projection on the north shore. The entire north shore of Hurepiti Bay is lined with coral reaching almost half-way across the bay beyond the anchorage. Three moorings of "Vanilla Tours" are nearby, for information call Alain on VHF 9. Excellent anchorage is also available about .2 miles north of the southernmost tip (Pte. Toamaru) of Baie Apu. Marina Iti has four moorings along the shore.

A cruise around Tahaa can be easily done for reef projections are marked with beacons. On the north coast is the main village of Patio where there is a bank, post office, shops and a Gendarmerie. Good anchorage can be taken east of the village or 1.25 miles north of Patio, south of Ilot Poaraara in 7 fathoms, sand.

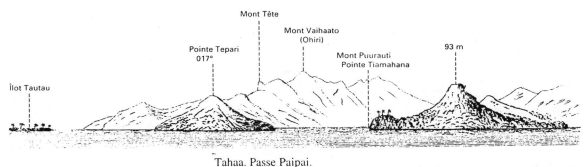

Tahaa. Passe Paipai.

Instructions Nautiques, Vol. K9.1 - FR.

Passe Toahotu is easily recognized by two islets, Mahea and Toahotu, marking the northern and southern tips of the reef. It is about 275m (300 yards) wide and is free of dangers. When entering the pass bring Mont Purauti on a range of 293° with the hill on Pointe Patai.

Good anchorage can be found toward the northwestern end of Baie Haamene. Take care to avoid coral banks lining the bay; some extend well into the bay and are marked by beacons.

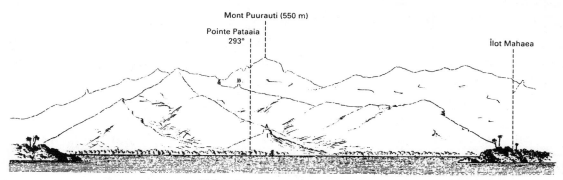

Tahaa. Passe Tohahotu.

Instructions Nautiques, Vol. K9.1 - FR.

ILE BORA-BORA

The spectacular volcanic peaks surrounded by an extensive lagoon of varied hues of blue make this one of the world's most beautiful islands.

Passe Teavanui is the only entrance into the lagoon. Located on the western side, it is wide, clearly marked and easily traversed. A leading line of 104° taken on shore markers leads through the pass. The front marker is a conspicuous red column with a white top 10m (33') high and the rear marker, not easily seen amidst the trees high on the hillside, is about 27m (90') high. Lighted buoys mark the channel and the edge of the reef can be seen on either side. The current is almost always ebbing.

Directly behind the pass is the Bora-Bora Yacht Club where anchorage may be taken. Yachts whose crews patronize the restaurant may tie to the mooring buoys, shower and take on water at no charge. This is the only source of water on the island where there is always a water shortage.

The town of Vaitape is in the next bay to the south where another favorite anchorage is located in 27m (15 fathoms), sand. It is possible to temporarily tie to the south side of the large commercial wharf when taking on fuel or supplies. The gendarmerie is located at the head of the wharf, and banks, a grocery store, post office and hospital are located nearby. The concrete wharves where inter-island freighters land cargo is around the point of land to the north. Directly across from the wharf in **Baie de Faanui** is an excellent, but small, hurricane harbor.

Vessels having a draft of less than 2.1m (8') draft can follow a well marked channel which takes you around the northern end of the island and down the east coast as far as Club Med. Use **French Chart #6002** to follow the marked route which threads through coral patches and passes through an area where coral was blasted to make a channel   When circling an island within a lagoon the red cylindrical markers are on the island side of the channel and green cones are on the sea side of the channel. In settled weather anchorage within the lagoon may be taken in 2 - 3 fathoms in areas free of coral found off the motus to the east.

Other anchorages have some limitations. On the southern point of Baie de Povai is the luxurious Bora-Bora Hotel off which is an exposed anchorage. A first-rate spot for snorkeling is between the hotel and Topua-Iti. Patrons of the bar may use their dinghy dock. Further south, around Pointe Matira the barrier reef is attached to a point of land and forms a secluded little bay where anchorage may be taken in 5 fathoms, sand. Entry to this spot is through a narrow corridor in the coral heads that must be negotiated only in the best visibility, thus requiring an overnight stay. It is best to locate the channel by dinghy prior to entering.

Shallow draft vessels can find a way around the south end of Ile Toopua and Toopua-lti to find anchorage on their western sides. Idyllic anchorages in 9 to 13m (5 to 7 fathoms) are just within the reef on either side of the pass. Between Motu Tapu and two semi-exposed coral areas to the east is a gap showing deep, blue water leading to a fair expanse of sandy bottom which is encircled by coral where temporary, day anchorage can be taken near excellent snorkeling. A similar spot lies between the southern end of Ile Teveiroa and Motu Ahuna on the north side of the pass which is shallower and less constricted by coral.

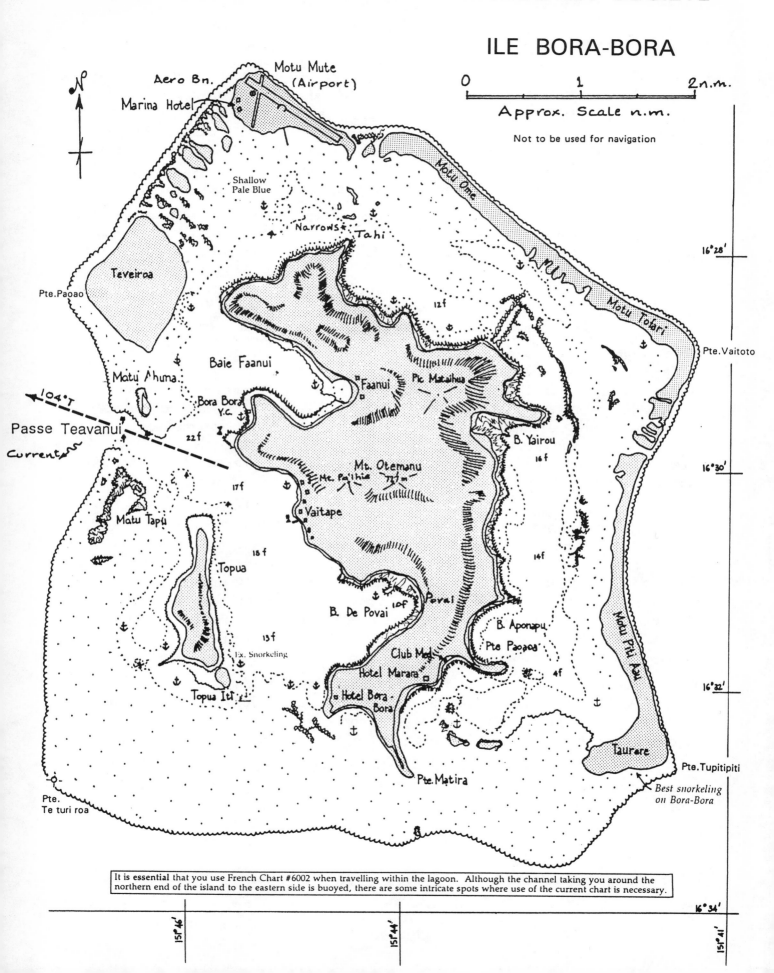

ILES DE LA SOCIETE

ILE BORA-BORA

0   1   2 n.m.

Approx. Scale n.m.

Not to be used for navigation

N

Aero Bn.

Marina Hotel

Motu Mute
(Airport)

Shallow
Pale Blue

Narrows — Tahi

Motu One

Motu Tofari

16°28'

Teveiroa

12 f

Pte. Paoao

Pte. Vaitoto

Baie Faanui

Motu Ahuna

Faanui

Pic Mataihua

B. Yairou

Bora Bora
Y.C.

104°T

16 f

Passe Teavanui

22 f

Mt. Pahia

Mt. Otemanu
727 m

16°30'

Currents

17 f

Motu Tapu

Vaitape

Topua

13 f

14 f

Ex. Snorkeling

15 f

B. De Povai

Povai

B. Aponapu

Pte. Paoaoa

Topua Iti

Club Med

Hotel Marara

4 f

16°32'

Hotel Bora
Bora

Motu Piti Aau

Taurere

Pte.
Te turi roa

Pte. Matira

Pte. Tupitipiti

Best snorkeling
on Bora-Bora

It is **essential** that you use French Chart #6002 when travelling within the lagoon. Although the channel taking you around the northern end of the island to the eastern side is buoyed, there are some intricate spots where use of the current chart is necessary.

16°34'

151°46'   151°44'   151°41'

ILE MAUPITI

This isolated, lofty island is the westernmost of the Society Group, and it lies 27 miles northwest of Bora-Bora. It is a remnant of a volcanic peak that now has steep, vertical cliffs in a semicircle on the southwestern side. The highest point, at 381m (1,250'), is near the center of the island. A barrier reef completely encircles the island, the northern side having one short and two long motus. At the southernmost point is Passe Onoiau, located between two small islets, Pitiahe (Motu-Iti-Ahe) and Tiapaa (Motu-Te-Apaa). The population is about 1,200.

Passe Onoiau has a poor reputation because in rough conditions it is hazardous to enter and numerous vessels have come to grief here. Not only is it winding and narrow but a strong outgoing current also adds to the difficulties in negotiating the channel. With a southerly swell large amounts of water come over the low and poorly defined reef on the southwest side. This water flows out of the pass constantly, reaching speeds of 9 knots. This results in heavy breakers across the entrance; some vessels have been trapped within the lagoon for up to two weeks. Breakers on the southern reef of Bora-Bora are a good indication of conditions at Maupiti.

High slack water always occurs at noon in the Societies, so departure from Bora-Bora early in the morning is advised. Passe Onoiau is about 75m (250') wide at the entrance but the navigable channel is greatly reduced by a submerged projection of the reef's eastern edge. The sea usually breaks over this projection which has 3.5m (2 fathoms) of water where it drops off. When approaching the entrance you should line up the passage from a short distance out to sea, through the clear portion of the opening to the two islets where the entrance is marked with white beacons with a red band. The channel to the wharf at the village is marked with beacons; depths vary from 1.5 to 5 fathoms.

The village of Vai'ea is on the eastern shore of the island; it has a concrete wharf with a wide, level, coral playing field alongside. Anchorage can be taken in a fairly clear area south of the wharf or obtain permission to tie stern-to the wharf. There are about 3.5m (2 fathoms) alongside, but care is needed as the bottom shoals rapidly on its northern side. Numerous small stores are scattered throughout the town and some produce (mainly watermelons and cantaloupe) are available. Fresh bread is available before 7 a.m. at the blue-roofed bakery south of the wharf The post office is open from 0730 to 1230. The island is linked to Papeete with thrice weekly air service via Raiatea or Bora-Bora and weekly service by the passenger ferry *Meherio II* from Raiatea.

East of the village is a wide, whitish expanse of very shallow water beyond which is the curve of Motu Tuanai (Tuanae) where the airstrip connecting Maupiti to the rest of the Societies is located. A hike to the Haranae Valley in the northeastern part of the island leads to some interesting petroglyphs of turtles. The western side of the island has the remains of a marae.

The beauty of the island is twofold: the water's lovely shades of blue and the shoal's pale colors create a delightful contrast to the green palms, and the warm, friendly people make visitors feel very welcome.

ILES DE LA SOCIETE
ILE MAUPITI

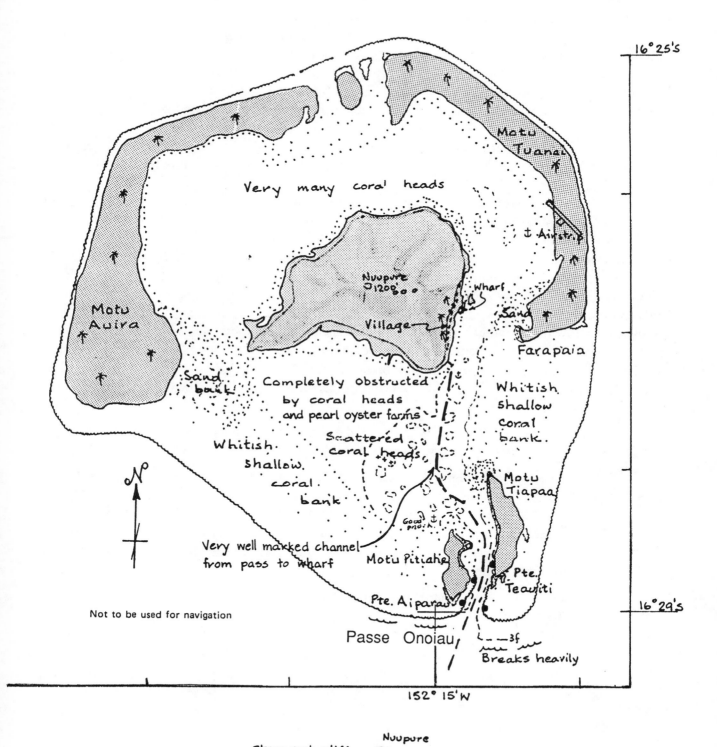

Approx. Scale n.m.

16°25'S

Motu Tuanai

‡ Airstrip

Very many coral heads

Nuupure ◯1200

Wharf

Village

Sand

Farapaia

Motu Auira

Sand bank

Completely obstructed
by coral heads
and pearl oyster farms

Whitish
Shallow
Coral
bank.

Scattered
coral heads

Whitish.
Shallow.
coral.
bank

Motu
Tiapaa

Good pnol‡

Very well marked channel
from pass to wharf

Motu Pitiahe

Pte.
Teauiti

Pte. Aiparau

Not to be used for navigation

16°29'S

Passe Onoiau

──3f

Breaks heavily

152° 15'W

Nuupure

Steep rock cliffs

Village

Entrance motus

Motu Tuanai
palms

Approaching Maupiti from W, distant about 5 miles

ILE MAUPIHAA (Mopelia)

This island lies 100 miles west of Ile Maupiti. Since it is an atoll that cannot be seen until close by, the approach should be timed to occur in daylight. Allowance must be made for the set of the current, and this can be established by using Maupiti as a mark as long as it is visible combined with GPS data. The atoll is roughly circular in shape, about 8 km (5 miles) across.

In 1998 Cyclone Martin swept over the island, destroying 75% of the trees and vegetation and completely destroyed all but one of the houses. Near the northern end of Motu Maupihaa all that remains is a concrete cistern where previously there were several houses. Three damaged houses and a cistern are visible a mile to the south and only one house and a cistern are left where there was once a village near the southern end of the motu. All navigational aids were destroyed and have not been replaced as of September, 1999. The inhabitants left the island and have not returned.

On the northwestern side of the atoll is the only pass which leads into the extensive, deep lagoon. A break in the coral shelf and agitated water indicates the location of the pass.

Passe Taihaaru Vahine is one of the trickiest passes in French Polynesia because it is very narrow and the constantly ebbing current can reach 6 knots or more at times, making a reliable engine and a good set of nerves necessary. Whirlpools occur in the vicinity of the coral patches where ebb currents meet inside the entrance. If there is a strong southerly swell or southeast trade wind blowing, water entering the lagoon on the south side will funnel out of the pass creating too much current for most yachts to negotiate safely. On the other hand, a northwesterly wind causes the waves to break across the pass and rips caused by opposing currents make the entrance impassable. During moderate easterly winds the current can decrease to 3 knots.

It is important to time your entry around noon when high tide occurs and the coral is plainly visible. Once the 27m (90') wide pass is in view, a bow look-out should be posted.

Three anchorages are available inside of the lagoon. The course must be set by visual means, with the clarity of the water making identification of coral heads relatively easy. Oyster floats are scattered throughout the lagoon at depths of over 17m (50'). Careful conning with good visibility is needed to find a route to the anchorage at the southeastern corner of the lagoon. Stay parallel to the beach in about 8 to 13m (25' to 40') to avoid oyster floats. During south and southeasterly winds this is the best anchorage.

Thousands of seabirds inhabit the small motus and the lagoon abounds with sharks, turtles and colorful tropical fish.

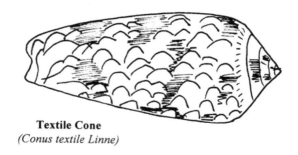

Textile Cone
(Conus textile Linne)

ILES DE LA SOCIETE

ILE MAUPIHAA (MOPELIA)

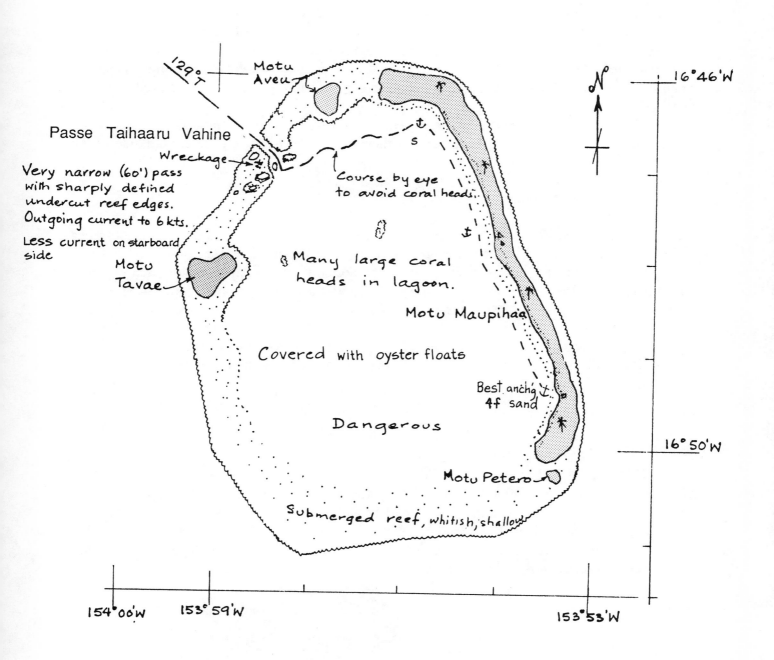

0 1000' ½ 1 2 3
Approx. Scale n.m.

Motu Aveu

129° T

Passe Taihaaru Vahine

Wreckage

Very narrow (60') pass
with sharply defined
undercut reef edges.
Outgoing current to 6 kts.

Less current on starboard
side

Motu
Tavae

N

16°46'W

Course by eye
to avoid coral heads.

Many large coral
heads in lagoon.

Motu Maupihaa

Covered with oyster floats

Best anch'g
4f sand

Dangerous

16°50'W

Motu Petero

Submerged reef, whitish, shallow

154°00'W   153°59'W   153°53'W

Not to be used for navigation

WESTERN ATOLLS of ILES SOUS LE VENT

The three atolls of Ile Tupai, Ile Manuae, and Motu One are described for information only since they are isolated and are not normally visited by cruising vessels because of the difficulty of landing and lack of anchorages and facilities.

ILE TUPAI (Motu Iti)

This is a pretty atoll, covered with palm trees, and is about 8 miles NNW of Bora-Bora. Since the traffic from Bora-Bora heads south or west, the island is seldom visited. Though it is approachable without danger, the fringing reef encloses the two islets of the atoll without an entry into the lagoon. A landing place with a small passage in the northwestern corner is used by small local vessels. About 50 people on the island support themselves with copra production. A small private airfield is on the island.

Chilean crew aboard the warship *Araucano* are said to have mutinied in 1822 and pillaged coastal towns in Peru before burying their treasure in marae on the eastern side of the island.

ILE MAUNAE (Scilly Island or Fenua Ura)

This is the westernmost island of the Iles Sous Le Vent group and it is about 40 miles WNW of Ile Maupihaa. The lagoon is about 6 miles in diameter and is accessible only to small boats by a pass located about .4 miles WSW of the northern point. Another pass used by small local vessels in calm conditions is on the east coast near a village. A reef borders the eastern coast which is composed of wooded motus; coral reefs are on the western and southern sides. The western coast is a dune more than 10 miles long and only about 50cm (20") high which is often inundated by seas washing over the reef. This is a dangerous atoll and should be avoided because it is visible mainly because of the surf on the western and southern sides.

Only about 10 people live on the island who support themselves with the harvest of copra. A visible wreck is located at 16°34.2'S —154° 43.0'W.

MOTU ONE (Bellinghausen Island)

This is the smallest atoll in the Iles Sous-le-Vent and it is about 40 miles WNW of Ile Manuae. It is composed of four wooded islets surrounding a shallow lagoon with depths of less than a fathom. The perimeter of the atoll is marked with rocks. There is no pass giving access to the lagoon though small local boats land on the west and south side of the atoll. Off these landing spots precarious anchorage can be taken in 10 to 20 fathoms. The small village is occasionally inhabited by seasonal workers harvesting copra.

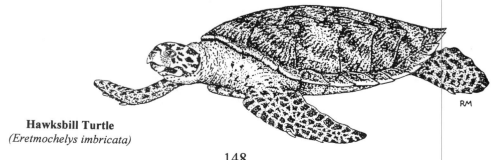

Hawksbill Turtle
(Eretmochelys imbricata)

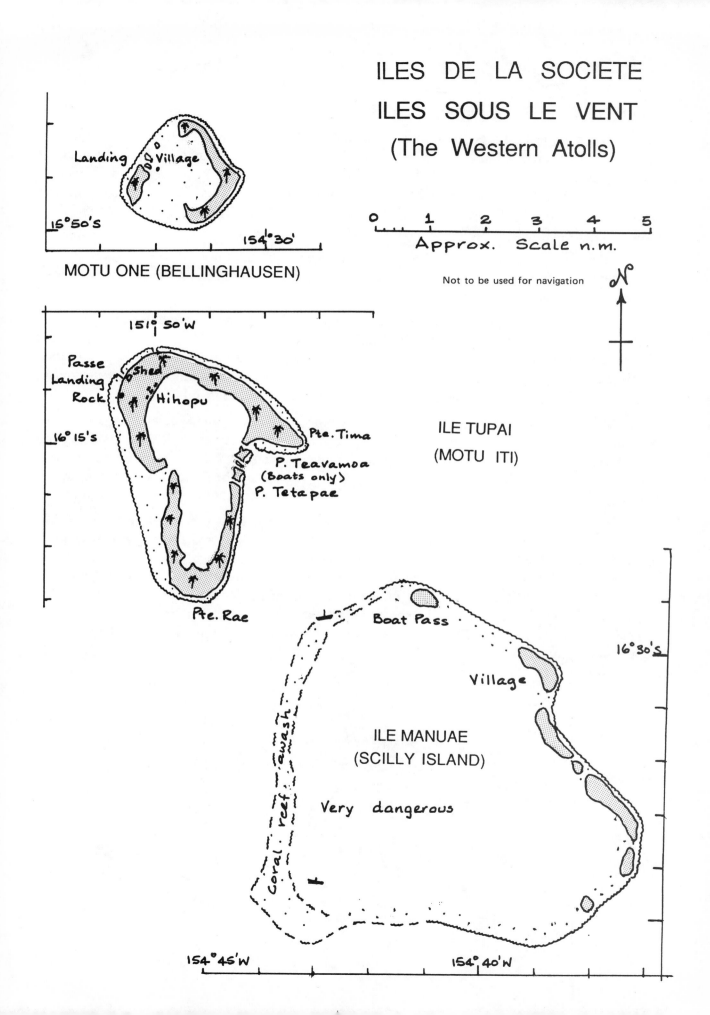

ILES DE LA SOCIETE
ILES SOUS LE VENT
(The Western Atolls)

0   1   2   3   4   5
Approx. Scale n.m.

Not to be used for navigation

N

MOTU ONE (BELLINGHAUSEN)

Landing   Village

15°50'S

154°30'

ILE TUPAI
(MOTU ITI)

151° 50'W

Passe
Landing
Rock

Shed

Hihopu

16° 15'S

Pte. Tima

P. Teavamoa
(Boats only)
P. Tetapae

Pte. Rae

Boat Pass

Village

16°30'S

ILE MANUAE
(SCILLY ISLAND)

Very dangerous

Coral reef awash

154°45'W

154°40'W

ILES AUSTRALES (ARCHIPEL TUBUAI)

This group of islands spreads over 800 miles in a WNW-ESE line across the Tropic of Capricorn, between 145°and 155°W longitude. It includes the islands of Maria, Rimatara, Rurutu, Tubuai and Raivavae. Ile de Rapa and Ilots Marotiri, located 300 miles SE of Raivavae, are under the jurisdiction of Raivavae. With the exception of Maria, which is an atoll, the islands are volcanically formed and resemble the Societies except for the lower altitude of their peaks. Approximately 5,200 people inhabit the islands.

Caution: Many of the beacons marking passages through the reefs around these islands are missing. Since the water is not clear, great caution must be exercised to avoid the numerous scattered coral patches.

These are high, volcanic islands, surrounded by fringing coral reefs close to the islands. There is no shelter behind the reefs, except at Tubuai and Raivavae. The islands are within the trade wind belt and have weather conditions similar to the rest of French Polynesia though they are slightly more humid. Their more southerly position gives them a wider temperature range, dropping to 10°C (5O°F) in winter. The strongest trade winds occur in July.

Permission to visit the group should be obtained in Papeete, and special permission must be obtained to visit Ile Rapa. An informal entry can be made at Tubuai or Raivavae. The main islands are fertile and support wild coffee and orange plantations. There are no facilities, and neither provisions nor fuel can be obtained in quantity. These are the most isolated of the French Polynesian Islands, although they are being brought out of this separation by air service to Tahiti.

The islands have had a turbulent past which is belied by today's quiet way of life. Agriculture was once well developed to support the warlike villages and a strong and aggressive population once lived here. Sadly, they were decimated by disease till only a few were left. They now have no cultural ties to their past. For example, Raivavae once had a social structure to rival Tahiti and had similar influence on the migrations of Polynesians. Tubuai once violently rejected the Bounty's mutineers and Rapa, the most exotic of all, still has the remains abandoned fortified villages on mountain peaks. For many years there was a disproportionately large female population living on the island.

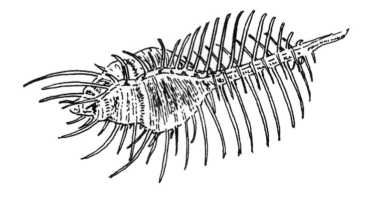

Comb of Venus
(Murex pecten Lightfoot)

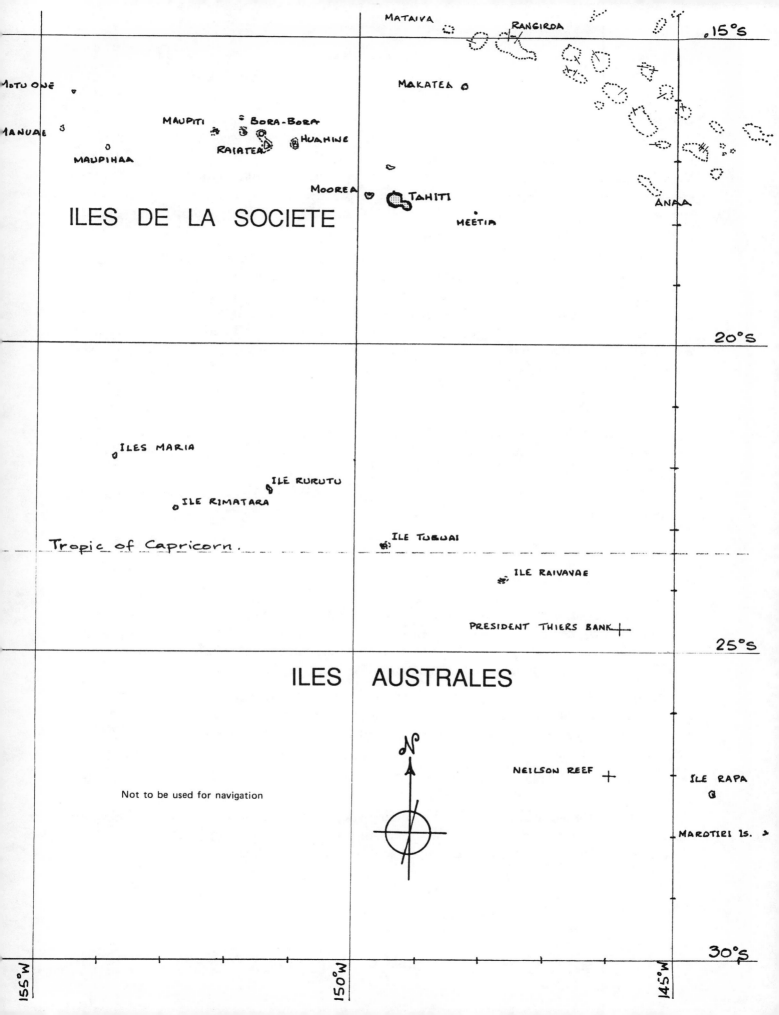

MATAIVA

RANGIROA

MAKATEA ○

○ MOTU ONE

MANUAE ○

MAUPITI ○ BORA-BORA

RAIATEA ○ HUAHINE

MAUPIHAA ○

MOOREA ○ ○ TAHITI

ANAA

MEETIA ·

ILES DE LA SOCIETE

15°S

20°S

ILES MARIA ○

ILE RURUTU ○

○ ILE RIMATARA

Tropic of Capricorn.

ILE TUBUAI

ILE RAIVAVAE

PRESIDENT THIERS BANK ┼

25°S

ILES   AUSTRALES

N

Not to be used for navigation

NEILSON REEF ┼

ILE RAPA ○

MAROTIRI IS. ○

30°S

155°W

150°W

145°W

ILE RURUTU

A fringing coral reef closely encircles this island and provides no protected anchorage within. The passages through the reef only allow small boats to have access to the shore. Vessels anchored outside the reef sometimes tie stern-to the stakes that mark the passages. On a northerly approach the main village of <u>Moerai</u> is prominent though its church is hidden by vegetation until close in. Two miles SSE of Moerai the red roof of the church in <u>Hauti</u> is clearly visible as is the church in the village of <u>Avera</u> on the west coast.

The island has a population of about 2,000 and the Government Administrator and gendarme reside here. Anchorage is possible off the passage at the village of Moerai but the holding is poor on hard, flat coral bottom, and strong trade winds make it an unsafe anchorage. There is a tiny harbor in front of the gendarmerie that can accommodate one yacht in <u>calm</u> conditions. Lighters unload cargo from the trading ships at the small harbor and pier one-half mile northwest of the gendarmerie, (in front of a large, white church). Harbor facilities were rebuilt in 1991 following a destructive cyclone. Although there is a lot of surge during E to SE winds, vessels can tie to the dock until the bi-weekly island freighter arrives. Water and some produce can be obtained. An airstrip gives the island access to Papeete.

The village of Avera is midway along the western side of the island where safe anchorage can be taken. Since the southwesterly swell causes high surf on this side, landing can be difficult making landing at Moerai preferable.

The most unique craft of the island are woven mats and bags with scallops and open work made from dried pandanus leaves.

ILE RIMATARA

This small island rises to about 85m (272') and has a population of about 1,000. It is encircled by a coral reef, cut by a few passages used for landings, but it does not have any sheltered anchorages. From seaward all that can be seen is a large graveyard (with tombs dating back to the 19th century) next to a green cement block boathouse above the beach. On the eastern side is the main village of <u>Amaru </u>which has a gendarmerie, radio station, stores, bakery and a school. The largest marae site in the Australs is found on this island.

Anchorage off the passage near Amaru is unwise due to poor holding. Better anchorage is found directly north of Passe Tahine in about 13m (6 - 7 fathoms), sand. In settled easterly weather, landing can be made at the concrete landing in the middle of the beach or on the sandy beach at Passe Tahine.

<u>Anapoto</u> is a village on the northwestern side of the island and its large church, school and concrete wharf are visible from offshore. Anchorage may be taken in the lee of the island in 9m (5 fathoms), sand and coral. Dinghy landing can be made at the wharf used by lighters to unload trading ships. Passe Hitiau, leading to Anapoto, may be the only usable one in strong prevailing winds. An average of one or two yachts per year visit Rimatara.

ILES AUSTRALES

ILE RIMATARA

& ILE RURUTU

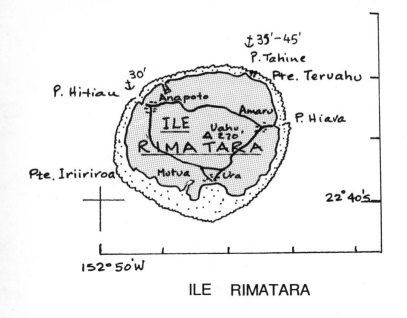

ILE RIMATARA

P. Hitiau 30'
P. Tahine 35'-45'
Pte. Teruahu
Anapoto
ILE
RIMATARA
Amaru
P. Hiava
Uahu 270'
Pte. Iriiriroa
Motua Ura
22°40'S
152°50'W

0 1 2 3
Approx. Scale n.m.

Not to be used for navigation

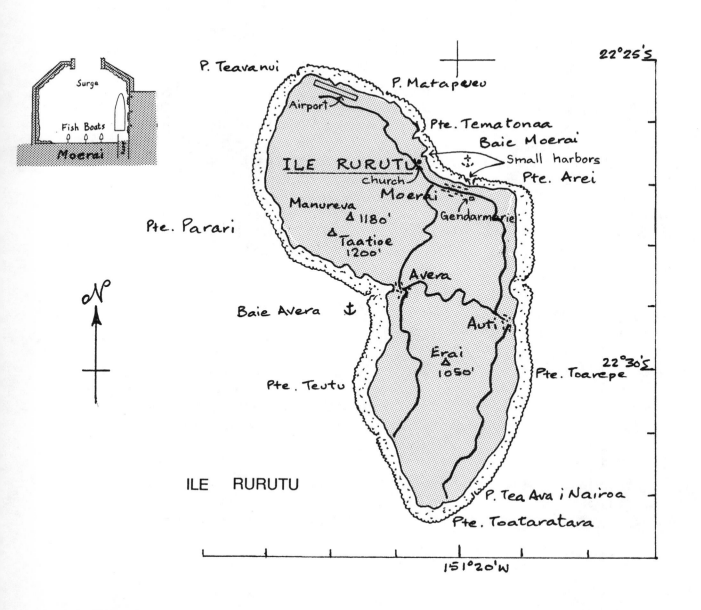

ILE RURUTU

Surge
Fish Boats
Moerai

P. Teavanui
Airport
P. Matapueu
Pte. Tematonaa
Baie Moerai
Small harbors
Pte. Arei
ILE RURUTU
church
Moerai
Manureva 1180'
Taatioe 1200'
Gendarmerie
Pte. Parari
Avera
Auti
Baie Avera
Erai 1050'
Pte. Teutu
Pte. Toarepe
22°30'S
P. Tea Ava i Nairoa
Pte. Toataratara
22°25'S
151°20'W

N

ILE TUBUAI

This volcanic island lies about 115 miles ESE of Rurutu, and 100 miles WNW of Raivavae. The largest of the Iles Australes, with a population of almost 2,000, it is the administrative center for Ile Tubuai, Raivavae and Rapa. From seaward it appears to be two separate islands since the mountains at both ends, Mount Taita (424m/1,390') and Mount Hanareho (312m/1,024'), are separated by a low-lying intermediate strip of land. The barrier reef lies up to 3 miles offshore. The channel through the reef is well marked and a bearing of 156° on the white beacons ashore assist entry. The lagoon is shallow and there are numerous coral heads that prevent travel around the island within the encircling reef. When traveling in the area keep a sharp look-out for FADS (Fish Aggregating Devices).

The only pass is on the northern side. Entry is made on a bearing of 156° taken on two red and white triangular beacons situated about one mile west of the village of <u>Mataura</u>. Once within the reef, a well-marked route to the east leads to the village where anchorage may be taken in about 6m (3 fathoms). If space is available and normal trades are blowing, the vessel may be tied to the concrete wharf east of the center of town. But check the schedule for the arrival of the freighter *Tuha'a Pae III* which comes every 2 weeks and avoid being tied up when it arrives. Surge may make it more prudent to anchor in the lee of the wharf rather than tying alongside; the bottom consists of rock and coral rubble left from dredging. Anchorage may also be taken after carefully threading your way through the coral heads to a spot off Motu Roa.

The Government Administrator and local Gendarme are in Mataura and they can authorize entry. Two white markers indicate a channel through the reef east of the wharf leading to a convenient spot for a dinghy landing. A population of about 1,500 inhabit the island's villages and a road circles the island linking the communities together. The airport gives the island access to the rest of Polynesia and the inhabitants have all conveniences such as electricity, television and telephones. Fuel and water may be available in limited quantities where indicated early in the morning and in the evening. Fresh produce and coffee are available in season and there are several well-stocked stores, a bakery, post office and infirmary in Mataura. The island produces quality potatoes, carrots and other fresh produce which is shipped to Papeete. For daily WeatherFax call at the Metro Weather Office. A worthwhile, 4-hour hike to the top of Mount Taitaa rewards you with some spectacular views.

Good anchorage can also be found by turning to the southwest after clearing the entrance, traveling south of Pointe Tepuu and anchoring between the southwestern end of the airport runway and the village of <u>Anua</u>. A well-stocked store is near the airport. Air service from Papeete operates Sunday, Monday, Wednesday and Friday.

The mutineers on *H.M.S. Bounty* attempted to land on Tubuai in May, 1789 but were forced back to the ship by a hail of stones. Fletcher Christian returned to Tahiti where some crew were left. He tried to land here a second time, failed, then went to Pitcairn Island. and founded a colony there.

ILE MARIA

This is a group of four small wooded islets within a coral reef. Two shallow passes on the western side are used by copra harvesters from Rimatara and Rurutu. Reports indicate that anchorage may be taken about a mile NW and SW of the reef in 6 - 15 fathoms, sand.

ILES AUSTRALES
ILE TUBUAI

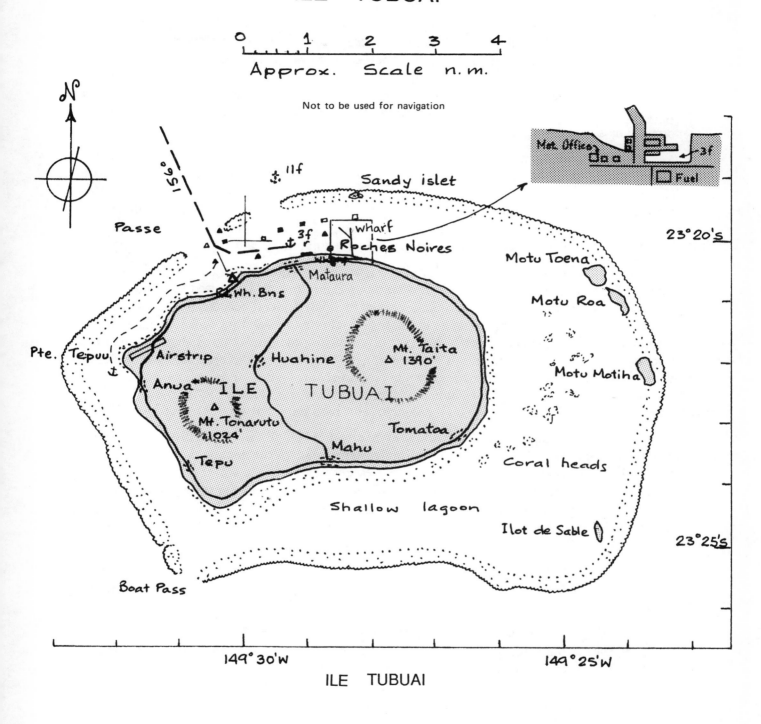

0   1   2   3   4

Approx. Scale n.m.

Not to be used for navigation

N

156°

11f

Passe

Sandy islet

Mt. Office   3f   Fuel

3f

wharf

Roches Noires

23°20'S

Mataura

Motu Toena

Wh. Bns

Motu Roa

Pte. Tepuu

Airstrip

Huahine

Mt. Taita
△ 1390'

Motu Motiha

Anua

ILE   TUBUAI

Mt. Tonarutu
△1024'

Tomatoa

Coral heads

Tepu

Mahu

Shallow lagoon

Ilot de Sable

23°25'S

Boat Pass

149°30'W   149°25'W

ILE   TUBUAI

Mt. Taita

Matura

Mt Tonarutu

Motu

Coral reef

Passe

APPROACHING FROM N, DISTANT ABOUT 2 MILES.

ILE RAIVAVAE

Raivavae lies about 100 miles ESE of Ile Tubuai and Ile Rapa is 200 miles further to the southeast. Near the northeastern end of the island is the highest point, Mont Hiro, 436m (1,430'); to the southwest is Mont Taraia, 305m (1,000'). The peaks are steep and precipitous, reaching out in two spurs at Pic Rouge and Presqu'ile Vainnana to enclose the main anchorage at Baie Rairue. Often described as one of the most beautiful islands in Polynesia, it has a barrier reef that is mostly awash and lies up to 2 miles offshore. Several motus lie along the south and east sides. The island is reported to be a good radar target for up to 25 miles.

Raivavae provides the best anchorages in the Australes, though visibility within the lagoon is not 'always as good as in the Tuamotu and Society Islands. After the anchor is set report to the gendarme even if you have just arrived from Papeete. The main entrance through the reef is **Passe Mahanatoa**; alongside to the east is Passe Teavarua, which should not be used because the beacons have been removed. Two other openings in the reef, Passe Teaoa on the south and Passe Teruapupuhi at the northeast corners are encumbered with coral heads and are not recommended.

Passe Mahanatoa provides a well marked channel through the reef on the north side of the island. The current is almost always outflowing and a sharp lookout is advised to avoid numerous shoal heads scattered about. The centerline is marked by lighted lateral beacons aligned with a range ashore bearing 167°. The entrance range consists of a tall white mast with a white square beyond. The minimum depth in the entrance is 4.7m (15.5') reducing to 4.3m (14') at the inner end for a distance of 35m (115') on each side of the centerline. After passing the beacons marking Roches Totoro proceed on a bearing of 261° on the white turret on Motu Tuitui. It has been reported that the tall white range marker on Motu Tuitui is overgrown and not visible. After passing Pointe Matoaitanata follow the route shown on the sketch. This pass should never be entered at night.

The best anchorage is about a cable (180m/200yds.) NE of the end of the <u>Rairua</u> wharf in 14m (8 fathoms), mud with good protection from easterly winds. The anchor should be well set as heavy squalls occasionally sweep down the hills. Vessels may tie to the wharf until the supply ship *Tuhaa Pae II* makes her visit every 2-3 weeks. When the wind becomes northerly, moorage at the wharf becomes very uncomfortable and anchoring is preferable as the barrier reef gives good protection. In Rairua a telephone is near the church. The generators stop at 2300 and recommence at 0800, making it too late to obtain the local weather report.

Another anchorage is off the village of Mahanatoa, but this location is exposed to the pass and it suffers from northerly winds. A safer anchorage is further to the east off the village of <u>Anatonu</u>.

According to the Gendarme it is unsafe to drink water piped to the end of the wharf but improvements are being made in the water supply. Edmond, a Frenchman who came to Raivavae 30 years ago, lives near the main pass range marker and enjoys supplying yachts with fruit and vegetables from his extensive gardens. The baker delivers fresh bread to the wharf at 0700 if it is ordered the day before. Satellite phone service is available at the post office and the infirmary is staffed by a French doctor. The inhabitants have turned down France's offer of an airport. Alcoholic beverges are not sold on the island. The road circling the island provides a long, scenic hike or a 45-minute walk takes you over the middle of the island.

Only one large stone tiki remains of the many which graced the maraes of the past. Located near Rairua, many believe that this tiki still has magical power (mana).

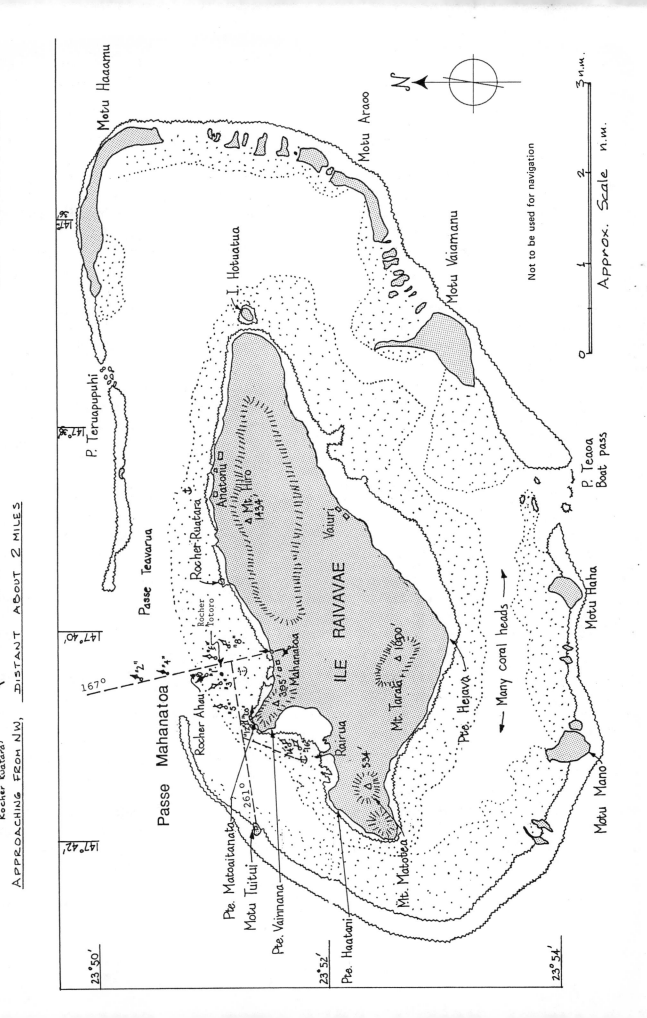

ILES AUSTRALES

ILE RAIVAVAE

Motu Haaamu

Motu Araoo

Motu Vaiamanu

Motu Haha

Motu Mano

P. Teaoa
Boat pass

Many coral heads →

Pte. Hejava

Mt Taraia 'Igoo'

ILE RAIVAVAE

Vaiuri

Mt. Matobea 534'

Anatonu

△ Mt. Hiro 1434

Rocher-Ruatara

Rocher Totoro

Mahanatoa 305'/αα

Rairua

Rocher Ahau

Pte. Haatani

Pte. Vainnana

Motu Tuitui

Pte. Matoaitanata

261°

Passe Mahanatoa

167°

Passe Teavarua

P. Teruapupuhi

I. Hotuatua

147°36'

147°38'

147°40'

147°42'

23°50'

23°52'

23°54'

N

Not to be used for navigation

Approx. Scale n.m.

0   1   2   3 n.m.

Mt. Hiro

White range markers
Mt. Taraia

Rocher Ruatara

Mt. Turivao

APPROACHING FROM NW, DISTANT ABOUT 2 MILES

ILE RAPA

This spectacular, but somewhat forbidding island lies well to the south of the rest of Iles Australes, about 300 miles from Ile Raivave and is administered by officials in Ile Tubuai. The island is composed of several steep, high, and jagged mountain peaks that drop to the sea in cliffs around much of the coast. The highest peak is Mont Perau, 650m (2,130'). Many of the other peaks exceed 365m (1,200'). The climate is temperate and humid, with frequent rain and sometimes fog. From October to April the prevailing winds are easterly though about once a month from December to February brief westerlies occur. The strongest winds from the west occur during July and August.

The steep coast has few offshore underwater dangers, except in the approaches to Baie de Ahurei, where the main villages and anchorages are located. The approach to, and actual entry into the bay is complex, and as the clarity of the water is not as good as elsewhere in Polynesia, the passage needs care. Shoals and spits block off much of the bay and extend well out from each of the seaward points, narrowing the entrance. This bay is impressive for it is the crater of a volcano which has been breached open to the sea.

Cruisers tie to the wharf to check in with the local official, a policeman (muto'i) who, when asked, will stamp your passport as proof of having visited the island. The bay is either very deep or shoal, making care and good sunlight necessary to find spots suitable for anchoring. The coral is mainly soft staghorn so damage to the vessel is negligible if you ground. Set the anchor well in the good holding coral, mud and rock for boisterous squalls funnel down the steep hillsides into the bay.

The island's 550 residents live on the most isolated spot in Polynesia and the supply boat, *Tuhaa Pae*, only visits the island every 6 to 8 weeks. The 3 or 4 small stores run low on inventory between shipments, "Fare Toa" usually has the best selection. Water is available behind the building on the main wharf. Crayfish are plentiful but the climate is not suitable for coconuts or other tropical fruits. Spear fishing is not allowed inside the harbor.

Since there is no road linking the two villages of Area and Ahurei, contact is by crossing the bay in long boats. For a small fee cruisers may be offered a ride ashore. A telephone is located near the post office on the main wharf. It requires a phone card which is available at the post office where money can be changed if the bank is closed. Electricity is available from 0800 to 1200 and from 1600 to 2400 and all day Saturday. The island is served by cable TV.

The trail to the forts is west from Ahurei village, past the soccer field. Proceed around the back of a bulldozed hill, turn left to an abandoned weather station and follow the trail. By turning right you will be on a longer walk but will arrive at a more interesting site, the restored fortress of Morongo Uta.

The island has had a colorful, and at times, violent history as evidenced by the fortifications and other remains on its green-clad, pointed hills. Wherever the hills appear terraced near the peak it indicates the remains of fortified mountain village strongholds which are now overgrown. These forts, built and faced with rock, were the home of warrior tribes which controlled the agriculture in the neighboring fertile lowlands. Then the usual pattern of European exploration and exploitation unfolded. The missionaries brought the people down from the healthy lifestyle in the forts, exposed them to disease, while the whalers and traders took the men and forced them to work elsewhere, until the island was one composed almost entirely of women. This led to a period when women became the work force and Rapa became known as the "Island of Amazons." Fortunately, this period has passed into history.

ILE RAPA

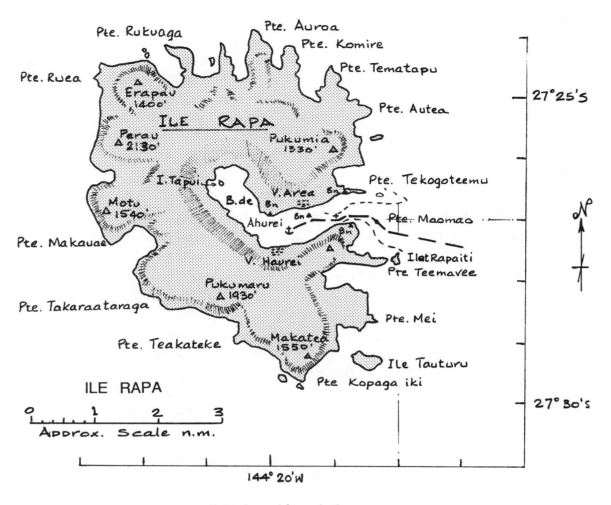

Pte. Rukuaga
Pte. Auroa
Pte. Komire
Pte. Ruea
Pte. Tematapu
Erapau
1400'
Pte. Autea
ILE RAPA
Perau
2130'
Pukumia
1530'
I. Tapui
Pte. Tekogoteemu
V. Area
B. de
Bn
Motu
1540'
Ahurei
Pte. Maomao
Pte. Makauae
Ilot Rapaiti
V. Haurei
Pte. Teemavee
Pukumaru
1930'
Pte. Takaraataraga
Pte. Mei
Pte. Teakateke
Makatea
1550'
Ile Tauturu
ILE RAPA
Pte. Kopaga iki

27°25'S

27°30'S

0   1   2   3
Approx. Scale n.m.

144° 20'W

Not to be used for navigation

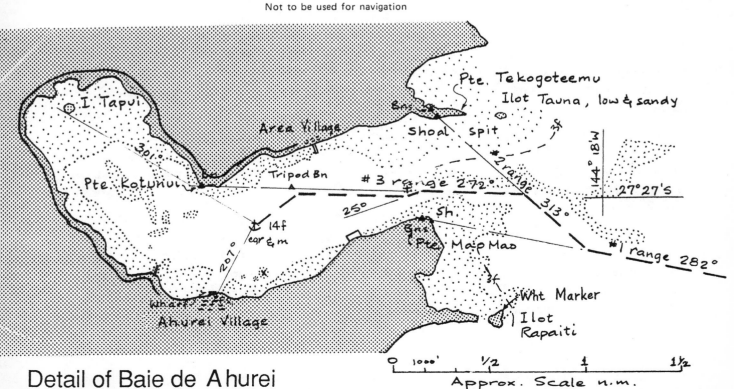

I. Tapui
Pte. Tekogoteemu
Ilot Tauna, low & sandy
Area Village
Bn
Shoal Spit
3f
301°
#2 range 313°
Pte. Kotunui
Tripod Bn
#3 range 272°
144° 18'W
27°27'S
250°
Sh.
14f
eqr & m
207°
Bns
Pte. Mao Mao
#1 range 282°
3f
Wharf
Wht Marker
Ahurei Village
Ilot Rapaiti

0   1000'   ½   1   1½
Approx. Scale n.m.

Detail of Baie de Ahurei

COOK ISLANDS

The flag of the Cook Islands has 15 white stars in a circle on a blue field, which represents the 15 small islands that lie scattered over a large area. The boundaries of the country include the land and sea between Latitudes 8°S and 23°S and Longitudes 156°W and 167°W. This is an area of over 750,000 square miles with a total land area of 93 square miles. The islands are flanked to the west by the Kingdom of Tonga and Samoa and to the east, French Polynesia. The weather is warm and sunny throughout the year with June to August being the cooler months. Rainfall is heaviest from November to March, the hottest season. Many of the islands were discovered by Captain Cook, after whom the islands are named.

The islands are divided into two geographic groups. The Southern, Lower Cook Islands, have volcanic origins with fringing coral reefs and include Rarotonga, Mangaia, Manke, Atiu, Mitiaro, Takutea and Manuae (Hervey Islands). The vegetation is sparse in comparison with the luxuriant growth of the Society Islands. The Northern Group are low-lying atolls and include Palmerston, Suvarov, Nassau, Pukapuka, Rakahanga, Manihiki and Penrhyn.

Entry formalities are handled at Rarotonga, Aitutaki, Penrhyn and Pukapuka (Danger Is.); permission to visit other islands can be requested on entry. The unit of currency is the New Zealand Dollar, supplemented by Cook Island currency which is not negotiable outside the Cook Islands. Entry rules and regulations are a result of the government's efforts to control the influx of disease and pests that might damage the country's agrarian economy. The boat will be sprayed for pests and will be visited by the harbormaster, customs and agriculture.. Note: Avoid entering or leaving the outer islands on a Sunday since it is strictly observed as the Sabbath.

The history of man's habitation on the islands is relatively brief. It is estimated that the first Polynesians probably arrived about 500 AD. The major migration to New Zealand, which culminated in the Maori culture began elsewhere in Polynesia. It was from Ngatangiia in about 135O AD that the intrepid seafarers set out in their great canoes on the last leg of the journey to Aetorea (now called New Zealand).

Since 1965 the Cook Islands have been a self-governing democratic commonwealth affiliated with New Zealand, which handles foreign affairs and defense, and subsidizes finances. Thus the Cook Islanders enjoy New Zealand citizenship and move freely to and from that country. The main language is Cook Island Maori, but English is also spoken with a strong New Zealand accent.

Cook Islanders are true, fun-loving Polynesians who are enthusiastic participants in both sports and dances. It is well worth attending one of their feasts which is sure to have entertainment in the form of dancing. Although there are many similarities in dance and language to those found in Tahiti, the Cook Island style is more closely related to the Maoris of New Zealand.

The London Missionary Society, now operating as the Cook Islands Christian Church, has had a major influence on the lives of the people. They avidly attend church and religion is a dominant factor in their lives. So as not to offend these friendly people, visitors should respect their dress code and dress modestly. Swim-wear should not be worn when visiting towns or villages. Tipping is contrary to local custom.

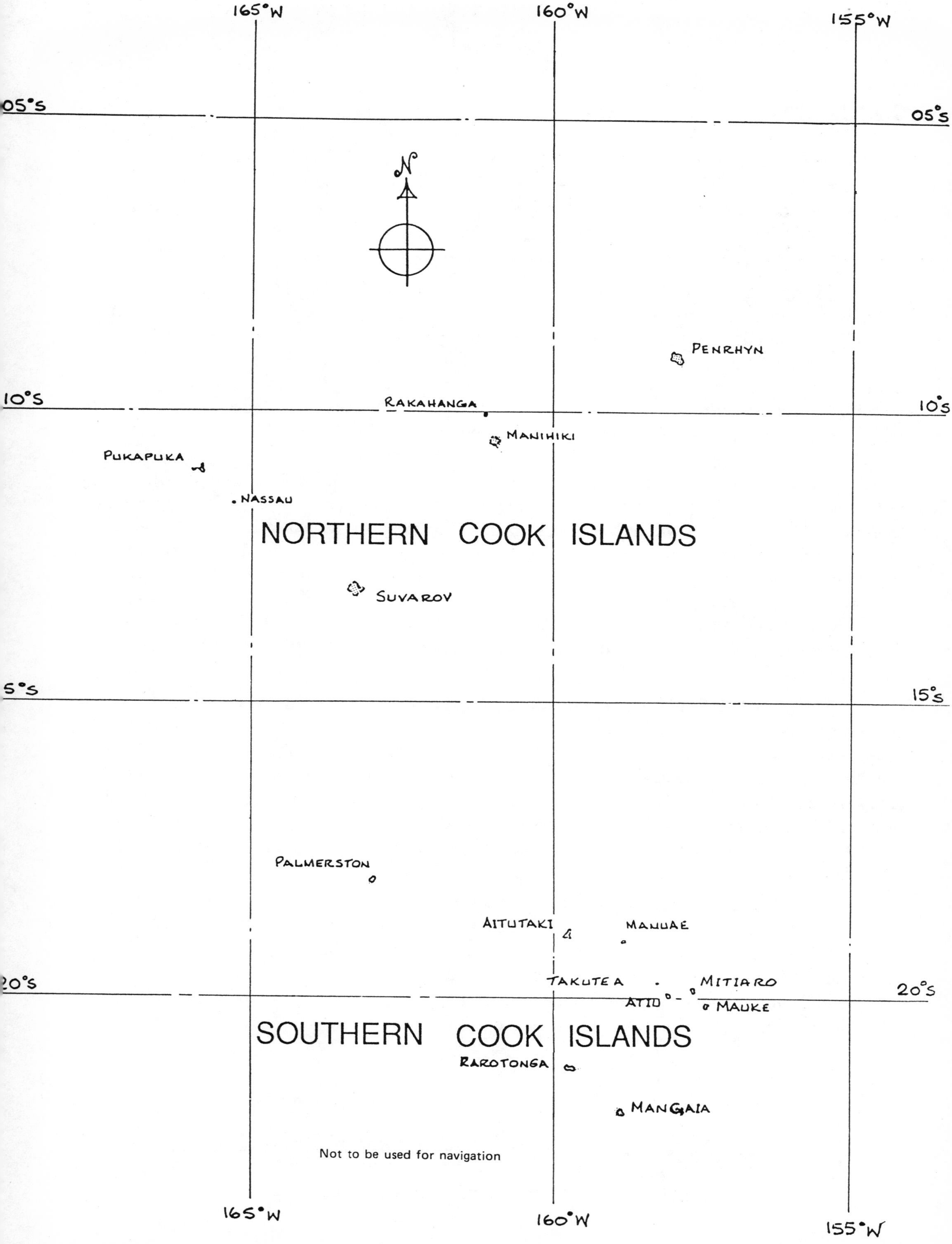

165°W   160°W   155°W

05°S   05°S

N

⊕

PENRHYN

10°S   RAKAHANGA   10°S

MANIHIKI

PUKAPUKA

NASSAU

NORTHERN COOK ISLANDS

SUVAROV

15°S   15°S

PALMERSTON

AITUTAKI   MANUAE

TAKUTEA   MITIARO

ATIU   MAUKE

20°S   20°S

SOUTHERN COOK ISLANDS

RAROTONGA

MANGAIA

Not to be used for navigation

165°W   160°W   155°W

RAROTONGA

Rarotonga is a beautiful and luxuriantly green, mountainous island within an encircling barrier reef. Often likened to a miniature Moorea, it is about 25 square miles in area. The rugged peaks of the interior reach to about 610m (2,000'), creating a sharp outline and are a spectacular scene from offshore. This is the most important of the Cook Islands; over half of the population reside here and it is the center of government. The main **Port of Entry** for the Cook Islands is at <u>Avatiu</u>. The island is a good radar target for up to 40 miles.

<u>Avatiu</u>, the only harbor on the island, is located in the middle of the north shore. It is extremely limited in space and access for the small, square basin is cut out of the reef with partially reclaimed areas on each side. Entrance during daylight is straightforward and there is a lighted range of vertical green lights. Local trading and fishing vessels have priority in the harbor. This can be a dangerous harbor to visit since deep-sea vessels maneuvering in the confined space sometimes collide with and damage yachts tied ashore. Cruising vessels must moor Med-style and be ready to move with short notice in the event of a ship arriving or strong winds from a northerly quarter which can make the harbor untenable. During the cyclone season, from the end of November to the end of March cruisers are not permitted to use the harbor.

Customs and Immigration are handled by the Harbormaster, whose office is alongside the harbor. When a vessel is within VHF range, contact the harbormaster on VHF Ch 16 or through ZKR, Radio Rarotonga and request berthing instructions. Vessels should fly the yellow Quarantine Flag while awaiting the Port Health officer who may spray the vessel with the insecticide used in aircraft arriving from foreign countries. Upon arrival a 31-day visa is granted; an extension can be obtained only at the immigration office in Rarotonga. To prevent the import of produce-borne bacteria, all fresh fruits and vegetables are seized. When departing the Cook Islands a $25NZ per person exit fee is charged, payable before port clearance papers are issued.

The harbor at Avatiu is in the middle of the residential and commercial area of the town of <u>Avarua</u> and stores and other facilities are within walking distance. The public market has a good selection of local vegetables and refrigerated and dried foods from New Zealand. Diesel and kerosene are available in Avarua. If large quantities of fuel are needed, arrangements can be made for a fuel truck to deliver it to Avatiu Harbor. Many cruisers congregate here for the annual 10-day Constitution Day celebrations at the beginning of August. Propane is available next to the Harbormaster's office. There are several international flights per week to Tahiti, Auckland, Fiji, Los Angeles and Honolulu.

A shallow entrance to the lagoon for vessels drawing less than 1.5m (5') is on the eastern side of Ngatangiia. Permission must be obtained to use this pass for it is constricted with fish traps. It is advisable to sound depths by dinghy or snorkeling before entry. It is best to anchor bow and stern in front of the condos. A heavy south or southeast swell produces a continuous strong ebb current, making maneuvering difficult at best. A local sailing club sails small dinghies in Muri Lagoon, which is a little further south.

APPROACHING RAROTONGA IS. APPROX. 3 MILES N. OF AIRPORT

SOUTHERN COOK ISLANDS
RAROTONGA ISLAND

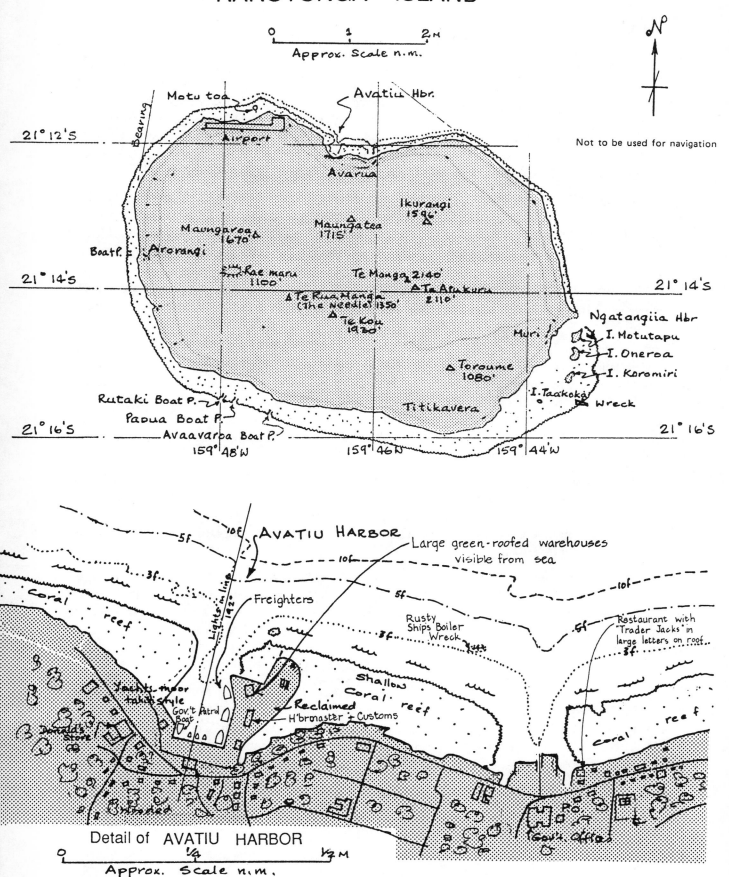

Approx. Scale n.m.

N

Not to be used for navigation

Motu toa
Avatiu Hbr.
21° 12'S
Airport
Avarua
Ikurangi
1596'
Maungatea
1715'
Maungaroa
1670'
Arorangi
Boat P.
21° 14'S   21° 14'S
Rae maru
1100'   Te Manga 2140'
Te Rua Manga   △ Te Atukura
(The Needle) 1350'   2110'
Te Kou
1920'
Muri
Ngatangiia Hbr
I. Motutapu
I. Oneroa
I. Koromiri
Toroume
1080'
Rutaki Boat P.   I. Taakoka
Papua Boat P.   Wreck
21° 16'S   Avaavaroa Boat P.   Titikavera   21° 16'S
159° 48'W   159° 46'W   159° 44'W

AVATIU HARBOR
5f   10f
10f
Large green-roofed warehouses
visible from sea
3f
10f
5f
Freighters
Lights in line
192°
Coral   reef
Rusty
Ships Boiler
Wreck
Restaurant with
"Trader Jacks" in
large letters on roof
3f
5f
3f
Yachts moor
tahiti style
Shallow
Coral   reef
Gov't Patrol
Boat
Reclaimed
H'brmaster + Customs
Coral   reef
Donald's Store
Gov't Office

Detail of AVATIU HARBOR
Approx. Scale n.m.

AITUTAKI

This is the northernmost island of the Lower Cook Islands and it lies 150 miles north of Rarotonga and about 55 miles northwest of the Hervey Islands. Its highest point is Mount Maungapu, 119m (390') high, where a light is located at the peak. A fringing reef borders the northern end of the island; on the south is a barrier reef on which a few tree-covered islets are scattered. A large, shallow lagoon (mostly .5m/18") with numerous coral heads is within the reef, creating a beautiful area that is reminiscent of Bora-Bora. Strong westerly setting currents south and east of the southern tip of the island must be considered when sailing in the vicinity. Several yachts have been shipwrecked near Motikitiu while approaching the island during poor visibility.

Arutunga Pass provides the only navigable channel through the reef. It is a well marked, long, narrow passage leading to a small basin on the western side of the island. The passage is less than 18m (40') wide and there is a shallow section where the maximum depth that can be carried at exactly high tide is 1.84m (6'). Current Tide Tables for Central and Western Pacific Ocean are required to determine the time of high slack water. Thus a vessel's draft prohibits many cruisers from visiting here. Because of very limited swinging space, it is best to anchor fore and aft or take a line ashore to a palm tree inside. Avoid the rock in the southern part of the harbor, covered .6m/2'. A nominal fee is charged for anchoring here.

The Port Captain occasionally monitors VHF Ch 16 during working hours and vessels may enter and clear through this Port of Entry. The Port Administration Authority Office is adjacent to the small basin where fumigation is done. A visa valid for 31 days is issued on arrival and can be extended for an additional period only in Rarotonga. In addition to a few stores with limited supplies on the island, there is a 19-ton mobile crane and a 11m (37') tugboat, *Orongo II*. A dinghy trip to the southern part of the lagoon is well worth the effort. The water is crystal clear and large variety of tropical fish are visible.

A tourist resort is located on Mangari Motu and the Rapae Motel doubles as the main bar where exuberant Friday night shows are put on by the islanders. Dancers from Aitutaki have been regular winners at contests held in Tahiti, though their performances are said to resemble the old style of dancing. Father Don welcomes cruisers and maintains guest logs of visiting yachts. He occasionally monitors VHF Ch 16.

A convenient spot for a mail drop is Cafe Tupuna, a short walk from the harbor, north on the main road in the village of Ureia, located on the west side of the road. E-mail sent to richards@aitutaki.net.ck will be printed and delivered to Cafe Tupuna. For a small fee E-mail can be sent. The postal address is "Name of Boat", C/O Cafe Tupuna, P.O. Box 56, Aitutaki, Cook Islands, South Pacific.

*****

The first European to weigh anchor here was Captain Bligh in the *Bounty*, just two weeks before the infamous mutiny in the waters off Samoa. In 1821 John Williams of the London Missionary Society arrived and immediately began converting the islands to Christianity. Though he met an ignominious end—stewed in a pot by the Big Nambas of Vanuatu—his church survives to this day as the Cook Islands Christian Church. The church in Arutunga, built in 1828, is the oldest church in the Cook Islands.

SOUTHERN COOK ISLANDS
AITUTAKI ISLAND

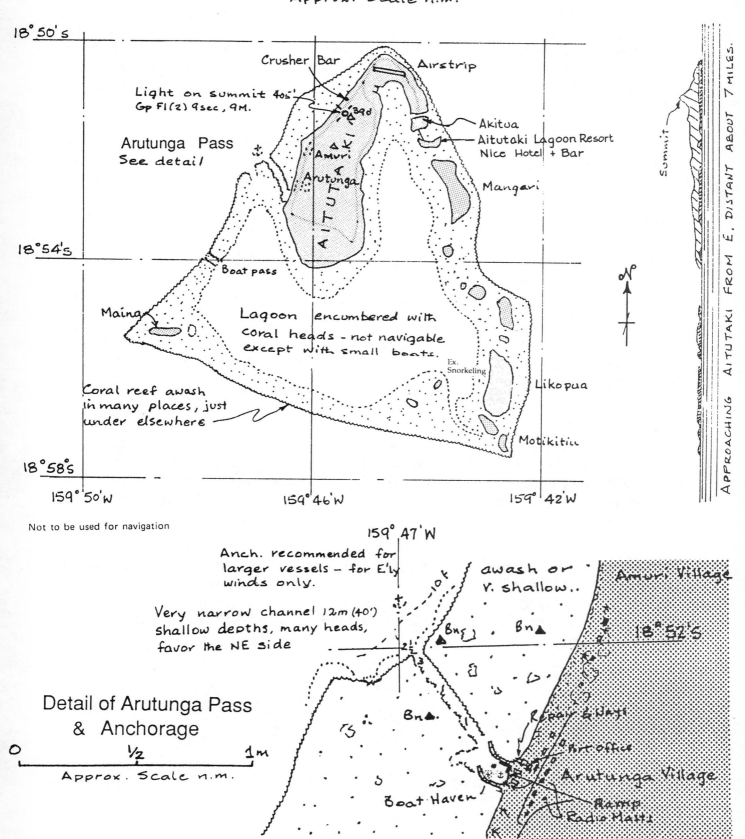

0   1   2   3   4
Approx. Scale n.m.

18°50's

Crusher Bar   Airstrip

Light on summit 405'
Gp Fl(2) 9sec, 9M.

Arutunga Pass
See detail

Akitua
Aitutaki Lagoon Resort
Nice Hotel + Bar

Amuri

Arutunga

AITUTAKI

Mangari

18°54's

Boat pass

Maina

Lagoon encumbered with
coral heads - not navigable
except with small boats.

Ex.
Snorkeling

Coral reef awash
in many places, just
under elsewhere

Likopua

Motikitiu

18°58's

159°50'W   159°46'W   159°42'W

Summit

APPROACHING AITUTAKI FROM E, DISTANT ABOUT 7 MILES.

Not to be used for navigation

159°47'W

Anch. recommended for
larger vessels - for E'ly
winds only.

awash or
v. shallow..

Amuri Village

Very narrow channel 12m (40')
shallow depths, many heads,
favor the NE side

Bn

Bn

18°52's

Bn

Detail of Arutunga Pass
& Anchorage

0   ½   1m
Approx. Scale n.m.

Bn

Repair & Natl

Art office

Arutunga Village

Boat Haven

Ramp
Radio Maiti

MANGAIA ISLAND

The most southerly of the Cook Islands, Mangaia Island is 176km (110 miles) ESE of Rarotonga. The island rises to a height of 169m (554') in the center but it is dominated by makatea, a formation of raised coral cliffs named after the high atoll in French Polynesia. These cliffs virtually encircle the island but are most prominent on the northern side where they vary between 45m (150') and 70m (230'). In places the raised wall is over one mile wide, and the coastal road around the island has to adjust to this feature. Caves once used as burial sites are in this formation.

A fringing coral reef, generally visible and extending up to .25 mile offshore, surrounds the island. There are no harbors, though boat passages or landings cut through the reef are used by small local vessels. Southwesterly swells affect these landings and at such times the northerly landing can be used. Someone must stay aboard the vessel at all times since anchorage is not possible at any of the landings. Currents in the area typically set to the west at about .5 knots.

Oneroa, the island's main village, is on the western side of the island and is clearly visible from a distance. A passage is located here but a better landing is at Avarua, about one mile to the north where a boat passage leading to a small wharf has been blasted out of the reef. A large shed marks the landing, and a light is sometimes shown if a cargo ship is expected. The swell and surge are such that it is best to use local vessels to go ashore.

The Lower Cook Islands are administered for the New Zealand government by a Resident Commissioner at Avarua in Rarotonga. Each island has a Resident Agent who is assisted by the Island Council.

MAUKE ISLAND

This is the most easterly of the Lower Cook Islands, and is about 150 miles ENE of Rarotonga. There is some makatea in the island's formation though its highest elevation is about 45m (150'), including the trees. It is encircled by a fringing coral reef that extends up to .25 mile offshore and is steep-to, allowing vessels to approach fairly closely if a landing party is to go ashore. There are no anchorages available. The island is reported to be visible on radar from a distance of 17 miles. The island has an airstrip.

A good landing place is at Taunganui, at the northwestern end of the island, located by sighting the village and its flagstaff. If the southerly swell is strong an alternative landing is on the northern side of Angataura. There are other locations but they are more difficult to negotiate. During shore visits someone should be left aboard the vessel and the trip ashore made in local boats.

Ancient Fish Hooks of Pearl Shell

SOUTHERN COOK ISLANDS
MANGAIA ISLAND & MAUKE ISLAND

0   1   2   3   4
Approx. Scale n.m.

Not to be used for navigation

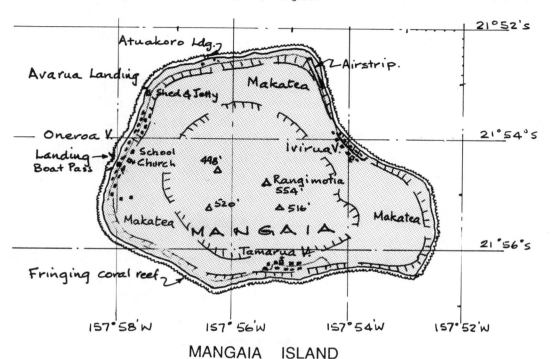

MANGAIA ISLAND

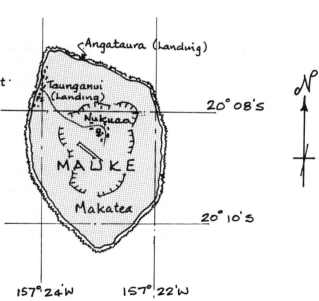

No anchorage is available; boats must remain hove-to near the coast and landing is best made with local small boat help.

Mauke Is. may lie 2½m further eastward than this position taken from the chart.

MAUKE ISLAND

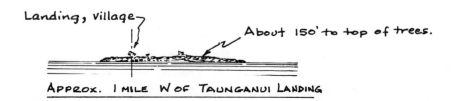

Landing, village

About 150' to top of trees.

APPROX. 1 MILE W OF TAUNGANUI LANDING

HERVEY ISLANDS

These two small, low islands—Manuae and Auoto—are within one encircling coral reef located 55 miles southeast of Aitutaki. There is no passage into the lagoon, though a landing can be made through Turakina Boat Passage on to Manuae Island. In the northwest part of Manuae there is a very small settlement augmented by people engaged in copra collection who work out of Aitutaki. An airstrip on the island provides connections to the rest of the Cook Islands.

MITIARO ISLAND (Mitiero Island)

This small, slightly raised coral island with traces of makatea, is about 22 miles northwest of Mauke. It is a green and fertile island with a small population. Although it is encircled by a fringing coral reef there is a landing place on the western side at Omutu, off the village of Atai. An interesting feature of the island is the brackish lake in the interior with edible eels.

ATIU ISLAND

Composed of raised coral and resembling Mangaia with its makatea, the small island of Atiu is 20 miles WSW of Mitiaro Island. The main villages are in the center of the island where the plateau has an elevation of 120m (394'). The village church is prominent from seaward. This is a subsidiary Port of Entry where clearance may be obtained when customs officers are present, otherwise you may have to pay for their transportation costs from Rarotonga.

The bold, raised, cliff-edged coast has several small bays where landing is possible. The fringing coral reef lies fairly close to the island, but landings are possible at Taunganui on the northwestern side or in suitable conditions, at Iotua Ika on the north. Other landings can be seen, but they are more difficult to use. The yacht must remain manned, and shore visits are best taken in local boats. Small amounts of fresh water may be obtained and some fresh produce is available in season. The island has a population of about 1,300 inhabitants and the Resident Agent resides at Taunganui.

TAKUTEA (Fenua Iti)

This is a very small, low, wooded island lying about 16km (10 miles) northwest of Atiu. It has a white coral sand beach and is surrounded by a fringing coral reef. A reef extends about 2 miles southeast from the southeastern end of the island, and occasionally the sea breaks heavily across it. There is also a shoal extending about .3 miles west of the western end of the island. Strong tide rips occur north of this shoal.

A possible landing site is on the north side but it is best avoided because of the dangers inherent in keeping a yacht in this area during a landing. The island is a bird and wild life sanctuary, though islanders from Atiu come here to harvest coconuts.

Interrupted Cone
Conus Ximenes (Gray)

SOUTHERN COOK ISLANDS

NOTE:- Hervey Is. may be about 5 miles
further N'ward than shown below
taken from charts.

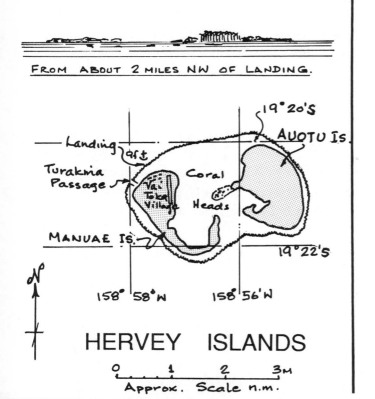

FROM ABOUT 2 MILES NW OF LANDING.

Landing
Turakina Passage
Va'i Toka Village
Coral Heads
19°20'S
AUOTU Is.
MANUAE IS.
19°22'S

158°58'W   158°56'W

HERVEY ISLANDS

0 . . . 1 . . . 2 . . . 3M
Approx. Scale n.m.

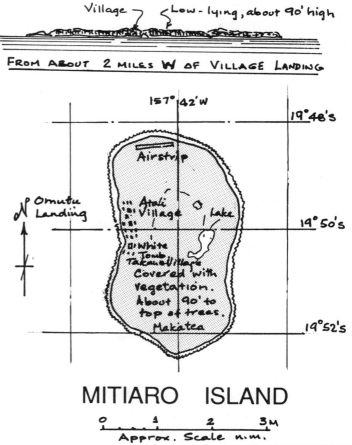

Village   Low-lying, about 90' high

FROM ABOUT 2 MILES W OF VILLAGE LANDING

157°42'W   19°48'S

Airstrip
Omutu Landing
Atali Village
Lake
White Tomb
Takauellaque
Covered with
vegetation.
About 90' to
top of trees.
Makatea
19°50'S
19°52'S

MITIARO ISLAND

0 . . . 1 . . . 2 . . . 3M
Approx. Scale n.m.

Not to be used for navigation

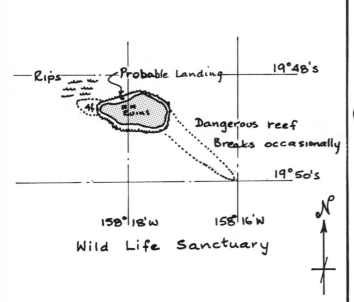

Rips
Probable Landing
19°48'S
High Point
Dangerous reef
Breaks occasionally
19°50'S

158°18'W   158°16'W

Wild Life Sanctuary

TAKUTEA ISLAND

0 . . . 1 . . . 2 . . . 3M
Approx. Scale n.m.

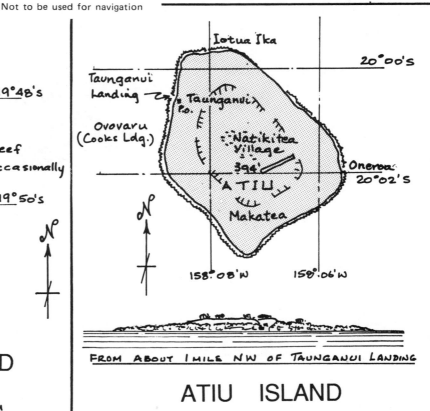

Iotua Ika
20°00'S
Taunganui Landing
Taunganui P.o.
Ovovaru (Cooks Ldg.)
Natikitea Village
394'
Oneroa
20°02'S
A T I U
Makatea

158°08'W   158°06'W

FROM ABOUT 1 MILE NW OF TAUNGANUI LANDING

ATIU ISLAND

0 . . . 1 . . . 2 . . . 3M
Approx. Scale n.m.

PALMERSTON ATOLL

This atoll lies about 200 miles WNW of Aitutaki. Six sandy islets are scattered along the coral reef surrounding the lagoon. All the islands are covered by coconut palms, yet the overall height of the island is barely over 15m (50'). On the northwesterly side of the most westerly islet is a settlement that is prominent from the west. A stranded wreck on the reef shows well on radar. Heavy gales from the NE to E are common in January and February, usually lasting 24 to 36 hours. The atoll is dangerous to approach at night.

There are several small boat passages into the lagoon, the largest of which is <u>Big Passage</u> on the western side. However, vessels drawing more than 1.2m (4') cannot enter the lagoon. The islanders usually come out in their skiffs as soon as they sight a yacht, show the crew the best anchorage spot, and offer a ride ashore. In settled trade wind weather, temporary day anchorage is possible a little to the south of Big Passage. An anchor watch must be maintained for this anchorage is safe only as long as an easterly wind holds the vessel away from the reef. When the wind subsides, the current may set the vessel on the reef.

The island's inhabitants have a unique history. They are the descendants of a patriarchal figure, William Marsters, a Lancashireman who settled here with three Penrhyn Island wives in 1862. He fathered 26 children, divided the islands and reefs into sections for each of the three "families" and established strict rules regarding intermarriage. The original home was built using massive beams salvaged from shipwrecks washed ashore. Although it still stands, it bears the scars of many hurricanes. Some of his descendants control the island while the rest live in New Zealand and elsewhere in the Cook Islands. The island has a population of about 50 inhabitants.

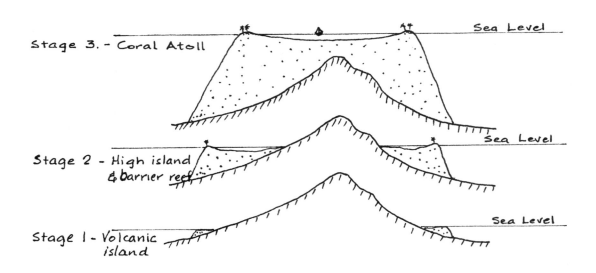

STAGES IN A DEVELOPING CORAL REEF (FROM DARWIN)
Imagine the sea level constant, but the land subsiding.

NORTHERN COOK ISLANDS
PALMERSTON ISLANDS

APPROX. SCALE N.M.

Not to be used for navigation

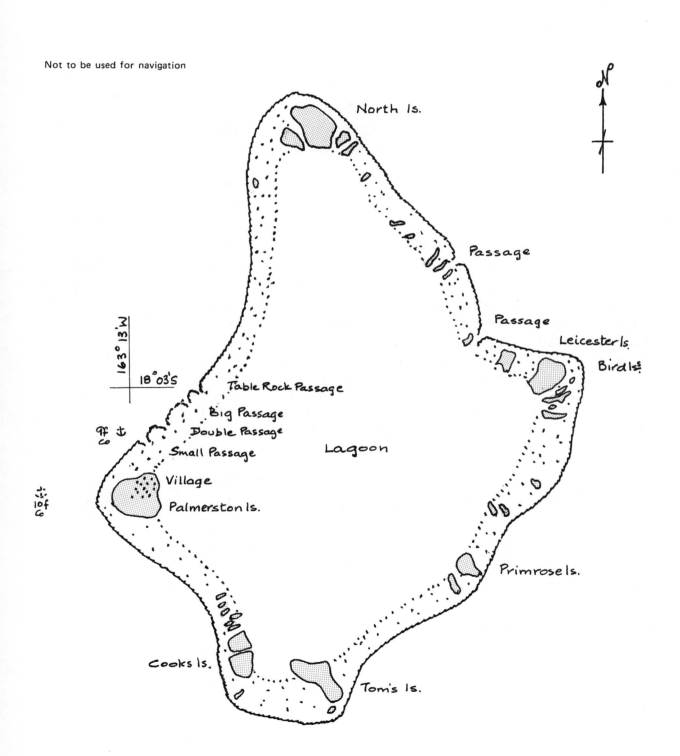

SUWARROW ISLANDS (SUVAROV)

Suwarrow is a fairly large atoll, about 11 miles across. A few small islands are scattered around the northern part of the reef, the largest being Anchorage Island which is visible from a distance of almost 7 miles. The southern part of the atoll is submerged and very dangerous to approach. A conspicuous wreck is situated near Seven Islands. Many vessels have been lost here and several have sunk within the lagoon where their wreckage is visible on the bottom. The anchorage is dangerous in anything but stable trade wind conditions.

The only pass into the lagoon is on the northeastern coast, between Anchorage Island and Northeast Reef. Several large coral heads (East Reef and South Reef) extend across part of the passage near Northeast Reef. A 3.6m (2-fathom) shoal extends southwest from Northeast Reef and this causes the entry to be slightly complicated.

Entry should be made only in good weather with a calm sea because the seas break over the shoal with any swell causing turbulence in the entrance. A bearing of 175° taken across the center of South Reef to Entrance Island on the southeast side of the barrier reef will lead past the shoal at the tip of Northeast Reef. Care must be taken to counter the effect of the ever-present current which has a strong set toward Anchorage Island. The vessel can pass on either side of South Reef, make the turn to the northwest, and enter the anchorage area. Tom's Place, a wooden shack, and a small pier he repaired, are midway along the island shore.

Suwarrow is a Nature Reserve and the caretaker resides on Anchorage Island. A nominal anchorage fee is charged (about NZ$5 per day). In addition, the Immigration Department charges a fee of about NZ$30 for vessels that have not first cleared into the Cook Islands at a designated Port of Entry. Permission is not normally given to anchor anywhere but off the pier at Anchorage Island, though sometimes the caretaker will allow visiting yachtsmen to anchor elsewhere in the lagoon such as in the lee of Seven Islands. However, this corner of the atoll has many coral heads that must be avoided when seeking an anchorage. By quietly rowing to the largest islet you will be rewarded by a view of thousands of birds in the air, on the ground, and in the trees. A maximum visit of three days is allowed on the atoll. With permission, it may be possible to obtain small amounts of water from the cistern.

The lagoon has many scattered coral heads. The clarity of the water and multitude of colorful fish make for excellent diving except for the profusion of aggressive sharks.

This atoll has also had a unique figure in its past, for it was here that Tom Neale, a New Zealander, lived as a hermit for periods totaling 16 years, from 1952 until his death from cancer in 1978. Many yachts visited during his time on the atoll and their crews were charmed by him. He wrote a book describing his experiences entitled, *An Island to Oneself.*

The first European to visit the atoll was the Russian explorer, Lazarev. He arrived in 1814 aboard the *Suvarov* and the island was so named. Following Cook Island independence the name was changed to "Suwarrow" so that it was more in tune with the Cook Island language. Many years ago the atoll became infested with termites and it can no longer be used for copra production.

NORTHERN COOK ISLANDS
SUVAROV ISLANDS
(SUWARROW)

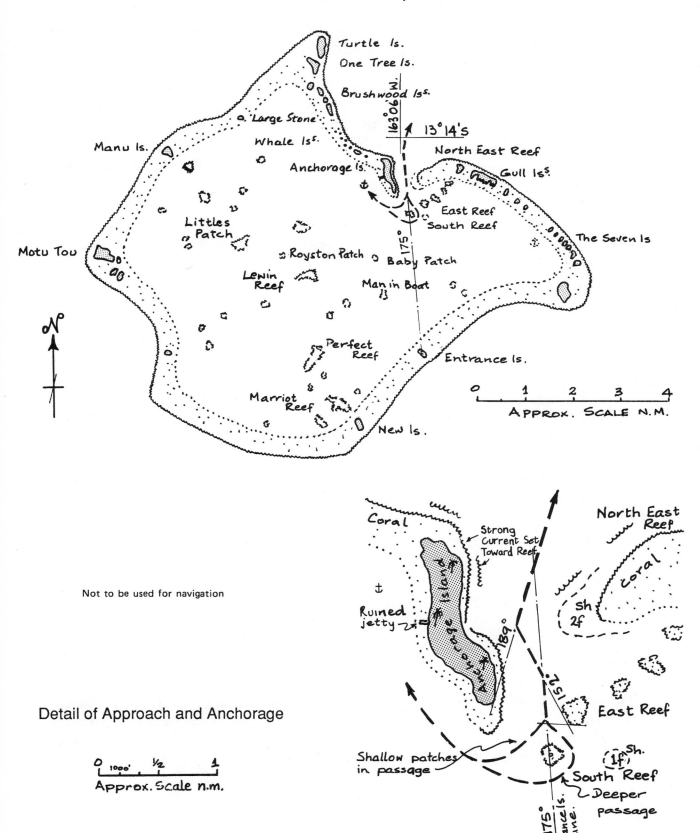

Turtle Is.

One Tree Is.

Brushwood Is^s.

Large Stone

Whale Is^s.

Manu Is.

Anchorage Is.

North East Reef

Gull Is^s.

East Reef
South Reef

Littles Patch

Motu Tou

Royston Patch

Baby Patch

The Seven Is

Lewin Reef

Man in Boat

N

Perfect Reef

Entrance Is.

Marriot Reef

New Is.

13°14'S

163°06'W.

175°

| 0 | 1 | 2 | 3 | 4 |

APPROX. SCALE N.M.

Not to be used for navigation

Coral

Strong Current Set Toward Reef

North East Reef

Coral

Sh 2f

Ruined jetty

189°

152°

East Reef

Shallow patches in passage

South Reef

Sh 1f

Deeper passage

Detail of Approach and Anchorage

175°
Entrance Is. in line.

| 0 | 1000' | ½ | 1 |

Approx. Scale n.m.

PUKAPUKA ATOLL (DANGER ISLANDS)

Pukapuka is the most western and isolated of this group and is a **Port of Entry**. It is a narrow atoll with a long, partially submerged coral reef (Terai Reef) extending from its western side for almost 3 miles. The palms on Motu Kotawa grow to about 38m (125'), while those on Pukapuka and Motu Ko reach about 30m (100'). A 3 to 5-knot current sets on to the eastern side of the atoll. This turns the stream so that it sets southward across Terai Reef on the ebb and northward on the flood. The reef and currents are the reason for its popular name of Danger Islands. Many downed airmen were carried by currents to the island during World War II. The island is featured in books by R. D. Frisbee and Professor Beaglehole.

A small whaleboat passage at the northern end near the village of Yato can be dangerous as the swell makes landing difficult unless you are using an inflatable. During easterly winds the anchor may be set in the pass with the aid of aluminum skiffs, with the current holding the vessel off. Otherwise you can anchor in the lee of the island on the western side where the current set must be kept in mind. Someone must be aboard the vessel at all times, maintaining a watch.

MANIHIKI ATOLL

This low-lying atoll has islets heavily treed with 21m (70') coconut palms scattered around much of the perimeter. The village of Tauhunu on the west side is marked by a sign, "Welcome to Manihiki," painted in huge letters on a corrugated iron shed at the head of a jetty. In settled conditions it is possible to land a dinghy at the jetty. There is no boat pass into the lagoon though anchorage (using two bow anchors) may be taken north of the landing in 13 to 18m (7 to 10 fathoms), coral or off the village of Tukao. Anchors may become fouled in the coral, making it necessary to dive in order to free the ground tackle. Vessels must be ready to leave at once if the wind leaves the easterly quadrant.

Since the atoll occasionally experiences droughts, water is used sparingly. With permission, water jugs may be filled at the cisterns behind the church. Bi-weekly air service links the island to Rarotonga and telephone service operates by means of satellite connections. The atoll has a population of about 500 inhabitants. The lagoon is the site of pearl farming activities and the local men are renowned divers.

RAKAHANGA

This atoll is 29 miles NNW of Manihiki. The main village, anchorage and boat pass lie near the SW end of the island. Because of its close proximity to the reef, this anchorage is safe to use only in periods of calm or settled easterly trade wind conditions. Post an anchor watch.

NASSAU ISLAND

This small island with its fringing reef is 155 miles northwest of the Suwarrow Islands. The only landing is on the reef at the northwestern corner of the island, and local advice is essential in getting ashore. A dangerous hazard in the area is Tema Reef, about 25 miles NNW of Nassau Island. The location of the reef is indicated by heavilly breakng seas.

NORTHERN COOK ISLANDS

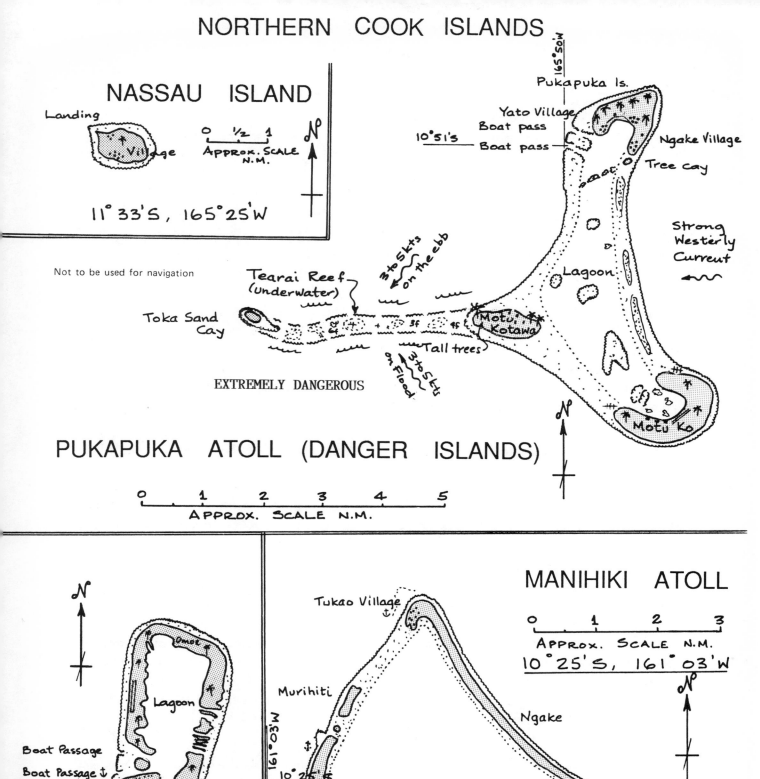

NASSAU ISLAND

Landing

Village

0 ½ 1
APPROX. SCALE N.M.

N

11°33'S, 165°25'W

Not to be used for navigation

Pukapuka Is.

165°50W

Yato Village
Boat pass

10°51'S

Boat pass

Ngake Village

Tree cay

Strong Westerly Current

Tearai Reef (underwater)

3 to 5kts on the ebb

Toka Sand Cay

3f 4f

Motu Kotawa

Lagoon

Tall trees

3 to 5kts on Flood

EXTREMELY DANGEROUS

Motu Ko

N

PUKAPUKA ATOLL (DANGER ISLANDS)

0 1 2 3 4 5
APPROX. SCALE N.M.

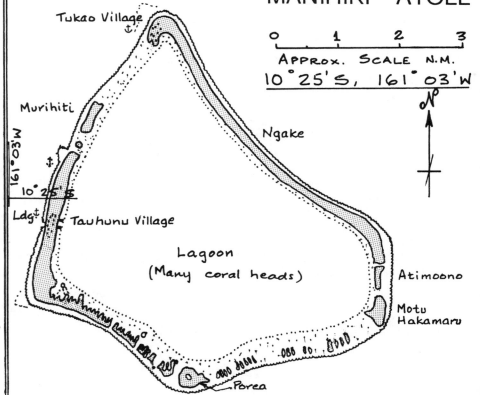

MANIHIKI ATOLL

N

Tukao Village

Omot

Lagoon

Murihiti

161°03W

Boat Passage

Boat Passage

10°02'S

161°01'W

Village

0 1 2 3
APPROX. SCALE N.M.

10°25'S

Ldg

Tauhunu Village

Ngake

0 1 2 3
APPROX. SCALE N.M.
10°25'S, 161°03'W

N

Lagoon
(Many coral heads)

Atimoono

Motu Hakamaru

Porea

RAKAHANGA ATOLL

0 1 2 3
APPROX. SCALE N.M.

PENRHYN ISLAND (TONGAREVA)

This is the northernmost of the Cook Islands, lying almost 745 miles NNE of Rarotonga and about 400 miles northeast of Suwarrow. It is an atoll with many low islets, most of which are topped with coconut palms. Three passes lead into a lagoon that has many large, visible coral heads and detached reefs with navigable water between. Black pearl farming in the lagoon makes it important to watch for and avoid the floats and lines of pearl shells, sometimes tethered just below the surface. Good anchorages are found in the lagoon.

Taruia Pass (West Pass), on the western side, is the best pass for use by cruising vessels. The channel has a depth of 5.8m (19') and is about 91m (300') wide at its narrowest part (where reef extensions on either side are visible). Tidal rips extending from the pass indicate the strength of the tidal currents which can reach 5 knots. The easiest entry is at slack water or with the first of the flood. The pass is entered on a bearing of 087° on Te Tautua village, on the eastern side of the lagoon. If the village is not clearly seen, the gap in the palms at the northern end of the village islet (between the long island and the smaller ones to the north) can be used. After entering the lagoon locate an anchorage either northeastward in the lagoon or southward off Omoka by visual navigation. **Siki Rangi (Northwest Pass)** is usable but shallower, and has a bank extending northwesterly that can cause rough seas.

The channel leading to Omoka turns to the south just east of the coral reef and a little islet, then leads through a clear passage between coral heads in the lagoon and the reef. Passage is easy in good light and poles usually mark the best route. Anchorage off the beach is preferable to tying to the rough rock wharf which has a depth of 4.2m (14') alongside. The 27m (90') coral fill dock is only 1.2m (4') deep alongside. The anchorage is studded with coral heads and an uncomfortable chop often develops during northeast to southeast winds.

Other anchorages include Ruahara, which is about midway along the north side of the atoll, about 4.5 miles northeast of Omoka; use caution because there are many coral pinnacles in this area. Many cruisers consider the spot across the lagoon, off the village of Te Tautua to be the best anchorage in the Cook Islands. There are fewer coral heads and less chop. Black pearl farming was initiated in the lagoon in 1994. It is important to watch for floats and strings of pearl oysters which are sometimes tethered just below the surface of the water. The local inhabitants are very friendly and enjoy visiting with cruisers. They often want to trade pearls for such hard to get items as sheets, towels, knives, tools and fishing gear. Takuna Pass is not recommended (except in calm conditions) because it is narrow and sometimes has breakers across the entrance.

Omoka is an official **Port of Entry** and you must check in with Health, Customs, and Agriculture officials, each of whom may wish to board the vessel. The Customs officer may keep the crew's passports until the vessel checks out and all fees have been paid. A nominal daily charge is made for anchorage in the lagoon as well as for spraying the vessel for insects by Agriculture officials. If the vessel is leaving the country an exit fee of $25 (NZ or Cook Is. currency) per person is charged. Weekly flights and sporadic shipping service connect the island to Rarotonga and worldwide telephone service operates by means of satellite connections.

Breadfruit, watermelon and fish are readily traded for. Fresh bread can be ordered from Christine early in the day for pickup at 1700.

NORTHERN COOK ISLANDS

PENRHYN ISLAND (TONGAREVA)

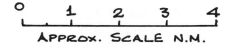

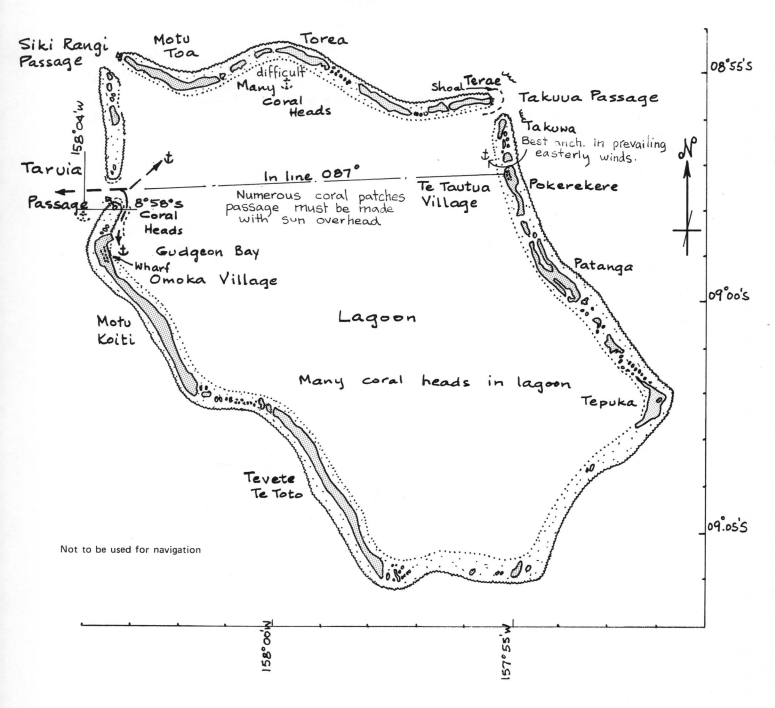

Siki Rangi Passage · Motu Toa · Torea · difficult · Many Coral Heads · Shoal Terae · Takuua Passage · Takuwa · Best anch. in prevailing easterly winds. · N · 158°04'W · Taruia · Passage · In line 087° · Numerous coral patches passage must be made with sun overhead · Te Tautua Village · Pokerekere · 8°58'S Coral Heads · Gudgeon Bay · Wharf · Omoka Village · Patanga · Motu Koiti · Lagoon · Many coral heads in lagoon · Tepuka · Tevete Te Toto · Not to be used for navigation · 08°55'S · 09°00'S · 09°.05'S · 158°00'W · 157°55'W

The islanders are devout Christians who welcome visitors to Sunday services which are worth attending to hear the haunting harmonies of their hymns. Photographs may not be taken inside the church and a dress code is strictly adhered to—women wearing dresses and hats, men in shirts and long pants.

NIUE*

First sighted by Captain Cook in 1774, this isolated island is 600 nautical miles WNW of Rarotonga and 1,100 West of Bora-Bora. It is composed of coral limestone, shaped like a two-tiered saucer that rises with thickly wooded hills to about 65m (200 ft.) above sea level. Affectionately known as "The Rock," Niue is dotted with numerous limestone caves, caverns and arches. Without streams or rivers, rainwater filters through the coral and passes into the sea completely devoid of any sediment, allowing the surrounding ocean to be crystal clear with visibility often up to 70m (230'). The dry season is from April to November and the wettest and hottest season is December to March.

Anchorage may be taken in the open roadstead on the western side of the island off the town of Alofi. Since there is no protection from westerly winds, yachts must be prepared to put to sea when a passing cold front turns the normal SE trades to the west. High winds can occur during the summer months but do not normally reach hurricane force since Niue is on the edge of the hurricane belt. The Niue Yacht Club has about 20 buoys moorings where cruisers may moor for a nominal fee (currently NZ$5/US$2.50). Because there is no sheltered harbor small boats are lifted in and out of the water by a crane located on the south side of the wharf. Dinghies from visiting yachts are also handled in this manner.

Niue is an independent nation in free association with New Zealand. The 2300 inhabitants have dual citizenship although the island administers its own affairs. "ZKN Niue Radio" monitors VHF Ch16 and 2182 from the Telecom office which operates 24 hour, facilitating reporting arrival before coming ashore.. Clearance must be completed by the captain before the rest of the crew goes ashore. The Customs office is in the town square above the landing. Customs fees are NZ$20 (about US$12) per person for both entry and departure. An Entry Permit is granted on arrival and is valid for 30 days; extensions are available from the Immigration Office. English and Nieuan are spoken. Air service to Tonga via Auckland has connections to Sidney. The currency is the New Zealand dollar. Provisions and supplies are available at supermarkets and specialty stores. Alofi also has a hospital, post office, hair salons banks and handicraft shops.

The Niue Yacht Club ZKN 4 has an operator monitoring VHF Ch 16, 60 or 61 most of the time. The Yacht Club is helpful in providing information regarding local services. To become a member of the Club and receive a burgee, there is a charge of NZ$20 (about US$12). Yacht Club members may have clean, untreated water (found on the far side of the wharf) and use toilet and shower facilities (half way up the wharf). The Niue Hotel hosts the Yacht Club and visiting cruisers are welcomed. The moorings have been established by the operators of Alofi Rentals where bikes, scooters and carscan be rented. Tel. 683-4017, e-mail: alofirenatals@sin.net.nu.

The town of Alofi is small but most services are available. Friday is market day but to get the best choice of goods plan to arrive at 0400. A small produce market is open on Tuesdays. To get the most benefit from a drive around the island it is advisable to hire a local guide. It is a full day's drive, especially if you wish to explore the caves and chasms. Before taking a guided tour ascertain the degree of physical stamina required, since visits to some caverns can be quite demanding. Niue is renowned for its spectacular diving because of the clarity of the water and wealth of marine life. Ask at Dive Niue or the Tourism Office for fishing regulations and the location of restricted areas before fishing or diving.

*Note: Niue lies west of the 165°W boundary of *Charlie's Charts of Polynesia*, but after hearing the glowing reports of cruisers about this lovely spot it has been included in this guide.

NIUE

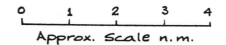

Approx. scale n.m.

Not to be used for navigation

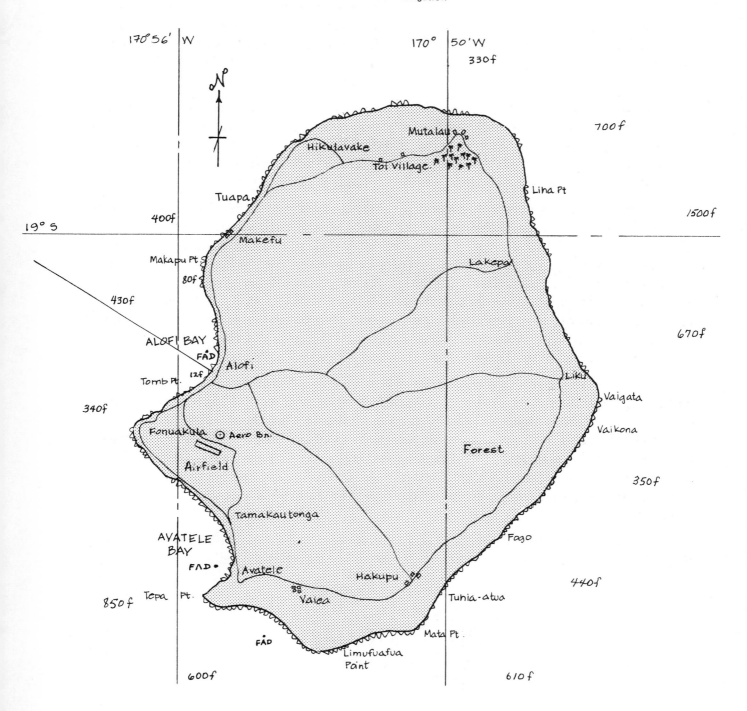

170°56′ W

170° 50′W

330f

700f

N

Hikutavake

Mutalau

Toi Village

Liha Pt

Tuapa

1500f

400f

19° S

Makefu

Makapu Pt

Lakepa

80f

430f

670f

ALOFI BAY

FÅD

Alofi

12f

Tomb Pt.

LIKU

Vaigata

340f

Vaikona

Fonuakula

Aero Bn.

Forest

350f

Airfield

Tamakautonga

Fago

AVATELE
BAY

FÅD

Avatele

Hakupu

440f

Tepa Pt.

Vaiea

Tuhia-atua

850f

600f

FÅD

Mata Pt.

Limufuafua
Point

610f

THE HAWAIIAN ISLANDS

The Hawaiian Islands lie well north of the equator but from a cultural, historic, and in an oceanic voyaging sense, they are linked to Polynesia and are therefore included in this guide. The information presented in the following section is an abbreviated version of *Charlie's Charts of the Hawaiian Islands.* Only islands having Ports of Entry are included here.

The chain of Hawaiian Islands is an extensive archipelago extending 1,500 miles consisting of 132 islands. Over 99% of the land mass is concentrated in 8 islands at the southeastern end, and of these, the island of Hawaii (the Big Island) is 60% of the total. The northwestern part has a few tiny islands with many shoals and reefs and is a wildlife preserve. Midway, a military base is the most northwesterly island.

The islands are a result of volcanic action which continues at a spot on the Pacific Plate now occupied by the Big Island. As the earth's crust has slid over this spot the other islands have moved northwesterly. Now only the Island of Hawaii is growing and in Mauna Kea and Mauna Loa its height exceeds 3,965m (13,000'). If measured from the ocean floor, their true origin, these are the tallest mountains on earth, well over 9,150m (30,000') high.

The prevailing winds are the northeast trades, which tend to be predominantly easterly. The trades are more consistent during summer months, though their velocity and direction can be affected by hurricanes or tropical disturbances in the vicinity of the islands. The trades are accelerated when passing through the channels between the islands, and this can make their transit unpleasant and sometimes difficult. The direction of the wind favors travel in a northwesterly direction up the chain, otherwise it is necessary to beat. Hilo, on the Island of Hawaii, is the most suitable departure or arrival point since travel to and from Tahiti requires the maximum easting. Hilo is the only **Port of Entry** on the Island of Hawaii, though others are located at Kahului on Maui, Honolulu on Oahu, and Nawiliwili on Kauai.

When traveling between Hawaii and the mainland of North America the most important meteorological feature is the Pacific High, a high pressure area west of North America. Sailing routes skirt this high which usually migrates northwesterly to about 38°N Latitude, 150°W Longitude in July and August, then southeasterly to about 30°N, 130° W by January and February. This is a statistical generalization and daily movements may vary. The best times for travel to and from the Hawaiian Islands are from June to August. From North America the route swings south, then west around the high; return trips to the mainland go north and then easterly around the high.

For emergency services and navigation information call the United States Coast Guard on VHF Channel 16 and change to a designated channel as request by the radio operator.

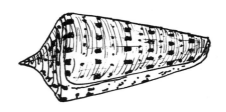

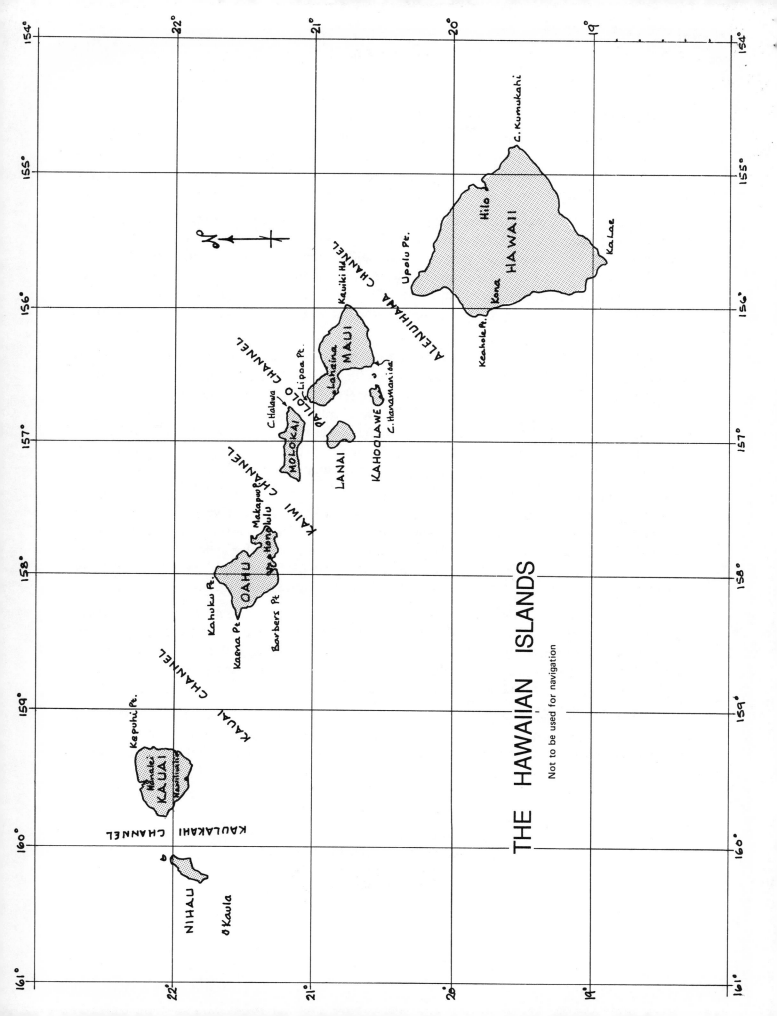

THE HAWAIIAN ISLANDS

Not to be used for navigation

THE ISLAND OF HAWAII (The Big Island)

This triangular island is the most attractive and interesting of the group. It has five volcanoes, three of which are dormant. Mauna Loa last erupted in 1975, but Kilauea's flank has erupted continuously since 1983. Bus tours operating out of both Hilo and Kailua-Kona visit Volcano National Park; this is a fascinating trip which also offers a good view of the countryside.

There is a distinct difference in climate between the two sides of the island. On the windward side, the regular rains give rise to lush green growth and create windy, cool and humid conditions. On the leeward side, it is dry, hot, and has gentle breezes, at times insufficient for sailing. In between, lie the volcanic uplands with winter snow on the highest slopes. Sugar cane, ranching and tourism are the main industries. The island, however, retains a rural charm that is missing in others of the group, and the people, particularly in Hilo, are very friendly and helpful.

The three main capes of the island are each important features. Cape Kumukahi is the easternmost point and is a low, black lava mass behind which are cinder cones and several craters. A light is shown from a tall mast tower on the point. The trade wind tends to split at this cape with part going southwesterly down the lower eastern side of the island, and the rest going northwesterly along the upper coast. The offshore current behaves in a similar fashion. From Cape Kumukahi to Upolu Point at the northern end of the island is a distance of 75 miles. The intervening coast is steep and bold; an offing of 2 miles avoids all dangers. Hilo Bay is about 19 miles northwest of Cape Kumukahi and is the major indentation on this coast.

It is best to work your way up the west side of the Big Island to Upolu before heading across the Alenuihaha Channel to Maui. Ka Lae, the southern cape, is about 63 miles southwest of Cape Kumukahi. It is a windy area with disturbed waters for the onshore current sets against the wind near the cape. Passage from Hilo to the Kona Coast generally means passing Ka Lae in the early morning hours. The cape should be given a berth of about 2.5 miles and the turn made in a slow, gradual fashion, as the seas allow, to avoid any chance of a knockdown.

Upolu Point is about 95 miles north of Ka Lae when the route follows the island's western coast. It resembles many of the nearby bluffs, but can be recognized by the radio towers, buildings and aero beacon. Alenuihaha Channel separates Upolu Point on Hawaii from the island of Maui, 426 miles to the north. When the trade winds are strong the crossing can be rough because the winds tend to accelerate at the channel's edges.

Historically, Hawaiian consolidation occurred under Chief Kamehameha I from the Kohala area. Honaunau is a restored City of Refuge and National Historical Park. Equally significant is Kealakekua Bay, where Captain Cook anchored, died and was later buried at sea.

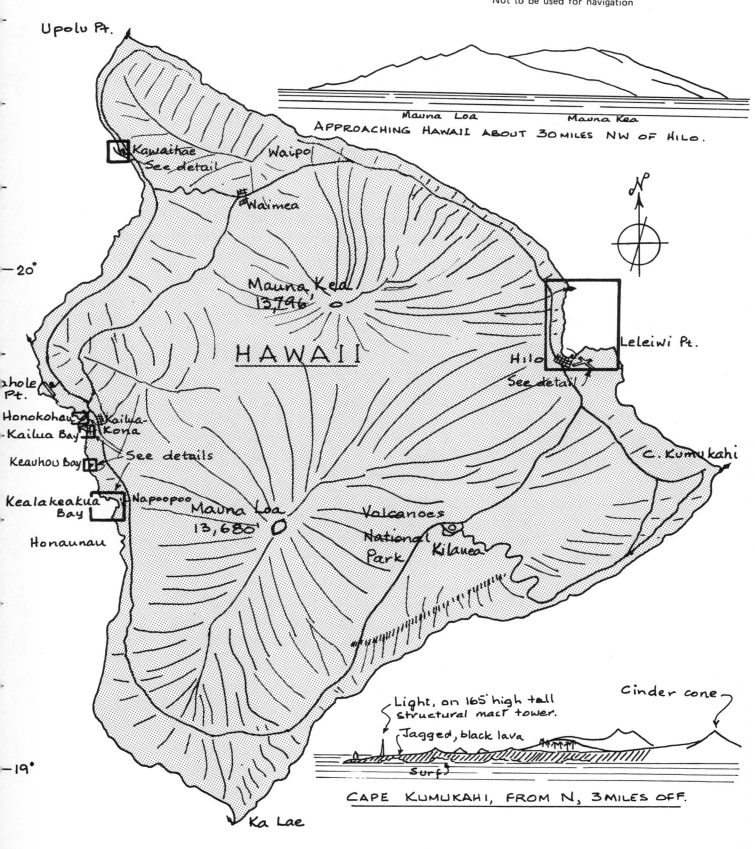

ISLAND OF HAWAII
(The Big Island)

Not to be used for navigation

Upolu Pt.

Mauna Loa   Mauna Kea
APPROACHING HAWAII ABOUT 30 MILES NW OF HILO.

Kawaihae
See detail

Waipo

Waimea

N

—20°

Mauna Kea
13,796'

HAWAII

Leleiwi Pt.

Hilo
See detail

ahole
Pt.

Honokohau
-Kailua Bay

Kailua-
Kona

See details

C. Kumukahi

Keauhou Bay

Kealakeakua
Bay

Napoopoo

Mauna Loa
13,680'

Volcanoes

Honaunau

National
Park

Kilauea

Light, on 165' high tall
structural mast tower.

Cinder cone

Jagged, black lava

—19°

Surf

CAPE KUMUKAHI, FROM N, 3 MILES OFF.

Ka Lae

156°   155°

HILO

This is a **Port of Entry,** the largest city and only port on the east side of the Island of Hawaii. If this is the vessel's first landfall in the islands it is mandatory that entrance be made at Hilo before proceeding further on the Big Island (whether the vessel is of foreign registry or not.)

Hilo Bay is the main indentation on the northeast side of Hawaii. About 1.5 miles north of the breakwater protected entrance is a lighthouse at Paukaa Point, another is about 5 miles further north at Pepeekeo Point, marking the northwestern point of Hilo Bay. The port of Hilo is protected by a long breakwater built on Blonde Reef. A weak light is at the end of the breakwater and a lighted bell buoy marks the end of the reef.

Your first entry to Hilo is best undertaken during daylight since the number of lights in the area can be confusing. In rainy weather, visibility is often greatly reduced and even on a hazy day landmarks are not clear until the island is closely approached. The swell breaks heavily on the reef and breakwater, especially when the trade winds are strong. Buoys mark the passage into the harbor behind the breakwater. Transient vessels should proceed to Radio Bay as Reed's Bay is restricted to use by local boats.

The small boat harbor is in Radio Bay, beyond the piers and big ship facilities; it is the only dedicated transient facility in the State. Moorage is available Med-style to the south wall or anchor; the holding is good and though the harbor is subject to some surge, it is the safest place to moor during storms. Most boaters pull the vessel a little farther off the quay during heavy weather to avoid any backwash.

Only the skipper is allowed to leave the vessel to report to the Harbormaster, Agriculture, and US Customs (which is located in a building just outside the port gates.) An entry fee of $25 US per boat is charged to foreign and US vessels (which have been out of the country.) Opposite the Customs Office is a small store; laundromat and shower facilities are near the docks. It is a pleasant walk to stores and restaurants downtown.

The Harbormaster controls the basin and collects moorage fees. Rates are set by the State and there is a 30-day maximum stay in any State-run harbor although time extensions are possible during the off season. A refundable $50 deposit is collected for keys to washroom and shower facilities.

Fuel may be purchased at service stations ashore and brought to the vessel in jerry cans. "Akin Petroleum" will deliver fuel to the dock if a minimum of 200 gallons is ordered. Several vessels may pool their needs and thereby avoid juggling jerry cans. Although equipment and repair facilities are limited, Honolulu and California can be contacted by telephone and needed items can be delivered by UPS directly to Radio Bay or in care of the Hilo Harbor Office which can also be used as a mail drop.

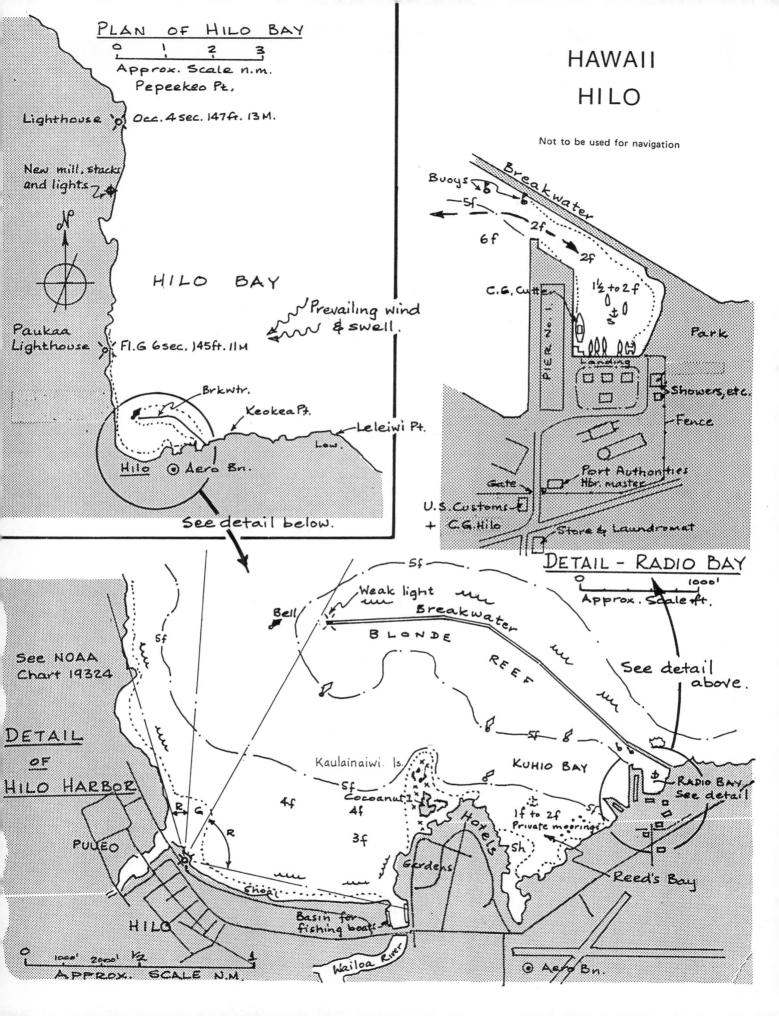

PLAN OF HILO BAY

0   1   2   3
Approx. Scale n.m.

Pepeekeo Pt.

Lighthouse Occ. 4 sec. 147 ft. 13 M.

New mill, stacks
and lights

N

HILO BAY

Prevailing wind
& swell.

Paukaa
Lighthouse Fl.G 6 sec. 145 ft. 11 M

Brkwtr.

Keokea Pt.

Leleiwi Pt.

Low.

Hilo   Aero Bn.

See detail below.

HAWAII
HILO

Not to be used for navigation

Buoys

Breakwater

5f

2f

6f   2f   2f

C.G. Cutter   1½ to 2f

Park

Pier No. 1

Landing

Showers, etc.

Fence

Port Authorities
Hbr. master

Gate

U.S. Customs
+ C.G. Hilo

Store & Laundromat

DETAIL – RADIO BAY

0   1000'
Approx. Scale ft.

5f

Weak light

Breakwater

Bell

B L O N D E   R E E F

See detail
above.

See NOAA
Chart 19324

5f

5f

DETAIL
OF
HILO HARBOR

Kaulainaiwi Is.

KUHIO BAY

5f

5f

Cocoanut I.

4f

4f

1f to 2f
Private moorings

RADIO BAY
See detail

R G

R

Hotels

PULEO

3f

Gardens

Sh

Reed's Bay

HILO

Shoal

Basin for
fishing boats

0   1000' 2000' ½
APPROX. SCALE N.M.

Wailoa River

Aero Bn.

KEALAKEKUA BAY (Kealakekua means "Pathway of the God")

This wide, open bay is dominated by steep, high cliffs along its northern side and the volcano's gentle slopes come down to the sea beyond. The cliffs are visible many miles to the south as one travels northward on the Kona Coast in normally calm conditions.

Much of the bay is a Marine Life Conservation District and Underwater Park and is divided into two zones. Though it is the best natural anchorage in the Hawaiian Islands, anchorage is no longer permitted inside the underwater park; visitors must anchor south of the park boundary. Two commercial cruise boats have permits to use the permanent moorings in Kaawaloa Cove near the Cook monument and commercial fishing boats belonging to a long established family have been granted special status in Zone B.

A concrete dock built at right angles to the beach allows easy access to the coastal road and village of Napoopoo where a walk up the hill leads to coffee plantations and mills. Dinghies must be lifted ashore or they bump heavily against the rough dock. Tourists snorkel off the dock but a better spot is in Kaawaloa Cove near <u>Captain Cook's Monument,</u> where a small dock allows shore access by dinghy. The nearby buoys are used by tourist boats from Kailua Pier and Keauhou Small Boat Harbor.

The paved road over lava beds to the south leads to the National Historical Park of Pu'uhonua 0 Honaunau: Place of Refuge of Honaunau. A visit to this fascinating park is well worth the long, hot walk but with luck, a kind motorist may offer a ride, or you can take a tour bus from Kailua. The informative presentation gives you an idea of what life was like on the islands prior to the arrival of Europeans in the 1700s. It is the site of a once sacred sanctuary for those who had broken the sacred laws (kapu) or were defeated warriors. Death was the price to be paid unless the accused could reach the refuge where a brief ceremony of absolution was performed by a priest and the offender could return to normal life at home. In the case of enemy warriors, they could wait until the battle was over and, provided allegiance was sworn to the victor, all was forgiven. A walk up the hill from Napoopoo leads to coffee plantations and mills.

Kaawaloa Cove has a tragic history. It was here that Captain Cook was killed in 1779. A monument erected in his honor is in the cove. It was the unfortunate chance of his landing here on the festival of Lono, and becoming associated with the god by the priests (for their own ends) that ultimately led to his death.

CAPTAIN COOK'S MEMORIAL, KAAWALOA COVE.

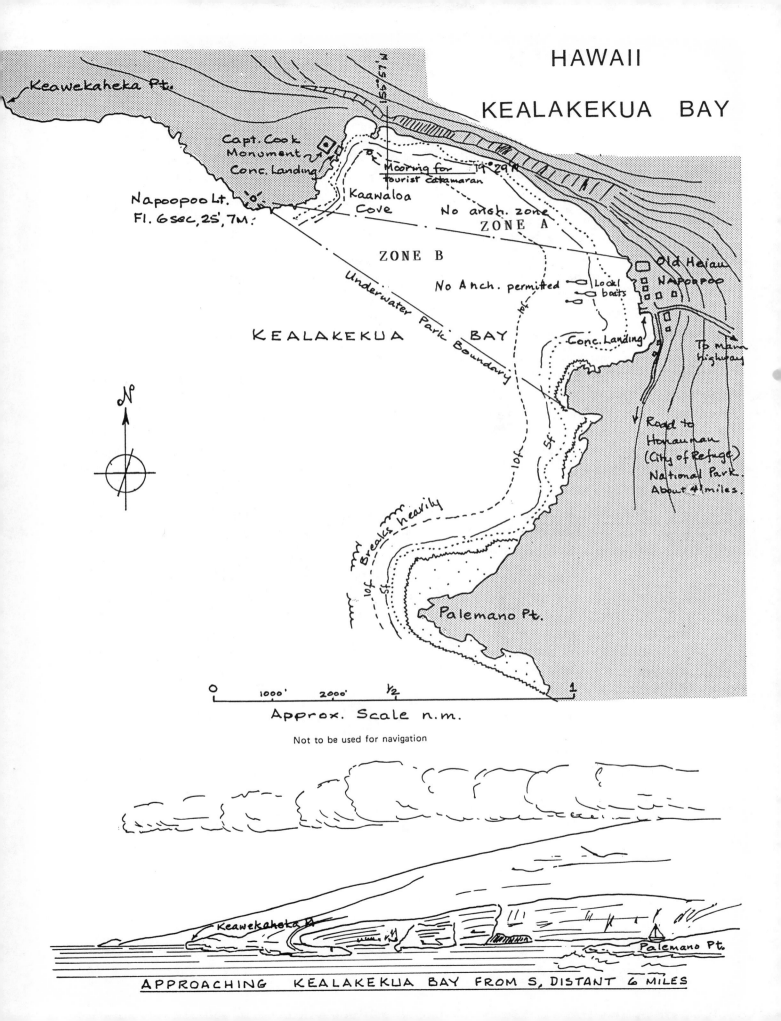

HAWAII

KEALAKEKUA BAY

Keawekaheka Pt.

Capt. Cook
Monument
Conc. Landing

Napoopoo Lt.
Fl. 6sec, 25', 7M.

155'57'W

14°29'N

Mooring for
tourist catamaran

Kaawaloa
Cove

No anch. zone
ZONE A

ZONE B

No Anch. permitted

Local
boats

Old Heiau

NAPOOPOO

KEALAKEKUA

Underwater Park Boundary

BAY

Conc. Landing

To Main
Highway

10f

5f

Road to
Honaunau
(City of Refuge)
National Park.
About 4½ miles.

Breaks heavily

10f

5f

Palemano Pt.

N

0   1000'   2000'   ½   1

Approx. Scale n.m.

Not to be used for navigation

Keawekaheka Pt.

Palemano Pt.

APPROACHING   KEALAKEKUA   BAY   FROM   S, DISTANT   6 MILES

KAILUA BAY and HONOKOHAU HARBOR

The "Gold Coast" of Kona, the tourist zone, commences soon after leaving Kealakekua Bay.   About 6.5 miles to the north is Keahou Bay, a small cove with the Kona Surf Hotel dominating its southern point.   The inner part of the cove is occupied by local boats, leaving only the somewhat exposed entrance for transient vessels.

Kailua Bay, 5.5 miles further north, is the site of the tourist Mecca of Kailua-Kona.   The 'harbor' is heavily used by tourist vessels, and its long pier is mainly for their use.   Other vessels may use the pier for up to one hour for loading.   Occasionally one may be allowed to stay longer, after hours, with permission from the Harbormaster's office at Honokohau.   A satellite harbor office is at the north end of the pier.   In addition to many visitor facilities there are tackle shops, hardware and marine repair services.   The only available area for anchorage is far from shore, exposed to the swell, and the holding is poor on rocky bottom; it is not recommended.

Two miles to the north around Kaiwi Point is the man~made harbor of **Honokohau** which was blasted out of the lava.   The harbor is entered from an offshore buoy on a leading light, with a sharp turn to starboard into a wave dissipating basin; then turn to port through a short channel to the main basin.   All slips are rented to local vessels, though the harbormaster rents space to transients on a temporary basis when space is available.   Thus, reservations are not possible and transients must call him on VHF Ch. 16 to check the availability of space.   Fueling is best done in the early part of the day, because after 1700 the sportsfishing fleet returns and the fuel dock area becomes congested.   A small convenience store is located above the fuel dock.

The building at the east end of the basin is shared by the office of the District Manager and the Harbormaster.   Restrooms are located adjacent to the harbor and a small building on the south side has barrels for oil disposal.

On the north side of the harbor is Kona Marlin Center which has a an excellent reputation as a shipyard.   Painting, welding, refrigeration service, electronic repairs and hull repairs on wood and fiberglass vessels are available in the yard or at a nearby industrial park.   Shops in the center have wide variety of boat supplies as well as some groceries, fishing gear, and tourist sundries.   Plans call for expansion of dry storage and repair facilities across the road to the northeast.   For information on the availability of dry storage space or shipyard work phone (808) 329-7896.

Kawaihae Harbor is about 19 miles north.   It has a small boat basin within the breakwater and an anchorage area is outside.   While getting there is usually easy, this is the area of the "Mumuku" winds.   These strong trade winds funnel through the mountain gap at the valley of Waimea and blow with great velocity in the vicinity of Kawaihae.   They can make the passage to Kawaihae impossible; winds may reach 60 knots or more and may last for a day.   In addition to the steep seas raised, a very strong northward current is created along the coast.

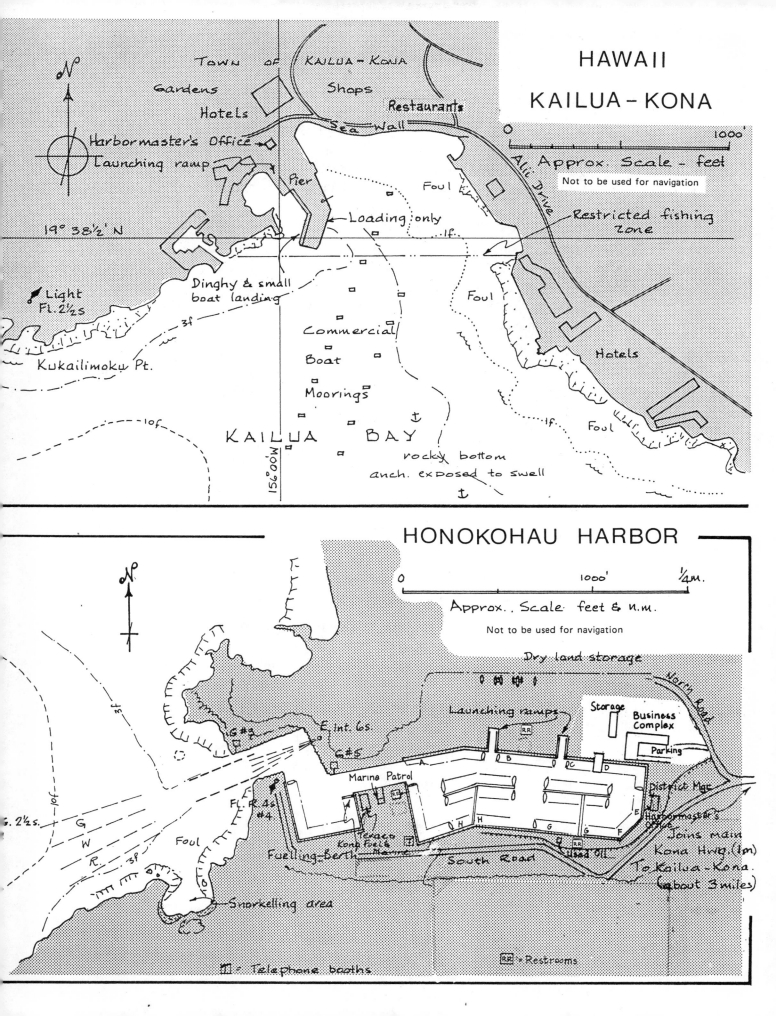

HAWAII
KAILUA - KONA

Town of KAILUA - KONA
Gardens   Shops
Hotels
Restaurants
Sea Wall

Harbormaster's Office
Launching ramp
Pier

Loading only

Foul

0   1000'
Approx. Scale - feet
Not to be used for navigation

Restricted fishing zone

Alii Drive

19° 38½' N

Light
Fl. 2½ s

Dinghy & small boat landing

Kukailimoku Pt.

3f

Commercial
Boat
Moorings

Foul

Hotels

Foul

10f

KAILUA   BAY

156°00'W

rocky bottom
anch. exposed to swell

HONOKOHAU HARBOR

0   1000'   ¼ M.
Approx. Scale feet & n.m.
Not to be used for navigation

Dry land storage

Launching ramps
Storage

Business Complex

Parking

North Road

3f

G #3

F Int. 6s

G #5

Marine Patrol

Fl. R 4s
#4

Kona Fuels

Texaco Marine

Fuelling Berth

A
B
C
D

District Mgr
Harbormaster's Office

s. 2½ s.
G
W
R   3f
10f

Foul

Telephone booths

E
H H
G
F

RR
Used Oil

South Road

Joins main Kona Hwy. (1m)
To Kailua - Kona (about 3 miles)

Snorkelling area

= Telephone booths

RR = Restrooms

MOLOKINI and MAUI

Since most vessels proceed from the Big Island of Hawaii to the bright lights of Honolulu on the island of Oahu, they will cross Alenuihaha Channel, and can visit Molokini and Lahaina enroute. The channel crossing can be eased by waiting for light trade winds. Staying in the lee of Hawaii until reaching Upolu Point, achieves the best angle to seas and winds in the channel.

Once the vessel has passed Cape Hanamainoa on the southwest corner of the Island of Maui, the wind's strength is reduced. A short distance further is Molokini Island, a remnant of a crater, where a temporary stop may be made to enjoy the diving. Seventeen day-use moorings are available on a first-come, first-serve basis. Unfortunately, some cruise boats behave as if they own certain moorings and they have been known to make cruisers feel like intruders. The island is a Bird Sanctuary and the waters are a Marine Life Conservation Area where fishing and coral collecting are prohibited.

Lahaina is about 17 miles northwest of Molokini. The entrance to the harbor has reefs on either side which are marked by privately maintained buoys. At the entrance there is a sharp turn to starboard which can be difficult to carry out in rough "Kona" weather. The (museum) brig, *Carthaginian II* occupies the outer berth of the wharf on the south side of the entrance. The small boat harbor is literally jammed from end to end with commercial and pleasure craft; space is seldom available for transient vessels. This is a crowded, tourist-oriented town, parts of which are maintained as a National Historic Landmark emphasizing its history during the days of whaling.

Most transient vessels anchor in the open roadstead off Lahaina, much as the whaling fleet did in the early 1800s. The designated anchorage area is too small, and is filled with many permanent moorings. Vessels anchor over a wide area in about 16m (9 fathoms), poor holding bottom, a little sand over rock or coral. Though summer trade winds are strong elsewhere, the anchorage is rolly, but reasonably secure; it is not uncommon for vessels to drag. During Kona storms marked by southerly winds, the roadstead is exposed and unsafe.

An alternative anchorage is about 1 mile to the northwest, around Puunoa Point, off the remains of Mala Wharf. This is sometimes preferred to the outer limits of the Lahaina Roadstead since there are several good sandy spots. Landing and boat launching facilities are maintained by the State in the lee of the old wharf. It is about a .5 mile walk to Lahaina.

The main attractions in Maui are its beautiful beaches and Haleakala National Park, the site of the largest crater in the world. This is an all-day trip by car up a steep and winding road to the crater's edge at an altitude of 3,056m (10,025'). Interesting varieties of vegetation are seen on a hike to the higher altitudes and on a clear day the view is spectacular. Bring a heavy sweater for cold winds are normal at the summit.

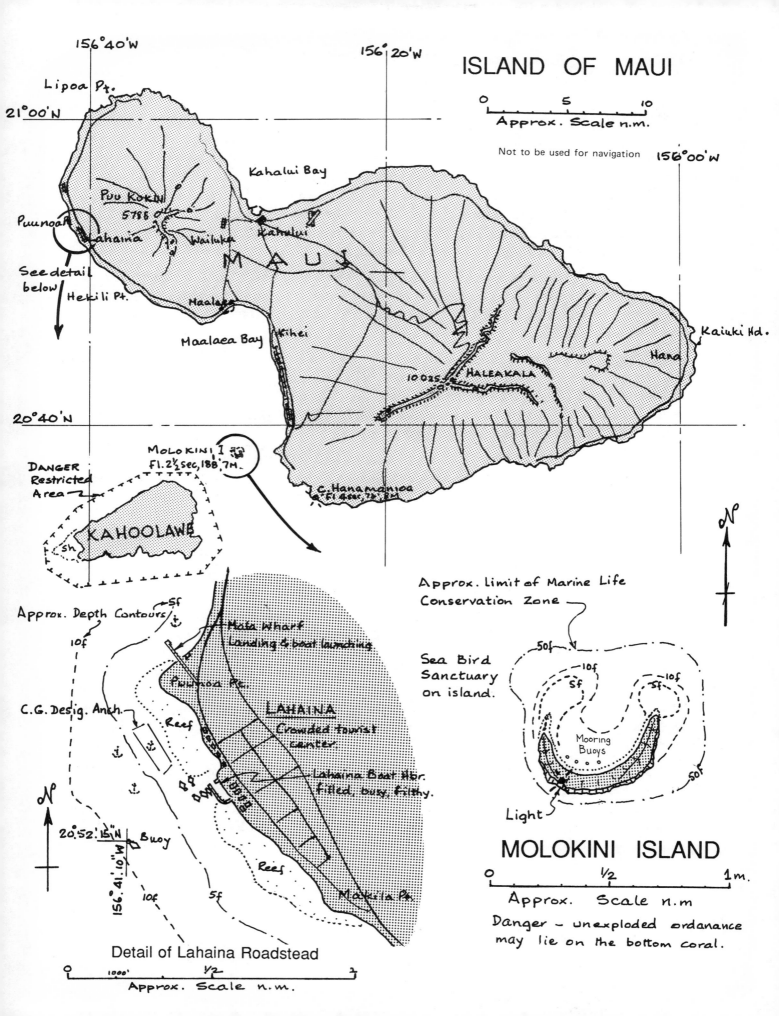

ISLAND OF MAUI

0   5   10
Approx. Scale n.m.

Not to be used for navigation

156°40'W

156°20'W

156°00'W

21°00'N

Lipoa Pt.

Kahalui Bay

Puu Kokini
5788

Puunoa
Lahaina

Wailuku

Kahului

MAUI

See detail
below

Hekili Pt.

Maalaea

Kihei

Kaiuki Hd.

Maalaea Bay

Hana

10025   HALEAKALA

20°40'N

MOLOKINI I
Fl. 2½ sec, 188', 7M.

DANGER
Restricted
Area

KAHOOLAWE

Sh

C. Hanamanioa
Fl. 4 sec, 72', 24

Detail of Lahaina Roadstead

Approx. Depth Contours

5f

10f

C.G. Desig. Anch.

Reef

Puunoa Pt.

Mala Wharf
Landing & boat launching

LAHAINA
Crowded tourist
center

Lahaina Boat Hbr.
filled, busy, filthy.

20.52.'15"N

Buoy

156° 41.'10"W

10f

5f

Reef

Makila Pt.

0   1000'   ½
Approx. Scale n.m.

MOLOKINI ISLAND

Approx. limit of Marine Life
Conservation Zone

Sea Bird
Sanctuary
on island.

50f

10f

10f

5f

5f

Mooring
Buoys

50f

Light

0   ½   1 m.
Approx. Scale n.m
Danger — unexploded ordanance
may lie on the bottom coral.

HONOLULU

The island of Oahu has less than 10% of the land area of the Hawaiian Islands but it is home for more than 80% of the population. The city of Honolulu accounts for much of the population as it is the state center for communications, transportation, and business and includes Waikiki Beach, which is a major tourist attraction. Crowded, rushed and extremely tourist oriented, it nevertheless attracts people from all over the world. Honolulu is a **Port of Entry**. Only a brief description follows; for greater details on lights, harbor regulations, mooring areas, etc. refer to the *US Coast Pilot* or *Charlie's Charts of the Hawaiian Islands*.

CAUTION: When approaching Honolulu it is essential not to confuse Koko Head for Diamond Head. To be on the safe side, it is prudent to approach during daylight so as not to add to the list of vessels which have been lost by entering Maunalua Bay instead of Mamala Bay where Honolulu is located.

Many vessels come to Honolulu where they may live aboard their vessel for up to 90 days if space is available and a permit has been issued. The two small boat harbors of Ala Wai Yacht Harbor and Keehi Lagoon have limited space for transient vessels. Kewalo Basin is a commercial basin and has fuel docks and repair yards where work can be done. A few small facilities are found outside Honolulu but these are usually filled with local vessels.

Ala Wai Yacht Harbor is 2.5 miles northwest of Diamond Head, a well-known landmark. The yacht harbor is entered through an angled channel. Within the main breakwater is a turning basin and fuel dock where one can complete check-in details and determine if any berths are vacant. Thirty transient slips are available on the outer dock on a first-come, first-serve basis. A permit must be obtained from the Harbormaster who collects moorage fees. A small repair yard is in the harbor. Behind the Ala Wai Harbor offices is a huge shopping center, Ala Moana Shopping Center. Easy access to an excellent bus system is on Ala Moana Boulevard, a major nearby thoroughfare.

Keehi Lagoon is a collecting spot for transient yachts since it is the only available large, designated anchorage area and has good holding mud. Access is through the reef at Kalihi Channel where a daylight entrance is strongly advised. Moorage in the Lagoon is controlled by the State Marina which has offices opposite the anchorage. A fee is charged for dinghy docking and may also he assessed for anchorage. Negative aspects of a stay here are the noise of air traffic from the adjacent airport and the dust and dirt of commercial operations along the busy waterfront. But since this is likely to be the only available place to moor, discomforts have to be tolerated.

A few miles to the west is the entrance to the excellent shelter at Pearl Harbor. The harbor is closed to civilian traffic and navigation in the proximity of the entrance channel is prohibited. Only retired military and those on active duty are allowed to moor at the Kaneohe Marine Corps Air Station (KMCAS) facilities.

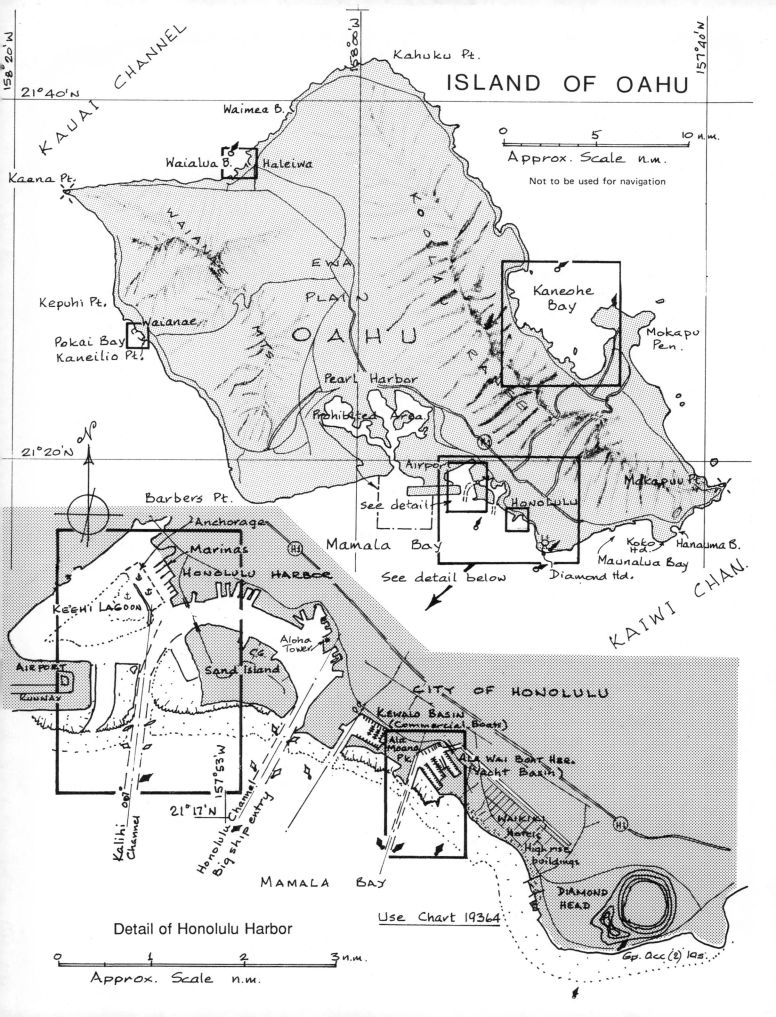

ISLAND OF OAHU

Kahuku Pt.

Waimea B.

KAUAI CHANNEL

Waialua B. Haleiwa

Kaena Pt.

Kepuhi Pt.

Waianae

Pokai Bay
Kaneilio Pt.

0   5   10 n.m.

Approx. Scale n.m.

Not to be used for navigation

WAIANAE

EWA

OAHU

PLAIN

Kaneohe
Bay

Mokapu
Pen.

Pearl Harbor

Prohibited Area.

21°20'N

Airport

see detail

HONOLULU

Makapuu Pt.

Koko
Hd.   Hanauma B.

Maunalua Bay

Diamond Hd.

Mamala Bay

See detail below

KAIWI CHAN.

Barbers Pt.

Anchorage

Marinas

HONOLULU HARBOR

KE'EHI LAGOON

AIRPORT

RUNWAY

Aloha
Tower

Sand Island

CITY OF HONOLULU

KEWALO BASIN
(Commercial Boats)

Ala
Moana
Pt.

ALA WAI BOAT HBR.
(Yacht Basin)

WAIKIKI
Hotels
High rise
buildings

Kalihi Channel

Honolulu Channel
Big ship entry

157°53'W

21°17'N

MAMALA BAY

Use Chart 19364

DIAMOND
HEAD

Gp. Occ (2) 10s.

Detail of Honolulu Harbor

0   1   2   3 n.m.

Approx. Scale n.m.

THE ISLAND of KAUAI

Kauai is 63 miles WNW of Oahu, across Kauai Channel. It is the northernmost major inhabited Hawaiian Island, only the tiny islands and rocks of the Northwestern Archipelago extend beyond it. It has a central high point of about 1,600m (5,250'); the gentle slopes and gulches of the south and east become steep and rugged ridges on the north and west sides. The average annual rainfall at Mount Waialeale is 1,173cm (460"), yet the coastal areas get only a fraction of that amount.

The trade winds that bring the rain impinge on and divide along the northeastern side of the island, then follow the north and south coasts to meet southwest of the island. Thus at Waimea on the southwest coast, there may be calms or land breezes while strong trades are blowing offshore. The acceleration of the trades is most often experienced off the northwestern coast where they are pinched against the steep Na Pali coast.

Vessels cruising the Hawaiian Island chain usually make their first stop on Kauai at Nawiliwili Harbor. This is the principal port of the island and is located on the southeastern coast. The main town of Lihue is 2 miles away and the airport is nearby.

Beautiful Hanalei Bay is on the north coast and it is often the last, most northerly stop before vessels leave the Islands to sail to the mainland. When entering this open bay, give a wide berth to the extensive reefs off the northeastern corner. Anchorage in 5 - 6 fathoms may be taken off the old wharf which is south of the massive Sheraton Hotel and Hanalei River mouth. To the west are the steep cliffs and narrow hidden valleys of the Na Pali Coast which offer spectacular views and intriguing hiking trails.

On the south coast of the island is Port Allen, the second port of the island, located in Hanapepe Bay. A small boat harbor is located here. A few miles further to the northwest at Waimea Bay, is the open roadstead where Captain Cook made his first landing in these islands in January, 1778. Behind the bay is Waimea Canyon with steep walls, deep gorges, and many waterfalls.

NIHAU

To the southwest, across 15 miles of Kaulakahi Channel lies Nihau, the Forbidden Island. The Robinson family owns and operates a cattle ranch on the entire island. They have forbidden intrusions for over a century in an effort to preserve the old Hawaiian way of life. Fewer than 300 people live on the island, while the Robinson family lives on Kauai on an estate surrounded by high barriers lined with bougainvillea.

Niihau has a 305m (1,000') tableland at the center, with lower coastal strips on each end. The small, steep island of Lehua lies off the northeast end, while Kaula Island, a military area, lies 19 miles southwest of Niihau and is a military area. The southern tip if Niihau is a small, steep hill often mistaken for Kaula Island. There are no harbors on the island, nor is landing permitted though fishing boats anchor and rest in the lee of the island.

ISLAND OF KAUAI

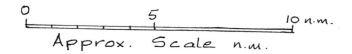

Approx. Scale n.m.

Not to be used for navigation

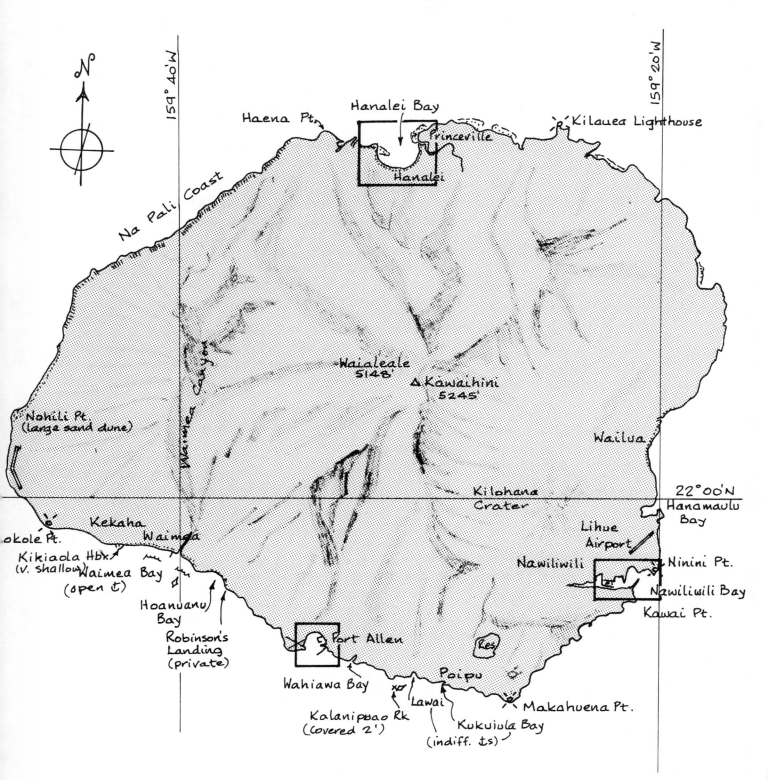

N

159° 40'W

159° 20'W

Hanalei Bay

Haena Pt.

Kilauea Lighthouse

Princeville

Hanalei

Na Pali Coast

Waimea Canyon

*Waialeale
5148'

△ Kawaihini
5245'

Nohili Pt.
(large sand dune)

Wailua

Kilohana
Crater

22° 00'N

Hanamaulu
Bay

Kekaha

okolē Pt.

Waimea

Lihue
Airport

Ninini Pt.

Kikiaola Hbr.
(v. shallow) Waimea Bay
(open ⊥)

Nawiliwili

Nawiliwili Bay

Kawai Pt.

Hoanuanu
Bay

Robinson's
Landing
(private)

Port Allen

Res.

Wahiawa Bay

Poipu

Lawai

Makahuena Pt.

Kalanipoao Rk
(covered 2')

Kukuiula Bay
(indiff. ⊥s)

NAWILIWILI HARBOR

This **Port of Entry** is located on the southeast side of Kauai and has a part-time Customs officer who can be called from the Harbormaster's office if a vessel is departing Hawaiian waters. The outer entrance to Nawiliwili Bay is between Carter Point and Ninini Point which is .75 miles to the northeast. The loom of the lighthouse at Ninini Point can he seen many miles at sea. The land runs westerly for .75 miles to Kukii Point where a smaller light is located on the shelf below the bluff.

Kukii Point lies north of Carter Point. A rock breakwater extends northeastward from Carter Point making the harbor entrance about .2 miles wide. A light is exhibited at the end of the breakwater where interlocking concrete bars give it a spiky appearance. Day range markers on two tanks within the harbor, and a large buttressed warehouse on a bluff above the wharf are clearly visible. A low sea wall in front of the wharf appears to run across the opening, but once past the entrance, a sharp turn to the south, then again to the west (after rounding the tip of the sea wall) takes a vessel deep into the harbor. This reversed "S" turn is not difficult for small vessels but can be challenging for skippers of large vessels. Approval for mooring rests with the harbormaster who works from the State Harbor Office behind the wharf area. He may be contacted on VHF 16.

The small craft basin lies behind a second breakwater about .5 miles into the harbor. The main pier with berths can accommodate up to 14 vessels, while multi-hulls and smaller vessels with shallow drafts can anchor in the wide space beyond.

Buoys for local charter boats are in line on the south side of the harbor, and vessels can also anchor behind them in Huleia Stream. Caution is needed in this area for the bottom shoals rapidly. When space is limited, a vessel may anchor in the bight north of the main breakwater, off the hotel and beach, though any place outside the small craft breakwater is subject to wind and surge.

Some shops, restaurants, and a small marine supply store are at the north end of the harbor. For major shopping or laundry and other services it is necessary to walk or hitch a ride for 2 miles up Rice Street to the town of Lihue.

The southern tip of Kauai at Makahuena Point, is 7 miles southwest of Nawiliwili. A light is shown here and a tall Loran tower is conspicuous. Avoid Koba Landing just beyond the point as it is not usable.

Kukuiula Bay, 3 miles west of Makahuena Point, has a small breakwater and can be used as an anchorage in good weather. It is affected by surge and is open to infrequent Kona storms from the south. Because seas break on the reef in front of and beyond the breakwater, on entry it is necessary to swing wide around it to keep to the center of the entrance. Local attractions are a blowhole and Lawai Bay which was featured in the TV series, "Fantasy Island."

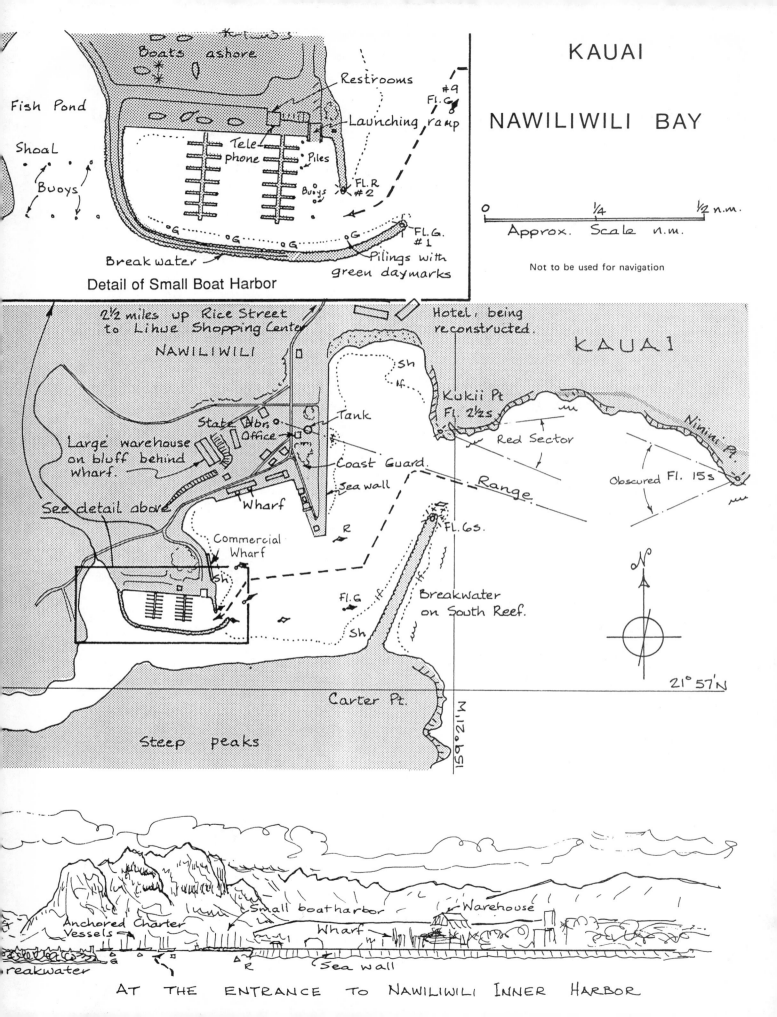

KAUAI

NAWILIWILI BAY

Detail of Small Boat Harbor

Boats ashore
Fish Pond
Shoal
Buoys
Restrooms
Launching ramp
Telephone
Piles
Buoys
Fl. R #2
#9 Fl. G
Fl. G. #1
Breakwater
Pilings with green daymarks
G G G G G

0   ¼   ½ n.m.
Approx. Scale n.m.

Not to be used for navigation

2½ miles up Rice Street to Lihue Shopping Center
NAWILIWILI
Hotel, being reconstructed.
KAUAI
Sh Hf
Kukii Pt Fl. 2½s
Red Sector
Ninini Pt.
Obscured Fl. 15s
State Hbr. Office
Tank
Large warehouse on bluff behind wharf.
Coast Guard.
Sea wall
Range
See detail above
Wharf
R
Fl. 6s.
Commercial Wharf
Sh
Fl. G Hf
Breakwater on South Reef.
Sh
N
21° 57'N
Carter Pt.
159° 21' W
Steep peaks

Anchored Charter Vessels
Small boat harbor
Warehouse
Wharf
Sea wall
R
reakwater

AT THE ENTRANCE TO NAWILIWILI INNER HARBOR

INDEX

APPENDIX I: UNIFORM LATERAL SYSTEM

Fairways and Channels

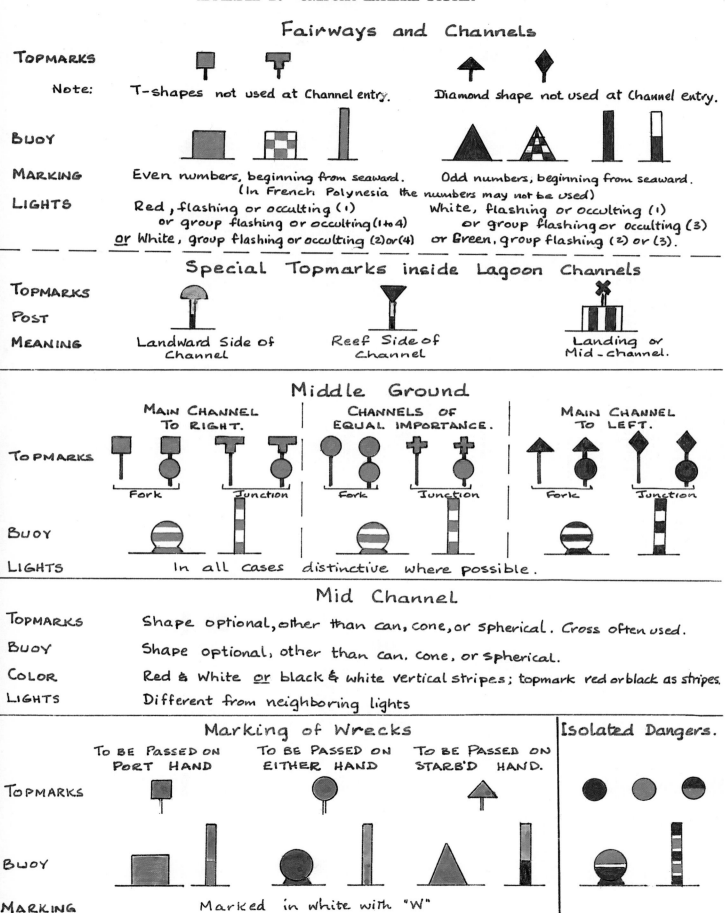

TOPMARKS

Note: T-shapes not used at Channel entry.   Diamond shape not used at Channel entry.

BUOY

MARKING   Even numbers, beginning from seaward.   Odd numbers, beginning from seaward.
(In French Polynesia the numbers may not be used)

LIGHTS   Red, flashing or occulting (1)   White, flashing or occulting (1)
or group flashing or occulting (1 to 4)   or group flashing or occulting (3)
<u>or</u> White, group flashing or occulting (2) or (4)   or Green, group flashing (2) or (3).

Special Topmarks inside Lagoon Channels

TOPMARKS
POST
MEANING   Landward Side of Channel   Reef Side of Channel   Landing or Mid-channel.

Middle Ground

	MAIN CHANNEL TO RIGHT.	CHANNELS OF EQUAL IMPORTANCE.	MAIN CHANNEL TO LEFT.

TOPMARKS   Fork   Junction   Fork   Junction   Fork   Junction

BUOY

LIGHTS   In all cases distinctive where possible.

Mid Channel

TOPMARKS   Shape optional, other than can, cone, or spherical. Cross often used.
BUOY   Shape optional, other than can, cone, or spherical.
COLOR   Red & White <u>or</u> black & white vertical stripes; topmark red or black as stripes.
LIGHTS   Different from neighboring lights

Marking of Wrecks   ## Isolated Dangers.

	TO BE PASSED ON PORT HAND	TO BE PASSED ON EITHER HAND	TO BE PASSED ON STARB'D HAND.	

TOPMARKS

BUOY

MARKING   Marked in white with "W"

LIGHTS   Green, Gp.Fl.(2)   Green, occulting(1)   Green, Gp.Fl.(3)   White or red, rhythmic.

APPENDIX II: U.S. AIDS TO NAVIGATION SYSTEM

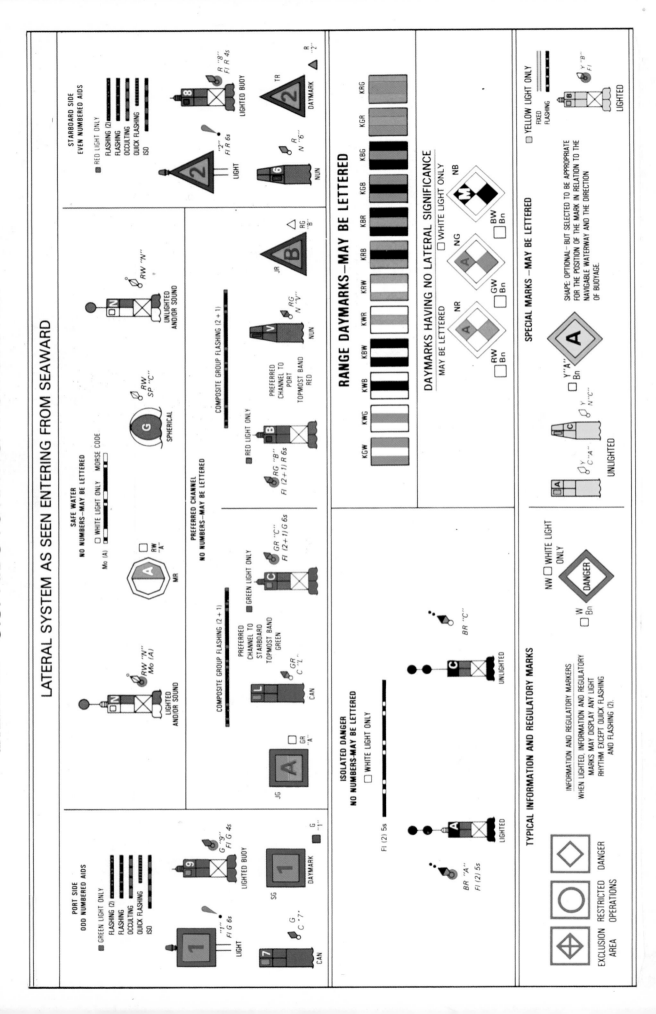

(Printed with the permission of the U.S. Coast Guard)